D1431374

Towards a Philosophy of Administration

Christopher Hodgkinson

St. Martin's Press · New York

© Basil Blackwell 1978

All rights reserved. For information, write:
St. Martin's Press, Inc., 175 Fifth Avenue, New York, N.Y. 10010
Printed in Great Britain
Library of Congress Catalog Card Number 78-676
ISBN 0-312-81036-9
First published in the United States of America in 1978

Library of Congress Cataloguing in Publication Data

Hodgkinson, Christopher.
　Towards a philosophy of administration.

　Bibliography: p. 228
　Includes index.
　1. Management.　2. Organization.　3. Social values.
I.　Title.
HD31.H558　　　658.4　　　78–676
ISBN 0-312-81036-9

Contents

Foreword

Ever since Max Weber it has been widely accepted that administration is a 'rational' subject, akin to science and economics. What these three sectors and carriers of modernity are said to share is a great measure of detachment, a separation of means and ends, a neutrality, a coolness. Thus, a scientist in the pursuit of truth shall not 'catch' any special finding, but remain open-minded about them; the marketplace functions because objects are subject to formal rules which put a measurable value on each, but leave the objects freely interchangeable. Only in primitive economics do people develop attachments to monetary units, e.g., individual shells. Finally, administrators are to treat all comers as equals, as strangers, disregarding friendship, kinship, emotional bonds and ideological affinities, using only relevant criteria in job assignment, promotion, award of contracts and so on.

Hodgkinson, in this important book, does not challenge the rational-modern quality of administration. But he masterfully lays aside the implication that administration is therefore valueless, neutral, aphilosophical, ethically free. He sets a philosophical agenda and vantage point for both the administrator (whom he views as a practising philosopher) and the student of administration.

Let me just illustrate one major implication of Hodgkinson's post-Weberian stance and then leave the reader to delve into this masterful volume. All people who act, especially those who act consciously in the sense that they reflect on what they are doing, as administrators cannot but do, rely on implicit or explicit assumptions about human nature. They see their subjects, superiors, and fellow persons as inherently 'good' in nature, or corrupt, or pliable. In the first case, they tend to encourage, to appeal to the sense of judgment and responsibility, and to see in inappropriate conduct either temporary lapses or the result of poor conditions, arrangements, or institutions, which can be changed. In the second case, they see people as seeking to maximize their own good even if it exacts costs from others, and tend to rely on supervision, verification, sanction, rules and regulations in their work. The third group wavers and waffles between these conceptions. Now this is not the place to elucidate what I consider 'the' correct answer. The point is that whatever philosophical assumption an administrator makes implicitly or explicitly about human nature, it cannot but deeply affect *his* conduct and that of the administration he helps shape. Hodgkinson will help the administrator here to be aware of his assumptions about human nature, that of others, and how those may be modified. He does the same necessary job for other dimensions of philosophy, from ethics to epistemology, in the following pages.

Amitai Etzioni
Professor of Sociology,
Columbia University
Director, Center for Policy Research

Preface

Administration is one of the most ancient and pervasive of human behaviours. Directly and indirectly, through the mode of increasingly complex organizations, it affects the quality of our lives. Well done, it enriches, liberates, civilizes; badly done it can destroy, dehumanize, and degrade. But what philosophy informs the study of this activity? Is there or can there even be a 'philosophy of' or a defensible philosophical approach towards administrative studies or, as some authorities would have it, administrative science? This book seeks to address these concerns.

A further motivation for such a book arises from the observed and expressed need by administrative practitioners in a variety of fields and administrative students at all stages of their careers for some kind of analysis of the problem of *value* in administration which might reach a little beyond the banalities or, worse, the sterilities which so often tend to pass as values and ethical training in the preparation of administrators. There is therefore the hope and ambition that some rapprochement can be made through the efforts of the *readers* of this book towards a restoration of dialogue between administrators and philosophers and between their respective constellations of subject matter, the social sciences and the humanities. It is bad enough to have a putative cultural gap between scientists and literati, as Lord Snow has suggested, but worse by far to have divorce between those who propound philosophy and those who translate it into action.

That this last is a largish ambition is shown by the fact that with a few honourable exceptions in modern times, notably Chester Barnard on this side of the Atlantic and Sir Geoffrey Vickers on the other, there has been little interactive literature between these realms of discourse. There are to be sure certain bench marks at the political level. In antiquity Plato tried to talk to administrators and in the Renaissance Machiavelli tried to talk to philosophers. The former attempt collapsed in Syracuse and the latter has since been treated with that kind of closet respect appropriate to a particularly nasty family skeleton. The work of some modern philosophers (Oakeshott, Arendt, Peters) and some notable insights in the area of public administration (Simon, Smithburg, and Thompson) may weaken these generalizations, but by and large, contemporary philosophers have inclined towards an obsessive preoccupation with the cleanlinesses of logic and mathematics or a fixation with the convolutions of language. For their own part those social scientists and psychologists with an interest in administration have suffered from corresponding fascination with the simplifications and reductions of behaviourism and quantitative empiricism. Yet as every administrator knows, whether he be endowed with the benefits of any professional training or not, the day-to-day activity of administration is often downright imprecise, unclean, non-quantitative, emotionally taxing and painful. It makes demands upon his individual character which call for the exercise of wisdom as much or more than for the application of cleverness; in a word, for philosophy in the most ancient sense of the term. For such readers, whether they be embarking on an administrative career or whether they are already well out into the ocean, I have endeavoured to write—with underlying presumptions and prejudices, of course. Among the chief of these must be the belief that being an administrator is more than being a technician and a politician, those dual faces of conventional professional managerial expertise. Secondly, there is the conviction that the realms of politics and administration, of policy and execution, are not so immaculately distinct as some received theory might lead us to believe. And thirdly, there is the intuition that to some significant extent administration is the disease for which, in a special sense, philosophy must be the cure. This is a sense important for the quality of life inside and outside of organizations.

It may be helpful to the reader to note that the three parts which comprise the book have different functions and emphases. Although the work is intended to be read as a consecutive whole this necessitates some consequent shifts of treatment and style. The purpose of Part I is to examine the field of administration from the standpoint of logic and detached rationality, to show first the limited applicability of logic, second the special character of the constraints on rationality, and third the overwhelming impress of extra-logical and valuational components in administrative action. The leading question which lends form to this part of the book is somewhat different from that of orthodox administrative and organization theory: What are the special competencies of administrators? What is the virtue by which administrators can claim the right to administer? And is this right merely the common property of each of us as certain political practices might seem to imply? Blunter yet, can *anyone* administer? Or are there *professional* desiderata? In searching for the answers we shall argue that, while a knowledge of organization theory may be desirable gloss on the administrative escutcheon, and while skills in the acquisition and deployment of power are of the essence, the essential competence lies in the area of judgment. And this, it will be seen, has moral implications. The argument will also cast some shade upon the orthodox wisdom about leadership.

The purpose of Part II is to explore the philosophical problem of value from the standpoint of administration, to re-examine the ways in which values intrude in administrative process, and to clarify the value concept in this context as preliminary to a disquisition upon the *philosophy* of administration in the next part of the book. It is here that the concept of value so fundamental to administration is explicated, I believe for the first time, in a way which will enable administrators to classify their contextual values and the levels at which value problems can be resolved. The essential aim is to provide the reader with some clarity of conception in this conceptually tortured area.

In the third and final section we begin by examining some of the ways in which the value complexities of the administrative situation can be dysfunctional, including the value pathology of administrators themselves. This treatment is not intended to be exhaustive, but rather incisively illustrative of the value defects which can impair the quality of organizational life. It is suggested that the administrator's philosophical problem has two determining parameters: the metavaluational impress of his organization and the multivalent dynamics of his personal philosophic and motivational drives. This leads us finally to the notion of a continuum of interest and, more importantly, to a set of propositions of a special kind which are intended to be used auto-pedagogically and to be interpreted in the idiosyncratic light of the reader's status and experience as well as in conjunction with the arguments presented here. Only in this ultimately introspective way can a non-doctrinaire philosophy be conveyed. And it can only be in the dialectic between reader as representative of the wealth of actual administrative phenomenology and the propositions as representative of the poverty of administrative philosophy as it presently stands that a richer and more beneficent philosophy, a true administrative humanism, can come to be.

Acknowledgements

The kind permission of the following publishers is gratefully acknowledged: MacMillan, Inc. for the reproduction of the diagram on p. 71 from David Braybrooke & Charles E. Lindblom *A Strategy of Decision*; Phi Delta Kappa Publications for the diagram on p. 71 from Daniel Stufflebeam *et al. Educational Evaluation and Decision Making*; McGraw Hill for figures on pp. 31, 32 from Golembiewski, R. *Men, Management and Morality* and Likert, R. *The Human Organization*; John Wiley & Sons, Inc. for excerpts from Katz, D., and Kahn, R. L. *The Social Psychology of Organizations*; Harvard University Press for passages from Chester Barnard *The Functions of the Executive* and MacMillan, Inc. for quotations from Herbert A. Simon, *Administrative Behavior*.

In addition the author wishes to express his gratitude to the Canada Council for funding part of this study and to the many colleagues and students on both sides of the Atlantic with whom he consulted. A special acknowledgement is due to the author's wife, Madge, for her support, technical assistance, typing, and forbearance.

I
LOGIC

Logic seeks straightness in a bent world.

1
The General Nature
of Administration

ADMINISTRATION AND PHILOSOPHY

Administration is philosophy in action. This is the general definition of administration and it can only be asserted at this point. In the work which follows I seek to *show* this definition by an unfolding and explication of the two realms of discourse, philosophy and administration, as they bear upon and have relevance for each other. It is important to appreciate at the outset, however, that by philosophy I do not mean any given body of doctrine, any one world-view, world system, or articulation of a specific epistemology, axiology, or esthetic. By philosophy I mean in barest essence the process of correct thinking and the process of valuing: rationality, or logic, and values. These constitute the dual aspects of activity whereby administration becomes philosophical.

There is another way in which the set of activities classified as administration take on, directly or at one or more removes, a philosophical colouring. This has to do with the assumptions about man and the nature of man held by the administrator. The essential raw material of administration is men. Human nature is the basic stuff of organizations, those goal-seeking collectivities or purposive systems which create the demand for the functions which give rise to administration. The administrator's private philosophy and his model-of-man enter thus into the complex equation which determines collective action.

Administration can be conceived as 'rationality applied to social relations' and simultaneously as an 'artificial system and, therefore, always contentious.' (Thompson, 1975, 76). It is a domain for the proper exercise of applied logic but the practitioners in this domain simultaneously initiate values and practise ethics (Simon, Smithburg, Thompson, 1950, 539, 554). We shall, there-

Logic

fore, be concerned with the logical and value aspects of philosophical administration and administrative philosophy. And because it will be shown that the problem of value tends to preponderate in the actualities of administration, a proportional weighting will be given to value considerations in the structure of this book.

In the first part of the work I wish to treat the general and special components of administration from the standpoint of rationality. That is, the way in which these elements enter into a whole which can be said to possess a certain logic and integrity which would justify the notion that there is a body of knowledge which can properly be called administrative. In the second part of the book the value characteristics of administration will be stressed, and in the final part, I shall endeavour to draw together the several strands of argument into pedagogical propositions about this branch of human activity which can serve as elements for a philosophy of administration proper.

ADMINISTRATION AND MANAGEMENT

It is necessary to distinguish between the terms 'administration' and 'management'. Again, the fact that tight definitions cannot be presented for the work which follows in itself shows something of the meaning of these complex concepts. We can make use of a figure (Fig. 1).

Figure 1: Conceptual Continua for the Definition of Administration

	ADMINISTRATION			MANAGEMENT
		Art ————	Science	
		Policy ————	Execution	
		Values ————	Facts	
		Upper ————	Lower	
		Echelons ————	Echelons	
	ADMINISTRATION	Strategy ————	Tactics	MANAGEMENT
		Qualitative ————	Quantitative	
		Human ————	Material	
		Reflective ————	Active	
		Generalism ————	Specialism	

Without by any means exhausting the dimensions associated with these sets of activities it can be seen that any definition would have to allow for a continuum from the highest level of administration to the lowest level of management, the more so since, as Barnard points out (1972, 6), these functions are pervasive across organizations and across persons in organizations regardless of title or ostensible rank. In general then we mean by *administration* those aspects dealing more with the formulation of purpose, the value-laden issues, and the human component of organizations. By *management* we mean those aspects which are more routine, definitive, programmatic, and susceptible to quantitative methods. Curiously, the two terms have differing trans-Atlantic usages; the interpretation given here controverts, for example, that of Keeling (1972). It does, however, conform with the American authorities most relevant to this text (Simon, Barnard) and indeed with the nomenclature of the Royal Institute of Public Administration. By and large, administrators in our terms will tend to be located high in the organizational status hierarchy while managers will tend to the middle and lower levels of supervision and responsibility. Loosely, we can consider administration to be the art of influencing men to accomplish organizational goals while management is the ancillary and subordinate science of specifying and implementing means to accomplish the same ends. Administration is ends-oriented, management is means-oriented. The pure administrator is a philosopher, the pure manager a technologist. But there is no approximation to purity at either end of the spectrum in the fact and practice of administration or management. The distinction is obscured and sometimes deliberately so.

A confusion of sorts reigns in the language because of the blurring of this distinction. The terms are used in some language games (notably those of commerce) to denote the reverse of what is declared here. Elsewhere in the literature they are used interchangeably or as synonyms. Simon in his major text *Administrative Behavior* loosely refers to administration as 'the art of getting things done' (1957, 1) and then goes on to stress the decision-making aspects as opposed to the merely 'doing' aspects of such administration. He would centre his work on the problem of *choice* leading to activity. In this sense he supports the terminology here decided upon. In a later section of his book (53-4) Simon attempts rather unsuccessfully to disentangle *administrative* from policy decisions, concluding only that the distribution of fact and value differ in each but not definitely specifying the relative mix. In this book we shall propose that the more the mix approaches the valuational the more the decisional activity is administrative and the converse for managerial decisions. Also, the more general the value component in decisions and the more such decisions affect the formulation and definition of organizational purpose the more administrative as opposed to managerial they become and the more they are part of what Barnard would call an executive function (222, 223).

It is of incidental interest that Barnard, whose theories provide major inspiration for this book, himself abjured the terms administration and management[1] preferring instead the usage 'executive'. In what follows executive will be used synonymously with administrator or administrative.

It can be repeated that both categories of activity pervade any organization. The humblest employee engages in administration when he ponders whether to quit his job and the most exalted of executives is compelled to the performance of some managerial tasks. In general, however, under any distinction the concern with the ends, aims, and purposes of organization is the precinct of the administrator while the major concern of managers will be with effecting means to prescribed ends. And in the hard world outside of academic distinctions managers will persist in intrusion into the administrative ambit while administrators will persist in withdrawing from responsibilities by a 'retreat into management'.

THE VARIETIES OF ADMINISTRATION

Is it reasonable to discuss administration as a general class of activities when in fact the between-organization differences (school vs. factory) and within-organization differences (line foreman vs. board chairman), not to mention the differences implicit in the distinction just drawn between management and administration, are all so great as to defy general treatment? That is to say, is not administration *context-prescribed* to such a degree that the proper study is of, say, *educational* administration or of *business* administration?

It was a major proposition of Litchfield's work (1956) that administration and administrative processes occur in substantially the same generalized form in industrial, commercial, educational, military, and hospital organizations. To my knowledge this proposition, though it attaches logically to a reductionist view of administration as a decisional process, has not been refuted by empirical evidence since it was first set out as a postulate for a theory of administration. In this book I concur with the notion of a generalized form of activity, administration-management, which obtains across the variety of organizational settings in which it occurs. Our interest lies in administration as both a discernible profession and a class of acts which can be conventionally prescribed by organizational context but not restricted or determined in essential nature by any given set of organizational boundaries. (It is a much finer philosophical point, and one which we can gratefully elide, as to whether individuals themselves constitute systems amenable to administration as implied, for example, in such lines as, 'I am the master of my soul, the captain of my fate.')

None of this denies the important modification which will derive from organizational settings. It would be interesting to speculate, for example, on the ways in which some organizations tend towards one end or the other of the administrative-managerial continuum. Thus, one would expect a departmental sub-unit of a large bureaucracy with a clearly specified mission and well-comprehended and task-adequate technology to be more 'managerial' and an educational institution with broadly defined goals and imprecise methodologies to be more 'administrative'. Both, however, would have necessary administrative subsystems and both would engage in administrative acts.

This study is directed across the adjectival subsets of administration: educational administration, hospital administration, public and business administration to administration-in-general, that general form of human behaviour which defines and achieves ends through organizations. It follows, too, that at the more general levels of administration practitioners pass with relative ease from one general setting to another. Military men have assumed high academic offices and leaders in industry have taken on major governmental roles. There is a freemasonry in the upper echelons of administration, a commonality of problems encountered and strategies adopted (Barnard, xxvii) which seems to support the assertion that administration is a generalism.

Nevertheless it should be noted that this general quality of administration is not entirely reflected in the modes by which administrators are prepared. For a variety of reasons, some historical, some political, some merely expedient, schools of administration tend to be organized on adjectival lines with public administrators, business administrators, and educational administrators receiving their training in separate establishments. General schools of administration studies such as that at the Irvine campus of the University of California are the exception rather than the rule. One suspects, however, that the texts studied and the practices followed within the entire variety of adjectival schools would reveal marked commonalities. Still, the preparation of administrators *qua* administrators is presently unusual. Perhaps the last clear examples were provided by the mandarins and administration class of the bygone Chinese and British Civil Services respectively. Both groups were selected initially on the basis of proven ability in the study of the classics and the humanities. Both were also elitist in that they made use of the meritocratic criterion of examination performance. The modern French practice exemplified in the *Ecole Nationale Administrative* to some extent perpetuates this generalist tradition.

We need not enter at this time into the difficult questions surrounding administrative preparation. These will come under discussion later for they are certainly relevant to any philosophy of administration but they need not detract from the focus of this book upon administration in its general and non-adjectival sense.

THE DEVELOPMENT OF ADMINISTRATIVE THOUGHT

While administration as a practice is as ancient as man himself the emergence of a body of reflective thought about it expressed in a cohesive literature is a relatively modern phenomenon. There are works of antiquity in the East and the West, notably Plato's *Republic* in our own tradition, which have concerned themselves directly or indirectly with administration. To some of these I am greatly indebted and will have much recourse later. In Western Political science there is a tradition of *Fuerstenspiegel* writing, the 'mirror for Princes,' within which the classic Renaissance work of Machiavelli is outstanding and hypermodern in its implications. But, by and large, the bulk of scholarship and certainly the massive outpourings of empirical study have occurred within our own century. This work is now voluminous. It cannot be treated here in any but the most summary fashion, but nevertheless we need to take note, however cursorily, of the broad sweeps of traditional and contra-traditional dialectic which have already displayed themselves within the present epoch.

The Classical View of Administration. The early twentieth century spirit of administrative thought can be captured and illustrated in the work of two men who each approached the field of study from opposed directions and with opposed logics. The first, Frederick W. Taylor, is still eminent for his attempts to make a science of productive effort (Taylor, 1911; 1915; 1964). His ideas, later elaborated in the work of the Gilbreths (1916; 1917) and Gantt (1916, 1920; Rathe, 1961), stemmed from an inductive method based on work and worker observations. If, as Bertrand Russell once said, work is of two kinds: 'first, altering the position of matter at or near the earth's surface relatively to other such matter; second, telling other people to do so': and if we are given a criterion of productivity, then there might seem to be, on the face of it, one best way of organizing the performance of tasks. (Clayre, 1975) Taylor's work led to time and motion study and his ghost is still very present in the managerial machine. In a sense one could argue that automation is a culminating exemplification and logical product of the spirit of scientific management in that it transmutes human labour into purely machine terms. In Taylor's days, however, automation and its technological concomitants could only have been at best a dimly distant vision.

In contrast to this inductive worker-up approach Henry Fayol in France, like his American contemporary a very successful practical administrator, chose to approach the study of administration from a more deductive standpoint. His thesis took the form of rational analyses and taxonomies of organizational function and structure (Fayol, 1916). The organization chart was born as was the progenitor of that peculiarly administrative mantram, POSDCORB (Planning, Organizing, Staffing, Directing, Coordinating, Record-Keeping, Budgetting).[2] Fayol's work has stood the test of time remarkably well and it is consistent with the more general theory of bureaucracy developed later by Max Weber, a theory based in part on sociological observation and speculation. In any event Fayol shares with Weber and Taylor in the early attempts to rationalize or scientize administrative thought.

This pioneering work, inductive and deductive, was followed in this classical tradition by a search for *principles* of administration and organization (Gulick and Urwick, 1937; Mooney, 1939). The search proved vain (Simon, 1965) but the faith in an inherent rationality, an underlying logic which could be exposed and reconstructed in a scientifically respectable manner, this has persisted. A characteristic of the classical view is that it is highly dependent upon certain *given* premises. Given (1) organizational purposes, given (2) organizational members (that is, men as quantifiable variables), and given (3) a set of technologies, then it should be possible to order these components upon given criteria of productivity and efficiency and such an ordering would constitute a scientific administration. The fact that only the third of these givens has proven amenable to rationalization would not have been clear at the time these authorities were writing. In the interbellum period the complexities attaching to the second set of givens, the human element, were increasingly the object of study and hence increasingly less of a logically given character while, finally, in contemporary literature the first set of premises, having to do with purposes and goals, has come under critical assault (Chaps. 2, 8).

The Humanist Reaction. It has been suggested that the fault of classical thought lay in the protean nature of its assumptions. Time and history as reflected in continuously changing ideologies and scientific-technological contexts result in a degree of variability to ends, means, and human resources which can often preclude any simple logic. From the time of the early 1930's there has persisted in the administrative literature a human relations movement (Mayo, 1933; 1949) or personality theory school (McGregor, 1960; Argyris, 1957; 1973) which has directed its attention to the human variable, most particularly as it appears in the role of the worker.

A philosophical base for this movement was established by the work of Mary Parker Follett between 1924–33 (Follett, 1924; Pollard, 1974, 161–176), and this work was remarkably well received. An important contributing factor must also have been the general, Pre-Depression industrial climate which, though paternalistic, permitted such elaborate and prolonged researches as the

Western Electric (Hawthorne) studies to be undertaken (Roethlisberger, 1939). It is uncertain to this day just what this remarkable socio-psychological investigation uncovered (Carey, 1974) but without doubt it led to reappraisal of the elusive and subtle relationship between organization members and organization administration. What went unchallenged was the criterion variable of productivity against which the human element was measured. Certainly the Hawthorne studies countervailed against if they did not entirely upset the classical tendency to take the human variable as a simple given and certainly they spawned an outpouring of study and literature upon the theme of work motivation (Steers and Porters, 1975). In consequence a large part of the body of administrative thought is given over to consideration of the findings of social science on motivation. Administration of the 'human system' preponderates over or at least looms as large as administration and mangement of the technical system. Moreover, the implicit model-of-man undergoes important shifts and alterations. (Miles, 1975, 32–43)

A leading contemporary exponent of the humanist reaction is Professor Argyris. In an extensive review of the research literature bearing on his favoured logic he could find only continuing support for his position (1973). This position would entail an ethic or philosophy of administration which would result in the reconstruction of organizations with a view to allowing increasing opportunities for organizational members to grow towards fuller and more-fulfilling maturity. Such a maturity would be similar to what the psychologist Maslow named *self-actualization*. Self-actualization is a *summum bonum* in Maslow's scheme of values[3] and he entered it into the literature of administration with his book *Eupsychian Management* (1965). The principle of hierarchical motivation is also elaborated in the work of Herzberg (1959, 1968) whose research led him to discriminate between lower level (hygienic, security) and higher level (job, motivational) needs and satisfactions. Taken to an extreme this logic can lead to a view in which business firms exist not, as classically understood, to make a profit but to provide opportunities for growth and self-fulfillment, the profit motive then becoming a necessary but not sufficient condition for the organizational existence. Overall, it can be said that this school of thought coalesces about demands for improvement in work conditions and work organization. Its proponents would have work become more of an end in itself and less, as implied under classical productivity-efficiency reasoning, a means to ulterior and extra-organizational values.

The premises of this school in turn are open to critique. Not all empirical researchers subscribe to its tenets (Carey, 1974; Dubin, 1956, Vollmer, 1960) but from our more philosophical standpoint it would seem that human relations thinking has a tendency to elide first the problem of organizational goals, that is, the first given of the classical logic, and second, the character and characteristics of administrators and administration, a premise also largely taken for granted by the classicists.

In sum, the thrust of the humanist reaction is against the untenable classical assumption of the human factor as a quantifiable and predictable variable. Such an assumption may be tenable within limits, but the early study of human work motivation led to some simplistic and perhaps exaggerated modelling as expressed, for example, in the Theory X and Theory Y of Douglas McGregor (1960). Stereotyping earlier thought, Theory X depicts man as essentially resistant to organization and work while Theory Y comes close to adulation in showing him to be full of creative resources and thwarted potential. McGregor stressed the point that these quasi-philosophical orientations referred to underlying beliefs about the nature of man which influence administrators in their behaviour (McGregor & Bennis, 1967, 77). Man becomes the measure of administrative things but the measure of man is premised upon philosophical bases which often seem to tend if not to the utopian then to the eupsychian.

NEO-CLASSICISM AND NEO-HUMANISM

Two great contributions to administrative thought were written in the decade between 1935 and 1945. Both are American and both, on the evidence of publication record alone, persist as classics in the administrative literature and are familiar to all serious students of administration. These works are Chester Barnard's *The Functions of the Executive* and H. A. Simon's *Administrative Behaviour*. Both are logical and scholarly assessments of the general nature of administration. They are both analytic and synthetic, and they treat administration as a special subsystem within a larger organizational systems complex. It is not unreasonable to treat them as complementary pillars of the received wisdom.

Simon is a logical positivist by declaration. His primary concern is with the limits of rationality which bound administrative process, a process which he sees as fundamentally one of *making decisions*. His analysis of administration remains essentially unassailed within the ground rules laid down, but the philosophical posture he chose to adopt forces the presumption of administrative man as some kind of value-neutral or moral cipher, at least to the extent that he is an organizational artifact. The administrator's values are taken to be those of the organization, and are irrelevant in the same way that an actor's are to those of a theatrical performance. Value considerations are exported, by the invocation of the productivity criterion, out of the organization: administration approaches play-acting. 'The task of the good actor is to know and play his role, although different roles vary greatly in content. The effectiveness of the performance will depend on the effectiveness of the play and the effectiveness with which it is played. The effectiveness of the administrative process will vary with the effectiveness of the organization and the effectiveness with which its members play their parts.' (Simon, 252). By *good* what apparently is meant here is subscription to the organizational metavalues (Chap. 11, below). That the argument about administrative value neutrality is not merely academic is obvious from the evidence of polemic even in such prestigious arenas as the upper levels of the British Civil Service (Report of first division Association, 1972, 168).

Barnard, writing out of his own administrative experience, is distinctively different in that he is greatly concerned with the *moral* component in executive behaviour. This moral aspect is linked to his concepts of responsibility and leadership (Barnard, Ch. XVII) and would seem to imply that the closer the administrator approximated ideal performance of executive functions the more he would take on the necessary paragon proportions. Barnard's executive elite is a moral elite, a secular priesthood, one within which Dostoevsky's Grand Inquisitor would feel quite at home. This preoccupation with morality renders him somewhat unique in this field of thought (but cf. Golombiewski, 1965). His analysis of organizational communications both comprehends the human relations movement and presages the emergent systems approach.

The theoretical and descriptive work of Simon and Barnard was followed and augmented by extensive and intensive contributions from the social sciences. The insights of sociology, social psychology, psychology, economics, and political science were eagerly commissioned in an attempt to render administration a 'science.' Simon's caveats on rational limits and Barnard's humanism may often have been discounted in this endeavour. The interdisciplinary thrust did, however, give rise to General Systems Theory, a quasi-scientific formulation springing from the natural science of biology (von Bertalanffy, 1956) and occasionally having near-religious overtones (Granger, 1971). The systems approach to administration was not sterile. Offshoots such as PERT (Program Evaluation and Review Technique) and MARS (Model Analysis and Redesign System) scored notable successes in such collective efforts as landing a man on the moon and building a nuclear submarine (Granger, 1971, 115, 139–155). Moreover, systems theory through its cybernetic 'black box' and feedback principles had a nice and clever way of treating imponderables such as the human variable. In a way systems thinking and its logical derivatives such as Operations Research and the variety of quantitative methods dependent on computer technology can be thought of as a return, at a more sophisticated level, to the classical position of scientific management.

The other arm of dialectic in administrative thought has now taken on the form of an organizational development or human resources school. (Blake and Mouton, 1964; Miles, 1975; Argyris, 1971; French and Bell, 1973). This view is represented as an advance on the human relations theory of management which now is held to be manipulative and unauthentic and to some large extent corrupted by administrative practice. While it de-emphasizes the group dependencies and social ethic of Whyte's *Organization Man* (1957) it elaborates upon the possibilities for more creative organizational structures (Likert, 1967) and a more fulfilling work environment.

Overall, what seems to have happened by the latter decades of the twentieth century is that most of the social sciences and most of the humanities (with the notable exception of philosophy) have been engaged to a greater or lesser extent with the topic of administration. Yet the attempt to create a science of administration has failed (Dunsire, 1973). But if the pretensions to administrative science fail then what is the study of administration? The answer seems to be that it is a great interdisciplinary nexus into which the streams of social science spasmodically flow. It continues to provide grist for a variety of disciplinary mills, notably sociology, social psychology, and political science. It provides source material for the novelist and dramatist and thus intrudes itself indirectly into the humanities[4] but curiously it has not come under the concentrated scrutiny of philosophers. A search of the literature in professional philosophy from 1945 to the time of writing reveals few entries bearing directly upon administration proper (cf. Lessem, 1973; Ladd, 1970; Subramanian, 1963; 1971; Suppes, 1961; Cooper, 1968 for characteristic approaches). Administrative science would seem to have misconceived while administrative philosophy failed to conceive at all.

This last fact is curious. Why the philosophical excommunication? What is it that attracts social scientists whilst deterring philosophers? Is it that it is philosophically unmanageable (*pace* Plato, *pace* Machiavelli)? Are the two realms of discourse, philosophy and administration, mutually irrelevant and disjunctive? Whatever the answers, this book is an attempt to effect a conjunction and restore a lost dialogue. And its initial argument is that administration is rightly to be considered as one of the humanities and as such a ground for philosophy.

To support this argument the underlying form of logic of administrative practice must be sought, first in a general and later in more directed ways. What is the general nature of administration (and administrators); what are the broad characteristics and attributes of the field and the actors in the field?

CHARACTERISTICS OF ADMINISTRATION

Administrative-managerial work—what it is that administrators of various kinds do, whether they be United States presidents or school superintendents or leaders of street corner gangs—has been fairly thoroughly studied (Homans, 1950; Neustadt, 1960; Carlson, 1951; Stewart, 1967; Shartle, 1956; Stieglitz, 1969; Sayles, 1964). The studies cross organizational lines and also address the within-organizational variations. A summative study by Mintzberg (1973) derives conclusions about administration (managerial work in Mintzberg's terminology) which can be condensed as follows. The nature of administration is such that the administrator or manager is first, extremely busy, works long hours, and has little free or private time relative to other organizational members. His work is characterized by brevity, variety, and fragmentation. 'Superficiality is an occupational hazard of the manager's job' and he gravitates to the more active elements of his work—the current, the specific, the well-defined, the non-routine activities' (51, 52). Much time is consumed with the preferred non-written modes of communication, scheduled and unscheduled meetings, and informal contacts. The voice, in its range from confidential whisper to authoritative rasp, is mightier than the pen and correspondence tends to receive perfunctory, though regular treatment. Moreover, and perhaps more ominous, 'The manager actually appears to prefer brevity and interruption in his work. He becomes conditioned by his workload; he develops an appreciation for the opportunity cost of his own time; and he lives continuously with an awareness of what else might or must be done at any time'. (51).

Mintzberg's deductions from his empirical observations of five chief executives led him to postulate a number of roles for the managerial (administrative) function which in turn could be grouped into the three sets of *interpersonal* roles, *informational* roles, and *decisional* roles. (54–99). In the first of these sets he acts as figurehead, leader, and liaison, performs ceremonial and symbolic functions, defines 'organizational atmosphere', and maintains horizontal relationships with significant others outside the organization. His informational roles call on him to monitor and disseminate the internal flow of intelligence within the organization and to act externally as spokesman on the organization's behalf. Lastly, under the set of decision making he will initiate and design organizational change, take care of system disturbances, monitor and control the organizational reward system, together with the flow of resources, and act in negotiations on behalf of the organization (*ibid.*)

Though presented in synopsis, this reveals certain distinguishing attributes of administrative as contrasted with other organizational roles. First, the administrator is in an interface position. He stands at the nexus of organization and environment. Whether the environment be supportive or inimical, an onus is created which persuades the administrator to develop those skills which can enhance the organization's prospects for survival. These are the skills conventionally associated with diplomacy, and the diplomat is a species of the genus administrator.

Secondly, the administrator is continuously concerned with linguistic 'intelligence'—he is under an onus to develop skills of communication, both reception and transmission, a broad category which embraces many sets of behaviour from the ability to articulate with some fluency to refined skills of analysis which may be quasi-legalistic or philosophical in scope.

Thirdly, and this follows the accepted logic of administration, the executive is a generalist. From the organizational standpoint he is the specialist in generalism. This implies a decisional prerogative and a range of decision making functions from the rapid, the reflective, the 'tactical' to the laboured, the reflective, the 'strategic'. These are all characteristics of the *job* of administration. They refer to the demands arising from a *role*, and though heavily laden with implications, entailments, and connotations they say nothing of the actual *personality* of the role-incumbent. Mintzberg's observations give a hint of the latter in his finding of a certain distaste for the reflective or philosophical end of the range of functions, but Mintzberg has biases of his own, which to some extent are revealed in the following quotation:

Management science has extended its influence up the organizational hierarchy since Frederick Taylor began experimenting late in the last century with methods to improve efficiency at the factory level. But a shift in orientation in the last decade has slowed its progress. The management scientist has sought elegance in his techniques. This may have been appropriate so long as he was dealing with highly structured problems. But those found at the policy level are not so neat, and it will take time to learn how to structure them. In his search for elegance the management scientist must be prepared to forego elegance, to adjust his technique to the problem rather than searching for problems that fit the technique. Management science must become once again the application of basic analysis—clear, systematic thinking with a reliance on explicit data—to the problems of management. (196)

Let us defer judgment in the qualitative-quantitative dispute at this point. Whether or not administration is the better characterized as art or science need not detract from the general observation that there is, upon the evidence, a *distinctive* set of organizational activities which can be called administration. This set may be distinctive enough to warrant such expertise that it cannot be 'done by anyone'. It may indeed constitute a 'profession', full-blown or embryonic, a profession with a territorial claim to a body of unified knowledge and a putative claim to the possession of certain specialized skills. The logic of such a profession and its work would devolve upon the relationship of men in purposive collectivities. Moreover, professionalism would imply the desirability of, if not the strict need for, some kind of formalized preparation. And amateurs would be abjured.

CHARACTERS OF ADMINISTRATORS

The personality traits of administrators have been the subject of some extensive study, particularly in the attempt to explore the trait theory of leadership (Stogdill, 1948; Shartle, 1949). This explanation was ultimately abandoned, largely because of the absence of firm or incontestable findings and also because of the proliferation of personality traits which could be operationally defined. Recent work could, however, be interpreted as a return at a more complex and sophisticated level to the idea that there are identifiable personality characteristics which would bear significant and predictive relations for administrative activity (Reddin, 1970; Fiedler, 1966). The argument is still somehow persuasive that there must or should be some sort of character attributes which could be shown to be significantly correlated with administrative success and that persons possessing these attributes could be identified and groomed in some way or other for leadership office. The melody lingers. What is philosophically peculiar is that, in most or all of this empirical effort, the *moral* attributes and standing of administrators tended to elide any careful empirical study. (Golembiewski, 1965, fails to show otherwise, though the work of Schutz, 1955, is relevant and interesting). Hints and suggestions occur, of course, throughout the literature. The following quotation from a classic work in public administration is illustrative:

Highly mobile individuals—individuals with very strong personal ambitions—gravitate into positions of power. In order to mount the ladder of hierarchical success it is often necessary to take actions or make decisions of a somewhat cold-blooded kind. One must 'go to lunch with the right people.' Sometimes friends must be by-passed. Occasionally someone must be fired who badly needs his job. Yearnings and aspirations of incapable people must sometimes be disregarded. Most persons, except those who have strong personal ambitions or unusually strong attachments to a goal, find such behaviour difficult. Consequently, many highly mobile people climb upward in organizational hierarchies by a kind of self-selection. (Simon, Smithburg, Thompson, 1950, 395)

But *realpolitische* comment of this kind, though instructive, still leaves us unable to speak factually or scientifically about administrator's *characters* as opposed to their *characteristics*, despite the insights of Barnard and the importance he ascribed to the moral element in executive behaviour (330, 331).

The peculiarity intensifies when we admit that administrators occupy positions of power over other men. This is a basic characteristic of the administrative function. Of course, when the power aspects of administration manifest at the political level, the obviousness of the power element and its moral implications attract the attention of biographers, historians, and political scientists (Collins and Moore, 1970; Lewis and Stewart, 1958, direct their attention more modestly) but again there seems to be a kind of moral suspension. There is, as it were, a democracy of great men in which Hitler and Churchill, Ignatius Loyola and Lucrezia Borgia are coeval. They all share the common property of skill in the administration of men. Theirs is the confraternity of administrative elitism, the freemasonry of power.

Since empirical evidence is lacking on the character of administrators as a species, despite the exotic example of the political administrative arena (Clark, 1969), and since the empirical evidence of characteristics is complex and confused the philosopher of administration can be forgiven if he makes assumptions about these elements. Here a strange contrast is offered between the ancients and the moderns.

From my own researches it would seem that the ancients tend towards a generally pessimistic view of administrative man (see Ch. 9). Such modifiers as power-seeking, success-oriented, ruthless,

aggressive, amoral fit as predicates into propositions with the subject administrator. This view persists through the Greeks to
Machiavelli. Plato's *tour-de-force* in the *Republic* is itself evidence
of the overriding cynicism. Yet, by and large, in the modern literature this mood of scepticism and negativity disappears. For
example, in the works of Simon and March (1958, 1945) the
administrator would appear to be a kind of moral cipher, ethically
neutered so as to further the ends of the *organization*. That such
moral castrates do in fact have self-interests which might be potent
enough to subvert or pervert their organizations does not receive
great attention (Simon, 1957, 242) and is often left out of consideration altogether (*per contra* see Wright, 1973; Brittan,
1964).

Of course there may be strong reasons for the modern disinterest
in administrative character (as opposed to characteristics). Given
the breach between philosophy and administration, given a journal
literature struggling for an academic and scientific respectability
and hence itself given over to interminable empiricism, given an
emergent profession with large vested interests, given the political security of bland formulations, and given a historico-cultural
environment which is in pluralistic and conceptual confusion
about values; these things together make for disincentives to any
a priori speculation on the moral investment in administration.
La Porte attributes the disinterest to an eroding ethos and de-
plores the decline of philosophical consciousness in administrative
studies (Marini, 1971, 20). Barnard is one of the significant exceptions to this general trend and much of his work is directed
specifically to this problem (162, 200–201, 258–284 and *passim*).
At times, however, this gives an unusually elitist overtone and an
anti-egalitarian nuance to his interpretation of the administrative
character.

Yet despite Barnard and despite the ancient biases we shall in this
part of the work avoid the extreme positions which have been
adopted on moral character, namely, paragonship, obsessive corruption, and cipherhood; views which represent roughly and
respectively the standpoints of idealism (Plato-Barnard), realism
(Machiavelli), and positivism (Simon). For the time we shall merely
assume that though administration may make extraordinary moral
demands it is practised by ordinary men. Later this position can be

reexamined. Our present concern is with the general nature of logic of administration. Such logic can be recapitulated in a brief reconsideration of the administrative functions.

ADMINISTRATIVE FUNCTIONS

We have now surveyed in a general way the broad state of conventional wisdom on administration, and the question which emerges is this: is there a discernible logic or underlying form which distinguishes this branch of human action? Perhaps this essential nature of administration can be most easily and quickly grasped from the perspectives of Simon and Barnard.

The former authority, Simon, takes the position that administration is quintessentially the process of making decisions. Not all decisions are administrative, however, and those which are are distinguished by their effect on organizational members. 'The decisions which the organization makes for the individual ordinarily (1) specify his function, that is, the general scope and nature of his duties; (2) allocate authority, that is, determine who in the organization is to have power to make further decisions for the individual; and (3) set such limits to his choice as are needed to coordinate the activities of several individuals in the organization (p. 8). His subsequent treatment of what we have called the administrative-managerial continuum follows upon this, and is of interest. For Simon administrative decisions are those which are uniquely directed to the decision making process itself:

> The statement, then, that as we proceed upward in the hierarchy 'administrative' duties come to occupy more and more of the administrator's time, and 'technical' duties less, must be interpreted with considerable caution. It is not true if the term 'administrative duties' is taken to refer only to the organization-determining functions. It is true, if the broader decisional functions which fall to the administrator are considered as administrative duties.
>
> 'What is the difference between these latter functions and the "technical" functions at the lower levels of the hierarchy? Simply that the content decisions of the higher administrator deal with more ultimate purposes and more general processes than the decisions of the lower administrator. We might say that the lower administrator's purposes are the upper administrator's processes.' (245–6)

In this version of the received wisdom the central function of the administrator then becomes that of making organizational decisions and decision rules.

Barnard takes a broader perspective. His executive functions consist of (1) maintenance of the organizational communication system, (2) securing the essential organizational services from individuals and (3) formulating the organization's purposes and objectives (pp. 215–234). Barnard was a systems theorist before that appellation became widespread. His observations on information flow predate and presage the most modern findings (Mintzberg, 1973). Nor does he at all neglect the decision function and process.

Combining these two authorities the range of administration then extends from a surface concern with the managerial-technical to a depth concern with organizational purpose. From philosophy at the centre of the sphere to action at the surface.

The basic nature of administration has not changed over time, but the emergence of a profession with its special insignia—professional societies and professional schools—is a modern phenomenon. Men still become administrators out of a rich variety of motives and in an even richer variety of ways but professionalism implies at least two criteria, those of a special competence and a special and relatively esoteric body of knowledge. Whether these criteria are met and whether administrators by virtue of these other criteria, have a special claim to occupy those administrative roles which all organizations create, are awkward questions which are difficult to answer with precision. For the present we can take the position that claims for an administrative knowledge base must be examined at least in the areas of organization theory, decision making, and leadership.

But administration is more than knowing, it is doing; and it is often characterized by a marked action orientation. Thus, in other words, an administrator may claim he *is* a leader because he *makes* decisions and policy and *maintains* his organization in a sequence of self-justifying behaviours which are independent of any reflection upon or knowledge *about* them. He would be as surprised to learn that he was concomitantly doing philosophy as Molière's character was to discover that all his life he had been talking prose. On the other hand, he would unquestioningly assert (and thus at once make the point about philosophy) that he carried *responsibility* in a way which made him distinctive from other members in the organization. The form of administration then is action-focused and the stereotypical attitude of administration is pragmatic. Though this may account for some of the lack of interaction between the domains of philosophy and administration it is still a little strange in view of the fact that organizations and administration are pervasive—we are all directly or indirectly members of or affected by the work of organizations and we are all either administered or administering—and this pervasion has vast significance for the meaning and quality of life.

2
The Nature of Organizations

ORGANIZATION THEORY

A major presumption of an administrative profession would be that its members can be distinguished by their superior knowledge of organizations, superior, that is, to non-administrative organizational members. A concern of administrative philosophy, therefore, would be with the substance of this claim. What logic underlies and what values are implicated by the body of organizational theory? The phenomena of human organizations have attracted the energetic attention of scholars and researchers; the vast bulk of literature on organization theory and its correlatives, including *administrative* theory, is evidence enough of this. But social science is a subaltern in the confraternity of academe and some of its more recent offshoots, e.g. organizational psychology, information theory, and organizational development, are themselves junior to administration as a field of study. In contrast, public administration has long been established as a discipline under the aegis of political science; and Waldo has suggested (1961) that a trend is discernible away from *administrative* theory as such to *organization* theory, a shift which would be consistent with the mid-twentieth century vogue for behaviouralism. He also pointed out that administrative theory would suggest 'an engagement with the world, a striving after values' whereas organization theory has more factual connotations, and is less value-involved (*ibid*. 217, 218). Of course, organization theory does not escape, much less resolve, any of the value problems attaching to administrative action, but it does suggest the possibility of theory, of models, and conceptual aids-to-navigation which might invest administration with a special competence, a competence not immediately accessible to any man in the street or any member in the organization and one, moreover, which is 'science'-based and intellectually respectable.

What are the dimensions and viability of this claim? Is it possible to discern more sharply the logic of administration by directing our attention to the study of organizations? We shall explore the answer to the first question in this chapter. As for the second question, Waldo, from the perspective of political science, suggested *not*. Referring to the fable of the blind men describing an elephant, he said: 'In view of the inclusiveness, the diversity, the amorphousness of the materials put under the Organization Theory heading nowadays, one must conclude that, if they all concern the same elephant, it is a *very* large elephant with a generalized elephantiasis' (*ibid*. 216). Organizational theorists themselves would have to concur. Haas and Drabek, for example, distinguish no fewer than eight 'perspectives' upon the plethora of concepts, hypotheses, and data representative of organizational thinking and research: rational, classical, human relations, natural systems, conflict, exchange, technological, and open systems perspectives (1973, 23–93). Each of these perspectives can be characterized by a theoretical model, and each can serve to structure the researcher's perceptions and his selection of variables for study. And each 'explanation' reflects its own *Weltanschauung*. Yet none, according to the authors, can serve as an entirely adequate or discrete theoretical base (*ibid*.). In another standard text Hall discriminates between management, economics, and structuralist theories under a closed system perspective and group, individual, technological, and power theorists under an open system perspective (1972, 35). Again, however, there is the conclusion that the understanding of organizations is not yet sufficient to allow people in them 'to realize their own desires, to allow the organization to achieve its goals, nor to allow organizations to accomplish all they could for society' (38). La Porte talks of the 'babble' of the literature and commiserates with the 'student in search of a coherent field tempted to flee from the endless vistas of semantic variation and seeming infinity of concepts' (Marini, 1971, 26).

It would be an impossible task to recapitulate or even to survey the assemblage of findings, studies, and theoretical speculata which could be treated under this large rubric. What we shall try to do instead is consider briefly certain selected topics of organization theory which together may contribute to a firmer grasp of the underlying logic of administrative behaviour. If the subject matter of science is restricted to factual (and empirically verifiable) sentences then it follows that we shall also be concerned with the boundaries at which a science of organization could be expected to terminate.

The relationship between social science and administration has been a productive one. Public administration certainly, and private administration almost as surely, have benefited from the sociological insights of Max Weber and his theory of bureaucratic structures (1947). Theories of complex organizations by Parsons (1951), March and Simon (1958), Etzioni (1961), Blau and Scott (1962) and others have at the very least provided analyses of organizational logic, diagnoses of a variety of organizational dysfunctions, and conceptual models or interpretive systems which have enhanced the knowledge base for administrative competence. Of course, not every administrator will be *au fait* with the full range of these findings, but nevertheless there is a pattern to professionalization which does tend to unite in a sort of symbiosis the study arm and the practitioner arm of the given profession. There is a given and take of information and few executives of experience and rank will not have made some acquaintance with organization theory. Many indeed will be quite familiar with the jargon of one or more of the social sciences, and many will be familiar with several of the conceptual perspectives referred to above.

Another fruitful outcome of the interest in human organizations has been the development of general systems theory, a movement having its origins in biology (von Bertalanffy, 1950) and reaching all the way to synthetic philosophy (Laszlo, 1972). The systems approach to organizational thinking provides a framework for interdisciplinary contributions. The analogues from biology may occasionally be overdrawn and the definition of human organization may become blurred, shading off at one end into the macrosystem known to sociology as an institution and at the other end into the microsystem of the 'primary group'; but despite difficulties of boundary definition, the conception of open systems of energy and information flow has undoubtedly stimulated a direct intellectual interest in the phenomena of organizations and an indirect interest in the phenomenon of administration. Barnard, as already suggested, was a systems thinker in advance of his time.

Systems theory does extend beyond organizational concerns,

however, and it can easily become a philosophy or a way of looking at life (Allport, 1960; Boulding, 1956; Etzioni, 1968; Laszlo, 1972; de Chardin, 1959). Even when confined to the organizational domain, a domain which is itself circumscribed and constrained by the metavalues of efficiency and effectiveness, it can, value-free protestations to the contrary, be used in support of ideological positions. Thus there is some consensus in social psychology, and empirically supportive data, for organizational practices which can be considered democratic or participatory (Likert, 1961; Katz and Kahn, 1966, 470; Wiener, 1954). Again, organization theory if not system theory *per se* has been used to support, for example, a Judeo-Christian ethic (Golembiewski, 1965) and a 'human resources' model (Miles, 1975; Leavitt, 1972).

Organizations have been variously defined or left undefined (Waldo, 1961). Thus Simon has,

> Human organizations are systems of interdependent activity, encompassing at least several primary groups and usually characterized, at the level of consciousness of participants, by a high degree of rational direction of behaviour towards ends that are objects of common acknowledgement and expectation (Simon, 1954, 157).

As is typical of Simon, the emphasis is on the rational character of organizations. Bakke (1960, 37) is more elaborate:

> A social organization is a continuing system of differentiated and coordinated human activities utilizing, transforming, and welding together a specific set of human, material, capital, ideational, and natural resources into a unique problem-solving whole engaged in satisfying particular human needs in interaction with other systems of human activities and resources in its environment.

Here, organizations are problem-solving units and the *systems* emphasis is clear. Argyris, more succinctly, says, 'organizations are grand strategies individuals create to achieve objectives that require the effort of many' (1960, 24). Here one can detect a phenomenological bent, that is, a view of human organization which sees them finally as constructs of human experience grounded in the subjective life of *individuals*.

For our own purposes human organizations can be understood as systemic entities existing within a determining environment and having at least two human members. By systemic entity is meant a discernible integrity of structure associated with purpose, even though the shape, articulation, and locus of such purpose may be obscure, unconscious, or even deliberately hidden. It is to be noted that at least two members are a precondition of organization and hence there is by definition a presupposition of a social structure and a hierarchy. It is to be noted also that it is the coexistence of collective and individual purposes that create the fundamental organizational dynamic or tension. Even at the purely collective level organizational goals can be themselves in dynamic or dialectical conflict, and such conflict may be a conscious or unconscious dynamic in the administrator's field.

The purposeful aspect of organizations can be categorized in several ways. Perrow gives a fourfold classification:

(1) Output goals (goods and service),
(2) System goals (maintenance and growth),
(3) Product goals (having to do with quality, quantity, and demand for goods and services),
(4) Derived goals (e.g. Political aims, investment, employee development) (1970, 135).

Although the definition of human organization is not agreed upon by theorists—Simon is content to consider it 'as a level of human grouping somewhere above the primary group (the small face-to-face work or family grouping that is the basic unit of the 'human relations' schools) and somewhere below the entity he calls 'an institution'—of which examples might be 'the steel industry', 'the retail trade', 'public administration' '. (Dunsire, 1973, 112–13)—there is a consensus about the pre-eminence of purposive action in organizational behaviour; organizations have a purposive character. If, therefore, organization theory were to lead towards an organizational philosophy, or conversely, it would be from the impetus of this fact or this aspect of organizational logic.

ORGANIZATIONAL STRUCTURE

Membership in organizations dictates some form of *social structure*, that is, some form of status differentiation. What is less clear from the standpoint of logic, but overwhelmingly true as empirical fact—both across time and across cultures—is that it seems to dictate some form of what is conventionally known as line and staff. Exotic exceptions notwithstanding,[5] power and authority[6] are normally conceived as flowing *along a line* from the philosophical core of the organizational field to the action levels at the organizational periphery. This flow, and its associated line of flow, implicates a principle of hierarchy, an order or ordering which must be grounded ultimately in the organizational purpose. This in turn generates and is manifested by a system of subordinate-superordinate-coordinate relationships among organizational members. It is the special prerogative of administration to define, clarify, defend, extend, and embellish this arrangement. Organizational status and reward systems tend to isomorphic symmetry with the line of command, and this is considered in the conventional widom to be functional and beneficent (Barnard, 1946, 46). In consequence, every administrator and manager knows what is meant by line and, with some degree of nicety, his position in the line. Contemporary theorists acknowledge this principle and tend to find its clearest expression in the rational formal theories of bureaucracy of Max Weber:

Every empirical study and most theoretical summaries explicitly or implicitly rest on Weberian concepts of formal organization. Even Katz and Kahn's *Social Psychology of Organizations*, which is clearly the magnum opus of this decade, is tied to these ideas. The Weberian base is not immediately apparent in this case because the authors begin their treatise with a comprehensive survey of systems and role theory which leads one to believe that their formulation will be markedly different. However, it is not. The hierarchical pattern of bureaucracy which underlies their analysis is revealed in their conceptualization of leadership. In their framework, the introduction of structural change to achieve organizational goals is initiated at the apex of the role system; the middle leadership level is concerned with elaborating and adapting a given structure to achieve given goals (interpolation); and finally, the bottom of the leadership system is concerned with the use of the given structure. There are a number of empirical studies which explicitly utilize the Weberian model and demonstrate that organizational reality seldom correlates very closely with the parameters of the 'model.' Typically, the deviations from the 'pure' consequences of this arrangement are explored and conceptualized, but the basic paradigm is not fundamentally questioned. (Marini, 1971, 144).

Collateral to the line are organizational members whose functions are in the classic theory ancillary and supportive to the line personnel. In decision processes staff can advise but not command as, say, the College of Cardinals can advise a Pope but not subvene to instruct a bishop in the line which consists of pope-bishop-priest. But the concept of staff lacks the lucidity of the concept of line. Empirical observation would suggest that staff personnel either fluctuate in their role definition by moving into and out of the line or else they exercise a line authority which is *de facto* if not *de jure* (Thompson, 1961; Dalton, 1950, 342). This problem need not defy resolution. If the logic were accepted that organizations were purposive collectivities with a 'line' from philosophy (purpose) to action (organizational work) then it could be allowed that all members were somehow in this line. Such a suggestion would, however, raise difficult questions about the organizational reward system and, in fact, the logic is not generally accepted. Conventional wisdom persists in retaining the line-staff distinction with all its attendant concerns about span of control and the organization of work (Ouchi and Dowling, 1974; Blau and Schoenherr, 1970).

Staff and line structure create the conceptual pyramid which, we would submit, is now so deeply ingrained in administrative consciousness as to constitute an archetype. Pyramidal structure follows from related consequents of line and staff logic such as specialization and division of labour. Nevertheless, iconoclastic attempts at alternative structural arrangements have been made from time to time. Figure 2, drawing on the work of Likert and Miles, shows alternatives such as the linking-pin structure A, B, C; the project team D; and the collegial model E. It will be observed by simple inspection, however, that a line persists in each case (shown by illustrative dotted lines in the diagram) and that no member is simultaneously a member of more than two primary groups. It is also significant that, with the exception of the collegiate model E, the apex of the line is always divorced from the 'action levels' and can only communicate through managerial or supervisory intermediaries. Again, Figure 3, from Golembiewski, shows two methods of organizing work, neither of which seems to displace (though the unorthodox attempts to modify) the essential structural logic of line and staff, that is, of hierarchy and flow of organizational decision processes. Our point here is not to argue the relative merits of these arrangements—that has been cogently accomplished by the several authors involved—but to show the persistence and perdurance of underlying structure. This depth structure makes it difficult to find anything new under the sun in organizational arrangement, and doubtless goes to support the pyramidal archetype so fundamental to administrative attitudes.

Figure 2: Variants on the Line-Staff Theme

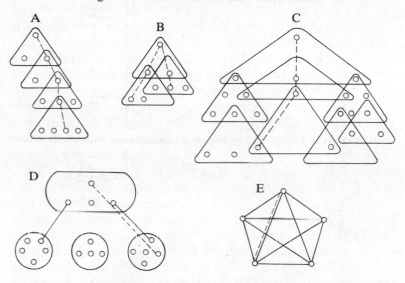

The conservative character of this structuralism does not at all imply that organizations have a static essence; on the contrary they are essentially compositions in goal-directed flux, essays in goal-achievement strategy. The other face of structure is function, the dynamic aspect of the arrangement of roles which are the constituents of structure. And structure returns us again to the element of purpose. Any organizational structure must in the last analysis be functional with respect to purpose. It is dynamic entity persisting over time. It must structure not simply its roles but its decisional procedures, and it has been suggested that the minima can be set at procedures for: (1) selecting leadership (administration), (2) structuring roles (job definitions), (3) setting goals (policy), (4) achieving goals (operations). (Morphet *et al.*, 1967, 88). This adumbrates

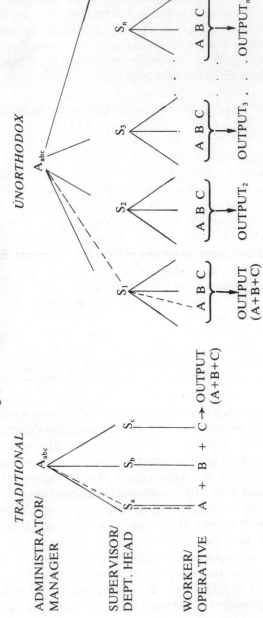

Figure 3: Alternative Production Structures

our original reduction of administration to a reflective complex of purposes, technologies, and men.

A number of serious attempts have been made to classify the genus organization by species, to deduce a typology or taxonomy of organizations, and these endeavours are important to our thesis, for the existence of discrete subsets of organization might militate against the possibility of a philosophy of administration grounded upon some commonality of organizational structure and function. A popular taxonomy is that of Blau and Scott (1962). They classify organizations as (a) *mutual benefit associations* (unions, churches), (b) *business concerns* (manufacturing firms, banks), (c) *service organizations* (hospitals, schools), (d) *commonweal organizations* (army, police).

The Blau and Scott taxonomy is clearly valuational in the sense that it is based on the notion of *cui bono*. That is to say, one of the ways in which organizations can be typified is by the nature and distribution of the rewards they produce. In other words, they can be typed by purpose and by beneficiary. Etzioni, from the sociological perspective, has typed organizations about the compliance-structure variable. Thus, organizations may be coercive, remunerative, or normative in their compliance structure while individual members respond in calculative, moral, or alienative ways—a school might be coercive-alienative, while a church is normative-moral (1961). Again the classification is clearly valuational.

Taking a social systems approach, Katz and Kahn again develop a four-way classification of organizations into (a) *productive* (b) *maintenance*, (c) *adaptive*, (d) *managerial-political* (1966, 112). Productive or economic organizations provide goods and services to society; maintenance organizations (schools, churches, political parties) maintain and support society by way of the latter's ideology and belief systems; adaptive organizations (hospitals, research units) solve social problems and provide society with new knowledge; and managerial-political organizations coordinate and adjudicate between competing social groups (e.g. labour unions and state bureaucracies) (147). Here the *cui bono* logic persists, but the overall recipient of benefit is taken to be society at large. Society is the synthesis within which the dialectic of organizations competing for their several advantage is worked out. The state, as representative of the social synthesis, retains the function of ultimate organizational arbiter.

Katz and Kahn also deduce a 'second order' set of classifying marks. These differentiate organizations on the basis of their end products—whether these have to do with persons or objects (e.g. schools vs. factories)—on the basis of the *kind* of organizational reward—whether this be expressive and intrinsic (terminal values) or extraneous and extrinsic (instrumental values); on the basis of whether the organization has a high or a low degree of bureaucratization; and on the basis of whether the organization tends towards stability or towards growth (*ibid*. 148).

It can be seen that organizations can be typologized in a wide variety of ways: first by genus, at which level of analysis the distinction blurs between organizations and institutions. Society, with its symbolic processes vested in the state, becomes the ultimate determiner of the organizational and administrative fields of action. Secondly, organizations vary by species and, while the choice of classification may be arbitrary or dialectical, there would appear to be some tendency amongst theoretical authorities to classify on bases which are related to interest or value. There would also seem to be nothing in these conventional taxonomies to deny Litchfield's major proposition of a commonality of administrative process across the variety of organizational forms. And finally, of course, organizations can be classified as individuals. In that each organization is its own unique phenomenological entity, bearing conditions which apply to it and it alone, and hence defining administrative action in that instance in the sharpest possible way.

There remains, however, one further subdivision which is internal or domestic and which has commanded much attention in organization theory, that is, the idea of formal and informal organizations. Each of the former is said to possess one or more of the latter. Barnard himself was the first great exponent of the informal organization (1972, 114–123). It has since become a near article of faith for administrators to 'know the informal organization'. The issue is still lively enough for Etzioni to label the work of March and Simon as classical (a term which tends to be dyslogistic as against the eulogistic 'modern') because of their prepossession with the formal organization, rational behaviour, and the 'search for the organizational tool most suited to serve a given set of goals, and not the organizational tool that keeps its participants most happy' (Etzioni, 1964, 31). Nevertheless, it seems fair to say that the relationship between informal and formal organization as affected by shifts in organizational type is at this stage of the development of theory not fully understood. What is understood is that the pattern of informal relationships within an organization, however construed, is of importance to the administrator on a variety of counts, especially under those heads variously described as organizational climate, morale, leadership, and communication. This domestic polity, and the polity extending amongst and between the organizational types, all share one quality, the factor of reward, interest, value. Organizations can be logically, typed but the logic itself will be valuational in base. Since there is nothing within the theory of organizational types to preclude a synthetic philosophy we can progress from the comparative anatomy of organizations to anatomy proper.

ORGANIZATIONAL BIOLOGY

The temptation to analogize between organizations and organisms is of long standing. And many the observer who has succumbed. Taking it at the largest possible level of analysis de Chardin talks of a 'biosphere' (1959) and, descending a note in the scale, Spencer has defended the organic analogy for society as a whole. Thus,

> . . . cells of an organism correspond to individuals in a society, tissues to simpler voluntary groups, organs to the more complex organizations. Economic, juridical, and political activities parallel the physiological, morphological, and unitary aspects of an organism. Merchandise in transition is tantamount to unassimilated food. Conquering races are male, the conquered are female; their struggle matches the struggle of spermatozoa around the ovum. (1910, 430 ff.)

Selznick, though distinguishing organizations from institutions, describes the latter as 'responsive, adaptive organisms' (1957, 5) and Michels (1915) and Parsons (1951) talk throughout of the organizational 'natural whole' as a living, responsive organism. The idea of organizations as systems with needs existing within environments and making adaptive changes for survival is well-entrenched, and could be traced as far back as Plato.

The contemporary version of this persistent analogue tends to be more abstract, more mechanical, more mathematicized. It is most simply expressed in the basic or core notions of general systems theory, a theoretical system for inter-disciplinary synthesis which itself originated in the maternal disciple of biology (von Bertalanffy, 1968). Figure 4 presents the essential elements. The form of a general system consists of an energic input, throughput, and output

Figure 4: A Cybernetic System

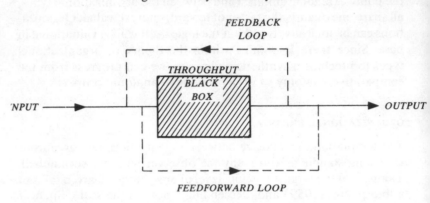

which is self-directing according to its targetting and feedback mechanisms. The conceptual system also provides the logical economy of a 'black box', since under many circumstances it may be unnecessary or impossible to know what actually goes on *inside* a system. It is enough to discern outputs, inputs, and their inferrable relations. Such a system as Fig. 4 is *open* in that it exchanges energy and information with its environment. And it is governed by the physical laws of thermodynamics. The first of these, that matter can neither be created nor destroyed, sets a limit to the quantum of energy in the universe. The second declares the tendency for energy systems to move, *ceteris paribus*, from states of order or complexity to states of disorder or randomness. To the extent that organisms, and organizations, confound this natural trend to disorder, chaos, and homogeneity, they exhibit the systems property of negentropy (negative entropy). A further postulate, this time of information theory, is that the degree of entropy contained in any system or organization stands in exactly inverse proportion to the quantity of information held there in (Shannon and Weaver, 1949).

Other characteristics of systems have been identified such as homeostasis, differentiation, and equifinality, all of which have clear biological analogues. Also, open systems are in constant commerce with their environment. This means that every system can be conceptualized as being a subsystem of a supersystem and being itself in turn a supersystem for its own subsystems. Carried to its logical extremities, this gives us a Chinese-box vision of the universe, one terminus of which is the closed energy system of the macrocosm and the other a terminus lost somewhere in the limits of subatomic infinity.

Let us return to the problem of biological isomorphism. Organizations may carry the analogy with organisms only so far. Though both are purposive entities they are not purposive in the same way or sense. An organization can have neither 'consciousness' nor 'will'. These can only be properties of its individual members. The implications of this distinction for administrative philosophy are crucial, for it bears heavily on problems of organizational morality and responsibility. Let us note that the forms of organization and organism differ. Katz and Kahn point out that

> . . . the basic systemic processes are energic and involve the flow, trans-formation, and exchange of energy. Human organizations have unique properties, however, which distinguish them from other categories of open systems. Perhaps the most basic of these unique properties is the absence of structure in the usual sense of the term—an identifiable, enduring, physical anatomy which is observable at rest as in motion and which in motion generates and performs those activities which comprise the systemic function. The human organization lacks structure in this anatomical sense; its land and buildings are trappings; its members come and go. Yet it has structure; it is not a formless aggregate of interacting individuals engaged in the creation of some random combination of events (453, 454).

In other words, a human organization is protean but has logical form, as a river exists by virtue of its banks, or a human being persists by virtue of the mystery of ego or 'I-ness', though in the former case one can never 'step into the same river twice' and in the latter case we are to believe that all of our cells are constantly dying or being replaced. A contemporary critic of the biologic fallacy puts it this way:

> . . . In systems theory, the prevailing image of the organization is that of an organism. Organizations exist; they are observable entities which have a life of their own. Organizations are like people although sometimes the image is more that of the recalcitrant child, rather than the mature adult. In any case, the theory endows organizations with many human properties. They have goals towards which they direct their activities; they respond and adapt to their environments. Nor can organizations escape the fate of organisms illadapted to their environments. Indeed, the fate of organizations depends upon their ability to adapt to an increasingly complex and turbulent environment. Following the Darwinian logic inherent in their image of the organization, systems theorists (Bennis, 1968) see small, quick-witted, democratic organizations replacing the ponderous, bureaucratic forms now expiring around us. The fact that bureaucratic organizations appear as large, robust, and formidable as ever does not appear to shake belief in organizations as living entities subject to stringent laws permitting only the fittest to survive. . . (Greenfield, 1974, 4)

A division opens up, then, in organization theory between those who would subscribe to a social science orientation and those leaning more towards a humanistic, phenomenological approach. The argument tends to hinge about the nature of social reality, the former group seeking scientific explanation, rational order, quantitative analysis while the latter tends to an emphasis on the individual, dialectical order, qualitative linguistic analysis. The dimensions of this debate are most sharply set out in Greenfield, 1975, a paper generating much instructive controversy. The author interprets the root philosophical distinction as being between realism and idealism with the 'scientific' school falling into the realist camp. From the standpoint of the present work, however, the dichotomy between realism and idealism is inadequate and could be misleading. It is sufficient to note that the dialectic of argument is between schools of thought (systems views) which incline towards treating organizations as real entities possessing a sort of 'life of their own' and contending schools (phenomenology) which lean to a view of organizations as social inventions, artifacts of a *cultural* nature created by their membership constituency. The party of the first part (Parsons, 1937; Parsons and Shils, 1962) with its emphasis on collectivity, runs the risk of committing the organismic fallacy, while the party of the second part (Greenfield, 1975; Filmer *et al*., 1972), with a corresponding emphasis on the individual, runs the risk of overlooking the possibilities inherent in the idea of organizational Gestalt. The organization is more than the sum of its parts; it has relative immortality in that it transcends the entries and exits of its members, and it has a quasi-personality or character to the extent that its symbolic life institutionalizes values and serves as a carrier of values across shifts in membership. Thus, in a sense the Christian Church can be properly analogized to a 'Mystical Body of Christ' quite as more mundane human organizations can become part of a 'body politic'. Organizations can indeed be logically analysed as is done in systems theory, but I shall argue throughout that it is the investing of this logical framework with a valuational 'life of its own' which is the special aegis of the administrator. That an organization does not 'die' when its administration is replaced means that the incoming administration have been able to direct not merely the logical system of energy, information, and decision flow but also, and more importantly, the valuational and interest complex which provides the true *raison d'etre* of the organization.[7]

It remains to be said that for an emergent profession, seeking rational, scientific, and intellectual bases, systems theory, with its range of suggestive metaphor, its foundations in biology and mathematics, and its capacity for permitting the transduction and translation of multidisciplinary jargon, is bound to prove attractive, even seductive.

ORGANIZATIONS AND HUMAN MOTIVATION

A criticism of the structuralist approach as well as the systems perspective has been that the individual and his motivations are inadequately considered. Nevertheless, there has now accumulated a voluminous literature of theory and research about the problem of work motivation (Steers and Porter, 1975; Vroom, 1964; Herzberg, 1968; Maslow, 1965 *inter alia*). Given the plethora of extant knowledge and supposition one might feel constrained against adding further to the 'babble of the literature'. The models presented below, however, are intended to be illustrative and typical of the present understanding—an attempt to show the consistency of pattern or syndrome across different levels analysis. Figure 5 shows the basic syndrome. An organization member represented by the dotted circle has his unique ego and value complex which is directed laterally towards seeking goals, incentives, or aspirations provided by the organizational reward system—pay, promotion, tenure. To achieve these goals he expends effort in the form of work to overcome impediments of various kinds as specified in the mid-part of the diagram. His commitment to these goals (C) will be a function of p (the probability of his attaining them) and v (his personal evaluation of them).

Logically, goals are either attained or the attainment of them is frustrated. If attained, the condition is termed success; the member finds a pleasureable release of tension, and is reinforced in his goal-seeking behaviour. His value-motivational complex is fortified.

If, on the other hand, the goals are not attained after due passage of time and expenditure of effort—if the promotion, for example, is not forthcoming, then there is the experience of failure and an arrival at the decision-point P_1. P_1 presents three alternatives: (1) exit or departure from the organization if this be feasible, (2) a renewed attempt at reaching the goal or a change in goal percept; perhaps a simple abandonment of the goal, (3) the various forms of behaviour classified in the bottom-most box in Figure 5 aggression . . . sabotage. Options (2) and (3) retain the member within the organization and have been arbitrarily labelled + positive and − negative, respectively. Each affects the value complex and, hence, the work-effort. Time, t_1, elapses in the repetitions of this cyclical pattern.

The same motivational logic applied at this micro level of analysis can be expanded to a medial level of analysis for group behaviour in organizations (Figure 6). Here the value complex is characteristic of a group rather than an individual and the group expends its effort through modes of organizational structure, task, and technology to reach organizational goals and group incentives. The commitment (C) to these goals is now a partial function of the metavalues of

Figure 5: Individual Value Behaviour Within Organizations
(*Micro-Analysis*)

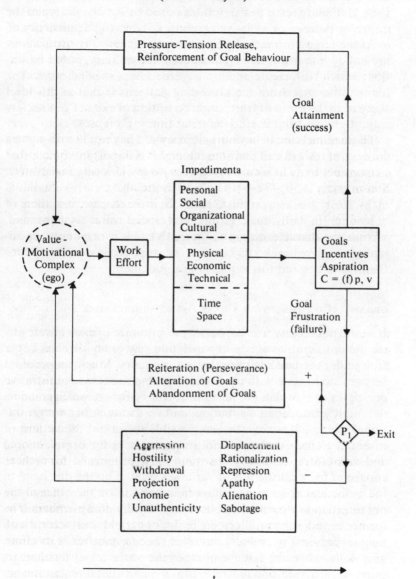

maintenance and growth (M_1, M_2, and see below, Chap. 11). Success is reinforced as before and further entrenches the metavalues (M_{1-4}). Failure leads to the options posed by P_2: dissolution of the group or positive or negative responses. Time (t_2) again elapses.

At the largest or macro level of analysis (Figure 7) organizations are linked into institutions (Commerce, the military, public education) which both create and are governed by a societal ethos. The major difference from the preceding patterns is that at this level there is, in the event of frustration, no option of exit at P_3. A society cannot escape from itself. Historical time, t_3, elapses.

These models are behaviouristic in style. They rest heavily upon a concept of reward and punishment, and it is important to note that persons act so as to secure rewards *or* to avoid losing rewards (cf. Simon *et al.*, 1950, 472–3). The models are also clearly valuational in at least two senses: first, there is in each case initiation of behaviour in individual, group, and social value systems and, second, the characterization of alternative failure responses as positive or negative implies that one sort of response is somehow better than the other and this is pure value judgment.

ORGANIZATION THEORY AS A BASE FOR ADMINISTRATIVE PHILOSOPHY

It would not be easy to encapsulate or epitomize or even to categorize the proliferation of labour which one way or another has borne fruit under the heading of organization theory. Much less would it be possible to state with precision just what are the administrative principles or postulates of an administrative theory which could be definitely grounded in the findings and verifications of an organizational science. It is nevertheless possible to set out the pattern of essential elements which establish parameters for organizational and administrative theory. In their most primordial form these consist of the dualistic sets of variables related on the one hand to the individual as an organization member and on the other to the organization as a purposive collectivity of individual members. The former includes the proliferating realm of variables associated with human personality, values, attitudes, needs, motives, capacities, and skills, while the latter embraces the variables of technology, purpose, structure, and function. Linking and attempting to synthesize these two sets is a third set of administrative variables, critical

Figure 6: Group Value Behaviour Within Organizations
(Medial-Analysis)

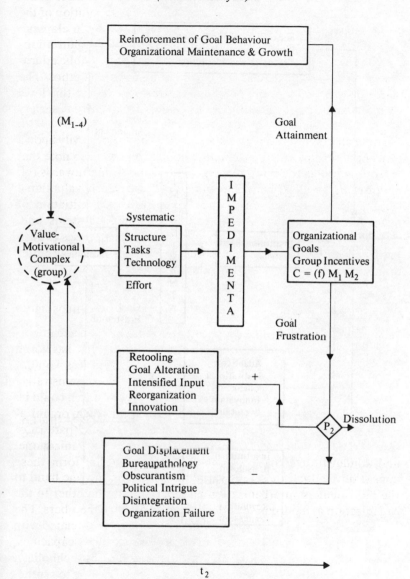

Logic

Figure 7: Organizational Value Behaviour Within Society
(*Macro-Analysis*)

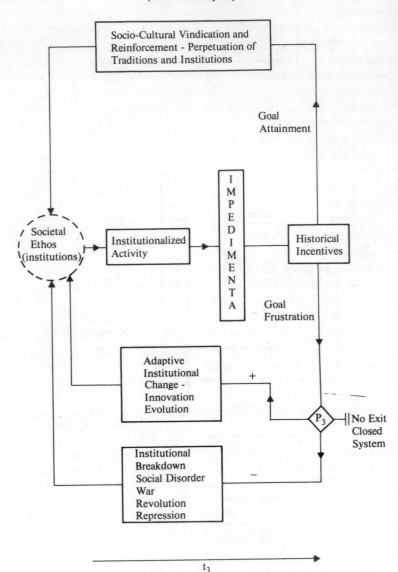

components of which are: the *effective* philosophy of administration, the level of administrative expertise, the resource flow, and the potency of metavalues. We have then a triad of clusters of variables representing respectively the membership, the collectivity, and the administration. Each cluster has been and is the source of empirical scrutiny. It cannot be said, however, that clearly incontestable general principles have yet emerged from the effort. Even such pseudo-laws of administration as 'organizational effectiveness is enhanced by having a single executive head' or 'organizational effectiveness is enhanced by delegation of authority' or 'organizations with a high division of labour will be more efficient than those with a low division of labour' are subject to contention (Miller, 1965, 403; March and Simon, 1958, 41–42; Haas and Drabek, 1973, 29 ff.). On the other hand, the subscription to 'science' and the 'scientific method' characterizing so much of this study has led to a devaluation of values in the sense of any form of ethical prescription for the administrative field of competence.

At other levels of analysis contention enters the realm of ideology, that is, of large-scale complexes and patterns of beliefs, attitudes, and values which cannot find any positivistic foothold within the limits of logic and rationality set by scientific method and empiricism. Thus there is the debate between the proponents of the monocratic-bureaucratic theory of organizational structure and the advocates of democratic-collegial counter-models. Max Weber is the grand exponent of the former position. The flavour of his polemic can be gleaned from the following quotation, and the strength of his argument can be gauged from the historical evidence of the persistence and growth of the bureaucratic form:

> Bureaucracy develops the more perfectly the more completely it succeeds in eliminating from official business love, hatred, and all purely personal, irrational, and emotional elements which escape calculation. The essence of bureaucratic arrangements is rationality. A spirit of formalistic impersonality is necessary to separate organizational rights and duties from the private lives of employees. Only by performing impersonally can officials assure rationality in decision making, and only thus can they assure equitable treatment for all subordinates. (Abbott and Lovell, 1965, 42–3)
> . . .
> Experience tends universally to show that the purely bureaucratic type of

administrative organization-that is, the monocratic variety of bureaucracy-is, from a purely technical point of view, capable of attaining the highest degree of efficiency and is in this sense formally the most rational known means of carrying out imperative control over human beings. It is superior to any other form in precision, in stability, in the stringency of its discipline, and in its reliability. It thus makes possible a particularly high degree of calculability of results for the heads of the organization and for those acting in relation to it. It is finally superior both in intensive efficiency and in the scope of its operation, and is formally capable of application to all kinds of administrative tasks. (Weber, 1947, 337).

The lists against Weber have been entered by many modern proponents of innovation, notably by Thompson (1961, 1965). We should note that a debate in organizational theory such as this must seek its resolution on grounds which are essentially valuational and extra-empirical. The resolution thus becomes philosophical in that it is dependent on value analysis and value bases. At the same time as it raises issues, organization theory is also a contributor to administrative philosophy along the logical dimension, to the extent that it makes factual discoveries and tests hypotheses against objective realities. It is in this way that the factual base for administrative philosophizing is extended. Clearly the study of human, and perhaps non-human, organizations is important to the manager, the executive, the administrator. To the extent that it is scientific by way of exploration of empirical data, and logical by way of conceptual manipulations, this activity provides a ground for administrative philosophy, and to the extent that organization theory is prescriptive, administrative philosophy must provide a ground for it.

In the end perhaps we can agree upon at least one thing, and that is that if there is to be any kind of coherent administrative philosophy it must take into account all the schools of opinion generated by organization theory and all of its empirical findings. That a literature of such a philosophy is yet hardly to be discerned is indeed a curious fact when one considers that the literatures of organizational sociology, social psychology, psychology, and systems theory flourish and proliferate in contrast. Science itself has a philosophy of science which is to science as, say, formal logic is to mathematics, but a corresponding philosophy of administration rooted in organization theory has yet to emerge. The disparity in this parallel has one obvious explanation; though the discourse of science and mathematics may be recondite and abstruse the underlying paradigms are simple and value-free. By contrast, administration and its field of exercise in human organizations constitutes a complexification which is to some extent irreducible, and, while its discourse may be simplified to the point of common property in the crystallizations of ordinary language, its underlying content is never value-free but always *more than objective*. This subjectivity enters organizational theorizing at a number of places, most notably in the discussion of organizational purposes and human motivation. It imparts to organizational theory a dualism which extends beyond structure and function, formal and informal, nomothetic and idiographic to the fundamental primordial split between value and fact, between what *is* and what *ought* to be.

3
Decision Making

The search for a knowledge base in organization theory which could serve to fund an administrative *profession* has proven to be, if not entirely elusive, then still falling short of any rigorous scientific ideal. The field would appear to be in some state of variously ordered disarray—polymorphous if not perverse. Administrators may nevertheless see in its study one pillar in an edifice of specialist professional competencies. Another pillar in that edifice would be the specialist competence of decision making.

The proper reference of organization theory is to the *field* of action within which administration is practised. Within this field in turn there exists a widespread, persistent consensus that there is a specifically administrative act—indeed, one which constitutes the pivotal function in administrative behaviour—and this is the act of decision making. The basic position was expounded by Litchfield in the first issue of *Administrative Science Quarterly*. In his article, "Notes on a General Theory of Administration' he analysed administrative action into a cycle of events which were initiated by decision making and then proceeded through programming, communicating, controlling, and reappraising back to decision making again. He also took care to stress that decision making could be 'rational, deliberative, discretionary, purposive' or 'irrational, habitual, obligatory, random', or 'any combination thereof'. Rational, that is, *logical*, decision making would follow a pattern which would include the steps: (1) Definition of issue, (2) Analysis of existing situation, (3) Calculation and delineation of alternatives, (4) Deliberation, and finally, (5) Choice. (*op. cit.*, 1956) It can be noted in passing that there are depths of ambiguity concealed even in this lucid exposition. How does one 'deliberate', for example? What is implicit in deliberation? And, in any event, is not the last step, choice, in some way redundant or at best recapitulative? For to choose *is* to decide and the act of decision making is that of deciding to choose among alternatives. Moreover, whether the choice is in some way *free* or in some way *dictated* plunges us at once into very muddy philosophical waters. The steps outlined by Litchfield are, however, still widely accepted and in high repute.

Another administrative theorist, Griffiths, writing a few years after Litchfield, continues the theme with some amplification but without contradiction:

(1) Administration is a generalized type of behavior to be found in all human organization.

(2) Administration is the process of directing and controlling life in a social organization.

(3) The specific function of administration is to develop and regulate the decision-making process in the most effective manner possible. (Griffiths, 1959, 91)

. . .

and, less axiomatically:

(1) The structure of an organization is determined by the nature of decision-making process. . .

. . .

(4) If the administrator confines his behavior to making decisions on the decision-making process rather than making terminal decisions for the organization, his behavior will be more acceptable to his subordinates. . .

(5) If the administrator perceives himself as the controller of the decision-making process, rather than the maker of the organization's decisions, the decision will be more effective. . . . (*ibid.*, 89–91)

He later sets out a model of the decision making process which is essentially identical with that of Litchfield's except that steps 3 and 4 (calculation and delineation of alternatives; deliberation) become more specific:

(3) Establish criteria or standards by which solution will be evaluated or judged as acceptable and adequate to the need; (4) Collect data (*ibid.*, 113).

The intrusion of value elements into the process is now definitely spelled out.

Of course, it can be said that decision making is a universal *Human* function in which all men are engaged at one time or another—perhaps even constantly. That such a function is not necessarily and intrinsically pleasureable may account by psychological displacement for some of the general animus towards administration expressed from time to time by the administered. But administrative decision making is distinctive in at least three ways. First, administrative decisions are made for and about other men and they are associated, as Barnard and Simon have shown, with degrees of freedom which have been *surrendered* by organization members (Barnard, 1972, 168–9; Simon, 1965, 12, 18). Second, these decisions have a special charge of *responsibility* or moral aspect to the extent that they relate to the organization, to the collectivity. Third, they are often second-order decisions or decisions-about-decisions insofar as they are concerned with the decision making process itself, within the organization. We can indeed conceive of organizations as patterns of decisional flow in which the critical or philosophical decisions having to do with organizational life and purposes are made by administrators and in which the subordinate technological *means* decisions having to do with organizational process are made by other organization members but are *designed* by administrators. It is almost beyond debate, then, that decision making is crucial to the administrative art. But do administrators possess any special expertise in this function which distinguishes them from their fellows in the organization? Again, is there a specialist body of knowledge, a component of science or technology which can prescribe in this domain? What is the logic of this critical process?

THE BASIC PARADIGM

Logically, decision making is a process whereby one arrives at a choice. It is the often quite agonizing business of making up one's mind, a task which Hamlet, for one, found quite intolerable. What is essential then for the process to commence is a choice point. This is a state of affairs wherein the decision maker faces alternative routes in the future flow of events. Though we call it a 'point', it represents an interval of time and is perhaps best envisioned spatially as a kind of crossroads. Within this interval a selection must be made between alternatives and one road followed to the exclusion of others. There must, therefore, be at least two alternatives. I would go further and argue that, finally, there must be *not more than* two alternatives. This must be so because it is logically impossible to choose between more than two things. What occurs when more than two alternatives are present in the choice situation is that binary options are successively and iteratively considered until, in the *final* analysis, the number of alternatives is reduced to two. It might appear on first face that one has options a, b, and c open but by the time of *taking* the decision either a or b or c will have been rejected so as to arrive at the final selection between ab, ac, or bc. Decision making becomes 'chattery' or 'dithering' only when rejected choices are inadvertently reintroduced into the process. Indeed, perhaps one might construe executive decision making as the fine art of sterilization and isolation of rejected options.

Complex decision situations can thus be analyzed in terms of an iterative binary comparison procedure which progressively narrows the field of choice. I do not, nor does anyone to my knowledge, claim that this complex process is properly understood at the psychological level and it is quite likely that conscious process is modified by unconscious intrusions. As J. F. Kennedy once remarked,

'The essence of ultimate decision remains impenetrable to the observer . . . often indeed, to the decider himself. . . There will always be the dark and tangled stretches of the decision making process—mysterious even to those most intimately involved' (1963).

Still, we need not resort either to political mysticism or to psychoanalytic obscurantism. If the business of decision were totally inscrutable, administrators might as well play dice with their universe and govern their organizations by means of tables of random numbers. In the practical world of organizational life, administrative decisions and choices have to be made continuously and at every organizational level, and logically each decision can be analyzed as an ultimate either-or, this-or-that, to be or not to be. This binary discrimination is entirely congruent with Aristotelian logic and modern science. A thing either is or it is not. Decisions are switches in the ramifying networks of possibility and even a decision *not* to decide is a decision, the binary alternative of which is the decision to decide. In the philosophy of administration there can be no escape from this ultimate dualism.

Faced with a choice, one is not of course compelled to react rationally. One may instead act on impulse, or toss a coin, or consult an astrologer. Or one may simply abdicate, by somehow leaving the decision to others but in this event the decision ceases to be a decision of the original decider in that the latter has decided to 'pass'. We may concede, however, that there is a presumption of rationality in the ordinary course of administrative behaviour and, on this presumption, the various models of decision making represent variants on the pattern set out below. This pattern or paradigm consists of the following sequence of steps.

(1) *Delineation of the ultimate binary alternative.*
'In the end it comes down to *this* or *this*'.
(2) *Assessment of the consequences of each alternative.*
This step can be subdivided as to fact and as to value. With regard to fact, the decision maker is constrained by the sources and extent of his information and knowledge as well as by his interpretation of information, the latter being a function of psychological factors, conscious and unconscious predispositions, as well as attributes of insight, competence, and experience. With regard to value this forms the preoccupation of most of this book, either directly or indirectly. It goes without saying that it is likewise a direct or indirect, tacit or explicit concern and preoccupation of the person having to make a decision.

Notwithstanding the enormous implicit difficulties the rational decider will attempt to determine the probabilities of selected outcomes (hereafter referred to as p's) and, in principle at least, assign to the alternative outcomes respective values (hereafter referred to as v's).
(3) *Calculation of expected values.*
With p's and v's assigned to outcomes the last phase of the decisional process becomes a matter of mere calculation since the quantified p's and v's can be multiplied to yield for any outcome an 'expected value'. The rational choice is then simply the highest expected value.

A simplified illustration should make this process plain. Consider an elemental administrative decision: To appoint or not to appoint a new member to the ranks of the organization. Let us assume that the information phase: collecting and studying curricula vitae, hearsay, interviews, gathering of impressions and opinions from colleagues, etc., has been exhausted. Let us further assume that the reduction of alternatives phase has reduced the selection process to a concentration upon one candidate.[1] It may then be assumed that if hired the new man would prove over times to be either adequate or inadequate in his role. Four logical outcomes then obtain: (0_1) *is engaged and proves to be adequate*, (0_2) *is engaged and proves to be inadequate*, (0_3) *is not engaged and would have proven to be adequate if engaged*, (0_4) *is not engaged and would not have proven to be adequate if engaged*. Suppose now that the administration is indifferent as between outcomes 0_1 and 0_4. The rationale for this assumption is that the whole point of the selection process is simply to avoid hiring failures and to hire successful personnel so these outcomes may be considered valuationally neutral as contrasted with 0_2 (hiring and failure) and 0_3 (failing to hire a success). Both 0_2 and 0_3 carry negative connotations since they could lead to organizational damage or detriment, especially if similar organizations were competing for similar personnel. Hence we ascribe tentative v's, say, -0.6 to 0_2 and -0.2 to 0_3, the range of v being from -1 for total negative evaluation, through 0 for evaluative indifference, to $+1$ for total positive evaluations.

We now make one last assumption to round out the illustration. This is that we are uncertain as to the likelihood of the candidate's proving adqequate or inadequate. Our statistical best estimate is therefore even chances of the one possibility or the other.[2] We now have the calculation matrix shown in Figure.[3]

Figure 8: Decisional Calculation

Outcome	p	v	$p \times v$
0_1	0.5	0	0
0_2	0.5	-0.6	-0.3
0_3	0.5	-0.2	-0.1
0_4	0.5	0	0

Expected Value $(0_1 + 0_2) = -0.3$
$(0_3 + 0_4) = -0.1$

The two expected values sum the respective possibilities for *hiring* $(0_1 + 0_2)$ and *not hiring* $(0_3 + 0_4)$. Since the highest expected value is for the latter combination, it follows that in this case, with these p's and v's, the rational decision is 'do not engage'. And in the practical situation it would be a case of 'back to the drawing board'. Obviously a different set of values could have been assigned to the variables in this calculus. The object here is merely to display the paradigm and its intrinsic reliance upon the essential factors of *analysis* (delineation of alternatives) and *imputation* (the ascription of p's and v's). Granted that the paradigm is immensely simplified—organizational context, socio-cultural, personal, and political elements constraining and affecting decision have, for example, been ignored—still it can be seen that the ultimate reduction, immediately prior to choice, is in the realms of probability and value. And it is further implied by the paradigm that, at least in principle, both of these elements can be quantified. That is, that essentially qualitative phenomena such as values are amenable to numerical representation. Thus the decision maker inhabits a world of uncertainty and value within which he struggles to analyze and impute.

It should be remarked that the omnipresent valuational component does not in itself admit the charge of irrationality. It is theoretically feasible to deduce rationally the value quantum from *a priori* sets of preferences such as those dictated by metavalues (see below) and organizational policy but the transformation from ordinal values (preferences) to cardinal values (decision v's) is by no means facile or understood even if feasible 'in principle'. We can note even here, however, that mere feasibility and rationality need not imply *justifiability*. And the question remains: Is the paradigm rational, logical, and amenable to science?

Writing at the beginning of the era of computerology and systems sophistication, Gore and Silander foresaw an imminent (it is now more immanent than imminent) management *science* in which both nonrationality and irrationality would be reduced to 'negligible factors' in decision making:

> One has the impression that there are those who look toward the time when numerical values, representing estimated outcomes, may be substituted for verbal symbols in a formula representing organizational goals, which would then be solved for a decision. Lest this seem incredible, it should be noted that it was done on a lathe operator's decisions long

ago by Frederick Taylor, and his expectations are becoming a reality through the application of today's more powerful tools to a manager's problems.

If it is accidental that the term management science is almost a simple reversal of scientific management, it is not without significance, for there is a sense in which the current scientific, rationalist movement is essentially scientific management with new, vastly more powerful tools. Where Taylor used algebra, arithmetic, engineering knowledge, and common sense, we find calculus, probability statistics, and the scientific method (Gore and Silander, 1959, 112).

Since those words were written nearly two very active decades have passed, and one can surely question whether much advance, if any, has been made on this particular front. Thus, for example, in a more recent work Thompson writes:

"The 'new science' has not spread greatly. In many places its promise has proved to be a false one, as, for example, in the use of Planning, Programming, Budgeting (PPB) as a device for achieving greater rationality in government decisions. PPB has been almost a total failure and has been dropped by state governments almost as fast as it was adopted after 1965 when President Lyndon Johnson ordered it installed throughout the federal government.' (1975, 95).

Scientific decision making continues to be elusive and chimerical.

MILITARY APPRECIATION

The basic paradigm is a logical reduction, but the essential form is implicit and concealed within all variants of the decisional process at whatever level of complexity. This can be shown in the example of military appreciation, a practical technique which involves elements of game theory (von Neumann and Morgenstern, 1947). The method, which can be employed within a variable time frame, can extend from a matter of minutes to a matter of months. It comprises the following steps.

First, the situation must be examined. By situation I mean the relevant context for action. The comprehensiveness of examination would of course depend upon the time, resources, and expertise available for the appreciation process. The situation is also to be examined with a specific intent, to determine any 'overriding factors'. These might be constraints such as time, weaponry on either side, fuel, logistics, morale, or political considerations. The isolation of overriding factors parallels Barnard's view of the decision process as 'opportunistic'.

'The ideal process of decision is to discriminate the strategic factors and to redefine or change purpose on the basis of the estimate of future results of action in the existing situation, in the light of history, experience, knowledge of the past' (209).

The technique of 'mixed scanning' as described by Etzioni (1976) and used in the Israeli army would also be appropriate for this step. Another example would be from space technology where spy or weather satellites have two cameras, one wide-angle covering large areas superficially and one scanning selected areas in greater detail, e.g. to detect hurricane cloud formations or missile installations. Implicit in the scanning process, of course, is a generalized aim (to win the game, battle, war, to solve the problem) which further implies an attitude or openness to the explorative possibilities and alternatives revealed in the primary appreciation or the generalized scanning process. Military appreciation cannot, however, be entirely speculative, entrepreneurial, or open-ended. It must be guided by strategic principles of selection. It must also be constrained by a higher level of specificity. Therefore:

The next step is to define the aim. The aim or 'object of the exercise' must be *simple, unequivocal*, and *singular*. Thus, 'Win the war!' is futile but 'Sink the Bismarck!' will do very nicely.

Third, the possible enemy courses of action must be explored and probabilities assigned, with a view to discovering the most likely enemy behaviour. This directly parallels the game of chess wherein the opponent's move must be carefully evaluated for future intent prior to proceeding with one's own plan or line of action. Poor chessplayers typically slur or elide this essential step of getting into the enemy's boots.

Fourth, it is now possible, in the light of the analysis resulting from the previous steps, to determine the options available to the decision maker. This, in effect, completes the analysis phase of the basic paradigm described in the preceding section.

Finally, these last alternatives are to be evaluated to determine one's own best course of action and a plan, i.e. the managerial side of the operation, drawn up. Once implemented, of course, and perhaps even if left unimplemented events would be altered, the dynamic context would change, and the need for further appreciations would revive.

I do not think I need to elaborate on the components of probability and value which permeate this process. Throughout, p's and v's are being guessed, figured, estimated, computed, intuited, and otherwise entered into the calculus. At all times rationality is assiduously sought, especially as there is a presumption identical to that of chess, whereby the most rational player is considered to be the one most likely to win.[8] Yet the difficulties and impediments to these analytic and imputational endeavours should be immediately obvious to the administrative mind.

Any non-machined, human decision involves p and v elements. Both p and v may be unstable and uncertain. In the case of machine-made or programmed decisions the machine or computer, or in some instances the human manager, can only *calculate* p's and v's. And certainly a machine cannot assign a p or v except by derivation from an already predetermined higher level p or v programme. Determination of programme or *policy*, like the true assignment of v's, is a prerogative reserved for human action and intention, it is a function of *consciousness*.

Simon is of the view that an individual can never possess enough knowledge of p or v ever to arrive at a truly rational decision. Only a 'closed system of variables' would permit approximation to a rational, objective, factual ideal (1957, 83). But even such an ideal, where decisions could be degraded to calculations, would presuppose a 'programme' of preferences or values which would derive from outside the system and would involve a logically different level of analysis.

CLOSED AND OPEN DECISIONS

The simplest classification of decision follows from the foregoing argument. Decisions can be thought of as primarily 'open' or 'closed'. The distinction rests on the degree of putative quantification and the feasibility or facility of such quantification. Closed decisions would approximate most nearly to the objective rational ideal. Operations Research, queueing theory, and linear programming provide instances in which the optimal solutions to decision problems can be obtained as with, say, airport and highway traffic control, crop rotation, inventory problems, and optimal bombing patterns. Such decisions are predominantly factual and managerial, values are 'given', goals are precise, alternatives are clearly identifiable, and outcomes are predictable. Moreover, it is possible to optimize or maximize the utilities or values which are given in the decision context and it is usually possible to employ sophisticated mathematical and computational techniques.[4] That such decision making is highly *rational* is attributable to the fact that it seeks a *best* solution. As Simon puts it,

'Roughly speaking, rationality is concerned with the selection of preferred behavior alternatives in terms of some system of values whereby the consequences of behavior can be evaluated'. (1957, 75)

Such a rough definition of rationality does of course imply at least another *level* of rationality, that which determines the 'some system of values', or else it implicitly sets a boundary to rationality itself, thereby casting the shadow of the irrational over the entire process.

In contrast, open decisions and open decision procedures are those which acknowledge the imponderability of the interaction effect between the decision maker and his environment. In the face of complexity and uncertainty the search for optimal solutions is yielded to adequate or 'satisficing' solutions, decisions which are pragmatically safe and in which the organizational cost benefit calculus is performed in some respects after the model of the punter or entrepreneurial risk-taker.

I would like to argue that the open model is the more typical of administrative decision making, and this is so because of the *a priori* limits to rationality. These include the following elements which by no means exhaust the specification: subjective and personal factors related to the decision maker or decision making group, historical factors in the form of organizational sunk costs and binding previous commitments, policy constraints and organizational decision rules, information communication and perception factors which may distort objective reality, unidentified consequences and unimagined alternatives (especially the latter), skills and competencies of the decision maker, elements of will and volition which are difficult to classify under either rational-cognitive or irrational-emotive psychological rubrics (See Chapter 6 *ff.*). Philosophically one could go even further and argue that only the open decisions are true decisions, on the grounds that in closed decision making all the essential *decisional* elements in the form of decision rules and values determination have already been established *prior* to the process. Thus, closed decisions would in fact be pseudo-decisions or calculations.

The point is essentially this. The intrusion of values into the decision making process is not merely inevitable, it is the very substance of decision. There is, however, yet another inevitability in the decision process and that is the presence of factual uncertainty, since the future states of affairs with which open decisions deal are always to some degree imponderable (otherwise there would be no scope for decision making at all!) We have indicated these twin inevitabilities by the symbols p and v. To the extent that p's and v's can be confidently specified, to that extent the process is closed, and conversely it is open. Quite apart from any vagaries of the existential situation within which a decision has to be taken, the process invokes two classes of act on the part of the decision maker: the cognitive determination of p's and the *trans*cognitive determination of v's. The meaning of transcognitive will be discussed below in Chapter 6, but it can be agreed now that the general significance of the qualitative element of value, directly in open models, indirectly in closed, is of prime importance. This irreducible element places the entire process beyond the dominion of logic. Wittgenstein (1961, 641 *ff.*) has denied the admissibility of value propositions in logical discourse, while other philosophers following Kaplan (1964, 6–11) would greatly extend the definition of logic. In the present work we are concerned to keep the distinction between logical propositions which can be assessed as true or false and value propositions for which the terms true or false are inappropriate.

To say this is to abandon neither the hope nor the norm of rationality in decision making. Rather, this hope and this norm should be retained as desirable prerequisites to greater sophistication about the process itself. For the time let us concede simply that the task of reducing uncertainty (specifying p's) is basically scientific in nature, while that of clarifying value (specifying v's) is philosophical and administrative.

In the desire to simplify the basic paradigm at the root of all decision making much has been left out. It is obvious, for example, that there are different kinds of decisions and that decisions are made, or reputed to be made, by groups of people as well as by individuals. Although our task is not to survey the literature on decision making, it may be advisable to note, in the general search for philosophical form, some of the complexities which immediately accumulate around the simplex and reductionist model described above.

First, there are the factors of personality which consciously or unconsciously may insert themselves into whatever range of discretion is left available for their exercise in the rational decision making process. It will make a difference to the calculus of p's and v's if self-interest, ideology, ambition, imagination, attitudinal predispositions, and prejudices become engaged. We have also left undiscussed the factor of *will* which is sometimes referred to by psychologists as ego-strength. Such a factor, I would suggest, though rather disreputable in academic psychology, is closely allied to notions of intention and commitment and can greatly influence decision making and decision taking at any point in the process. It can indeed prove crucial to the total complex of decision action. Since such a factor extends beyond logic and cognitive rationality, it may be reserved for later discussion.

But all these are merely psychological complications. In addition there is the important political question, not always easy to answer, as to *who* makes decisions. Who *really* decides? The responsibility for a decision is often collective. This may be formalized as where certain decisions are required to be made by specified groups. Sometimes advisory parties to the formal decision maker exercise suasion or they control vital data. Standing committees, self-selected and formally selected individuals, representatives of power-seeking factions within and without the formal decision making processes of the organization—all these and more compound the superstructure of decisional complexity and increase the difficulty of resolution and determination of the v-factors in the paradigm. While it is an ostensible function of administration to make decisions about who will make decisions, this regulatory function can be subverted in a complex organization in a variety of ways and any undermining, by default or otherwise, of this function is at the very best non-contributive to purity of logic in decision making.

Decisions will also complexify by setting, by contingency, and by type. Setting relates to our previous discussion of open and closed models. In a valuable review of the literature Stufflebeam and others have developed a fourfold classification of settings which will be discussed in the next chapter. The same authors also construct a fourfold typology of decisions, structuring decisions, implementing decisions, and recycling decisions (Stufflebeam *et al.*, 1971, 79–84). The logic of this typology is consistent with Litchfield's analysis and with our own conception of an organizational flow of decision-making from philosophical core to action periphery. Within this classification only the more technical and managerial *implementing* decisions could be considered even relatively value free.

Lastly, decisions never occur in a vacuum. Each decision is linked into an enormously complex web of contingency, interrelation, and means-ends concatenations. The web also embraces not merely the actual but the possible, and the possible is limited only by the range of human imagination. Each taken decision becomes both a constraint and a liberating potential for future decisions. Paradoxically, perhaps, the most rational decisions tend to be those which are the most constrained, for the fewer the degrees of freedom the greater the amenability to logical calculation and the greater the ease of determination of the p and v factors. But it should also be noted that, in line with our general thesis, the more contingent and determined decisions become the more they fall into the category of the managerial and technical. The truly great administrative decisions are those which tear apart and create anew whole patterns of contingency. Only when the vicious circle of causation can be broken does administrative or philosophical action become possible.

ABERRATIONS

Simon in a number of places (1955, 111; 1959, 272; 1965, 33) has abandoned the ideal of rationality in the sense of maximizing utilities in decision processes and has been inclined to settle for a reality-based paradigm in which the decision maker satisfices rather than optimizes. The satisficing decision maker is not irrational. He has merely modified his level of aspiration in coming to terms with complexity and has settled upon a practical administrative solution to the problems of (1) p and v calculus and (2) imaginative and creative search for alternative outcomes. It is pragmatic but not unreasonable. There are, however, other responses to decision making which can be considered irrational, aberrant, and philosophically suspect. Aberrant reactions are particularly likely in response to the valuational element in decision problem solving.

Because value propositions can never be labelled true or false in the same way as can propositions of logic or propositions which are empirically verifiable, they can be thought of as metafactual or metascientific, beyond the reach of quantitative methods. To deny this is to commit the naturalistic fallacy, the argument for which asserts that no amount of facts or 'is's' can 'prove' a value statement or an 'ought' (Moore, 1903, 10, 13–14). This means for administrators that no amount of fact-gathering or information seeking can ever *conclusively* put them 'in the *right*'. Factual bases may be desirable in arriving at value premises but in themselves they *prove* nothing. The naturalistic fallacy cannot, however, be allowed to create any state of philosophical vacuum or stasis. This would be anathema in the practical realm of action and so a variety of techniques have emerged to solve the problem of value resolution in the ongoing affairs of organizations. Among these we can consider the polar opposites of participation and evaluation, both of which are rational approaches to the values difficulty but both of which can easily degenerate.

Participation is the technique of consulting and co-opting interested or knowledgeable parties so as to enlarge the deliberative scope of the decision making process. It seeks essentially for a consensus on value issues, though if this is not obtainable, the v-factor may be determined by some form of vote or weighted ballot arrangement. The method can be strongly influenced by any overriding democratic ideology although this may manifest less as an Aristotelian faith in the wisdom of the masses than as a deep-seated lack of confidence or trust in the wisdom of a single administrator. (Consider the Soviet reliance upon collegiate decisions; the word 'soviet' itself means 'committee'.) Carried to extremes, the method becomes the aberration of determining values and making decisions on the basis not of rationality, but of political suasion. That participation can result in the 'settlement' of a value question is one thing, that it can 'prove' anything is quite another. And that it can be subverted by force or manipulation quite another yet again.

The opposite strategy to participation is that of assigning values problems to values experts. This may be done *ad hoc* through consultation or formally through the creation of an evaluator role[5] (Stufflebeam *et al.*, 1971, 43, 297–307). In either case a distinction is presupposed between deciders or decision takers, those who have the organizational responsibility for the decision, and advisers or decision makers, those whose role is to analyze and evaluate. That there may be, for the practical administrative philosopher, a whiff of the fallacy of immaculate perception in this distinction is not surprising. Its possible subversion has been succinctly expressed as follows:

> Thus it happens that great deference is paid to the recommendations of experts, and that these recommendations covertly introduce into administrative decisions values of which even the experts are unaware. Further, because nonexperts hesitate to contradict experts, experts may inject into administrative decisions value preferences of which they definitely are conscious. And because experts often learn their standardized solutions with little or no understanding of the basic reasons for them, they are often very inflexible and resistant to new ideas. (Simon *et al.*, 1950, 547)

In any event, this practice is a plain admission of the great difficulties attendant on the decisional process. There is also an element of illogic in the mere conception of an objective analyst because the ultimate choice point in the whole decision making process would still be when the *administrator* decided between the final alternatives presented. The adviser could not *then* presume to offer advice without tainting his own 'objectivity' and upsurping the administrator's function. On the other hand his very formulation of alternatives would include his 'evaluation' and would thus be unsurping the administrator's function at the critical part of the paradigm. The horns of an ancient dilemma begin to loom in the mist.

Another aberration might take the form of an overconcentration upon those aspects of the decision problem which were factual and quantitative. The advent of the computer hardware and its associated technology has greatly assisted this form of self-deception. Kaplan's law of the instrument (see Note 9) is pertinent to this kind of psychological retreat.

Yet another and more insidious mode of irrationality can occur through the practice of 'open' decision making, where 'open' is used in the sense of accessible to public or organization membership: 'Open decisions openly arrived at'. Such procedures are commonly constrained by a necessary measure of formality and this can incline them towards quasi-judicial solutions where value issues are resolved in terms of precedent and literal interpretation of policy rather than by any imaginative or creative resolution. Again, this in itself is not unreasonable and from the values standpoint may be beneficent to the extent that it invokes principles and the clarification of principles (see Chapter 6) but it may lead to conservatism or off-stage manoeuvering. Much worse, the open public forum may become merely a display for manipulative ends, the actual decision having been made prior to the forum, privately and covertly, by key parties in the process, thus nullifying the rationale for the procedure.

Lastly, illustrating but by no means exhausting the possibilities for aberrant reaction to decision difficulties, there can be a resort on the part of administrators to a pseudo-neutral or 'bureaucratic' posture wherein the difficult, valuational, qualitative aspects of the decision paradigm are treated as external constraints, givens, or are simply overlooked or denied altogether as being somehow outside the process (Tribe, 1972, 95). This might be called the 'not ours to question why' attitude, and though it is a form of retreat to managerialism it can extend to the roles of evaluators and consultants with dysfunctional organizational effect.

The concern throughout this chapter has been to show that the special body of knowledge dealing with decision making reveals that the process itself cannot be rigorously scientific. The presence of an internal value component assures the process of a philosophical status. Are administrators then more philosophically expert than their non-administrative fellows? At this point I would rather beg the question and simply assert that in this most difficult realm of human behaviour administrators have a very special interest. If the crucial knowledge for decisions has to do with human values then it would also seem to follow that administrators, those who make the organizational decisions, should at least desire to lay a claim to expertise on this topic. In a logical world they would be especially knowledgeable about the concept of value. Value knowledge for them would be a special competence.

4
Policy Making

Policy making is to decision making as strategy is to tactics. It may be considered as the making of decisions which bear heavily on the organizational life both as regards the organization's mission or purpose and the general *modus operandi*. Sir Geoffrey Vickers thinks of it specifically as 'the setting of governing relations or norms, rather than in the more usual terms as the setting of goals, objectives or ends...' (Vickers, 1965, 31). It has been described as a 'body of principle to guide action' and a 'design to shape the future by exerting influence upon trends that flow from the past into the present' (Lerner and Lasswell 1951, ix). Policy and philosophy coalesce. An organization is a potent thing. At any instant it represents in a complex fashion the sum total of its history and, simultaneously, its potential for the shaping of the future, its own and that of the entire fabric of circumstance within which it has its being. The quality of that being and its potential for the future is the manifestation of its philosophy, the synthesis of logic and value as crystallized in the accumulation and formulation of policy. And this highly philosophical business is a continuous and ongoing affair. As Barnard stressed, decisions and policy making never end. 'The ever-changing present generates ever new purposes in the continuing organization' (210). Katz and Kahn distinguish policy making on the basis of level of generality or abstraction. Policy decisions are those which are large in terms of organizational space and time and policy making is 'the decision aspect of that level of leadership which involves the alteration, origination, or elimination of organizational structure' (Katz and Kahn, 1966, 259). It is the formulation of substantive goals and objectives for the organization as well as procedures and devices for the achieving of goals and the evaluating of performance (*ibid.* 260).

Both logically and valuationally, policy making can be considered the epitome of administrative action—quintessential administration—philosophy-in-action. This brings us face to face with an important problem, a problem of ramifying implications and one which has to do with the definition of the term *administrator*. Who is it that makes policy? What I have already said implies that *whoever* does so is *ipso facto* an administrator, whether designated as such or not. It also implies that administration is a very pervasive form of organizational behaviour which cannot be strictly confined within the precincts of a formalized administrative role. In a sense, the parallel is with everyday extra-organizational life, where man is, by birthright, a philosopher—yet few choose to take the study seriously. If there were an administrative profession, however, the onus would be clear. Administrators would have to take the study of philosophy seriously.

The problem takes on a special form because of a powerful political dogma which is sometimes raised to ideological status in Anglo-Saxon cultures. This holds that the policy function belongs to amateurs or to lay or part-time members of the organization. 'The expert is on tap and not on top'. Or should be. The province of professionals is to do what they are told, they are the experts in means while the laymen are the experts in ends. Thus, legislatures of elected citizenry determine policy for nations or provinces, boards and trustees for hospitals and schools, boards of directors for firms.

It cannot be denied that these representative or political groups make policy, but it would be fallacious to assume that *only* they make policy and it would be naïve in the extreme to pretend that ranking administrators within organizations do *not* make policy. If they did not they would be in our terms mere managers, but to the extent that directly or indirectly, formally, or informally, by persuasion, control of information, or whatever means they determine policy decisions, they are executives or administrators. It follows then that administrators are of three kinds. First, there are those who come to their office by way of some form of political process; by appointment, election, or patronage. These are politician administrators. Their association with the organization may be temporary and transient, and they may have had no formal administrative preparation. Secondly, there are administrators with or without tenure who have some kind of a career pattern of preparation and are permanently affiliated members of their organizations. They occupy designated roles as administrators. These we may call professional administrators. Thirdly, there is an important hybrid category which is of increasing institutional importance in contemporary society, especially in those organizations which subscribe to the so-called collegiate principle. This type of administrator, the collegial administrator, is a career professional member of his organization but is elected or appointed from within the organization to occupy an administrative role for a specified term of tenure. Administration is not his ostensible or initial profession and he may have had no preparation in the field. Typical instances are deans of university faculties, some school principals and superintendents. This last grouping combines the attributes of amateur and professional but the latter term refers usually to a profession *other than* administration.

We shall have cause to refer to this classification later. Let us note, meanwhile, that only in the category of professional administrator is it reasonable to make the presumption of any preparation or training in the fields of administrative competence. And even here we cannot presuppose instruction in the philosophical skills of analysis and value clarification (Wiles, 1974; Hodgkinson, 1975). Yet all three groups are engaged in administration, make policy, are administrators. If rationality is to be a value in organizational life, and if rationality would require professionalism, then the present practice of administration, in Western societies at least, must be conceded to be irrational.

PLANNING AND GOALS

From the organizational standpoint policy refers either internally or externally. Internal policy establishes decision rules or parameters which determine and define whole realms of subordinate and contingent decisions. Examples are the allocation of budgetary discretion or the requiring employees below a certain rank to sign in each morning or, conversely, allowing employees to determine within set limits their own hours of work. This policy may be formally set down in written rules or informally developed through the modes of convention, custom, and tradition. It establishes, as it were, the game rules and the kinds of moves which may be made within the organizational game. The skilled administrator is the adroit game player, and through his skill both fixes and changes the game. External policy, on the other hand, has to do with planning. A course has to be set for the organization in a context of competing and conflicting environmental factors. This calls for a special kind of organizational perspective, a diplomatic as well as philosophical overview.

Policy making is 'high level' in a double sense; it is usually conducted at a high level in the organizational hierarchy and it is high level in that it is especially charged with values relating to the overall purpose, mission, or 'life' of the organization. It forms the organizational philosophy, and the term philosophy is often used loosely and casually by actors at the policy level. The decisions at this level are decisions writ large because the elements of the paradigm: alternatives, probabilities, and values take on a heightened collective significance. The search for alternatives may enlarge into a deliberate planning or research and development function along with a formal apparatus of investigation, research, study, and reporting. (This proactive luxury may, of course, be instantly deferred or swept aside in any reactive response to emergency). The p-factor will also become more significant because of the greater stakes of organizational investment. This fact may create a certain demand for an administrative attribute which can only be likened to a propensity for gambling or 'figuring the odds'. This risk-taking faculty would be counterbalanced, however, by organizational pressures towards caution and conservation. Not every administrator may possess the Hitlerian or Napoleonic genius for intuitive risk-taking. Finally, it is clear that the v-factor in the decision paradigm will at this level be enlarged because of the scope of policy decisions and their significance for other levels of the organization. In the extreme, sufficient bad policy will lead to organizational extinction. In sum, this general raising of *level* of decision making leads one, in the search for logical form, to look for ways of characterizing policy making *strategies*.

GENERAL STRATEGIES

Decision settings were briefly referred to in the previous chapter. They are of particular relevance to the problem of policy. The general elements of settings are shown in Figure 9. This diagram reproduces the original conception of Braybrooke and Lindblom and the reformulation of their ideas by Stufflebeam and his coauthors. Both sets of theorists make essentially the same point, that if decisions are analyzed two-dimensionally, by scope of change involved and by level of understanding, then purely rational paradigms are weakened to the point of defeat except in those instances (Quadrant 1) where the situation factors (p's and v's) are well understood and agreed upon. It is to be noted, however, that the selected dimensions of analysis blur the distinction between uncertainty and evaluation and between value and fact. In our terminology p's and v's pervade the entire field depicted in the arrangement of Figure 9 and it is only in the first quadrant that they could be specified with any precision. To put it another way, values and facts are inextricably intertwined in the fields of administrative action represented by Quadrants 2, 3, and 4, but in Quadrant 1 it might be possible to disentangle them enough to apply with some success the purely logical paradigm. Again, as we move towards the right in this conceptual scheme, uncertainties increase and it is as if values preponderate over facts, especially so in Quadrant 2, designated by the later authors as metamorphism. Below the horizontal axis, understanding or information grasp (presumably a compound of fact and value) is low and this reflects in policy strategies.

Large Change Strategies: Large changes affecting the organization (and remember that the organization may be a nation-state or even a nation-collectivity, OPEC for example) call for policy action to the right of the vertical axes in Figure 9. The original authors describe such action as revolutionary or utopian, and give examples of wars, crises, and 'grand opportunities' while the later writers call the activity utopian or innovative. And while Braybrooke and Lindblom could not confidently put forward any analytic method for decision making in these domains, Stufflebeam and his colleagues suggest that the basis for decision must be either overarching theory (e.g. Marxism) or 'conceptualization, heuristic investigation, and structured inquiry'. It would seem, then, that as risks and uncertainties magnify, as they do in any large-scale forward-reaching attempt to form the shape of things to come, the policymakers need reinforcement in the form of some kind of ideology. That ideology may be a philosophical, religious or politi-

Figure 9:   Change-based Analysis Formulation by Braybrooke and Lindblom

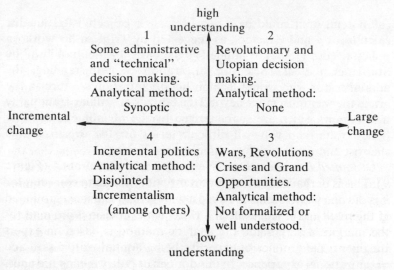

high
understanding

1	2
Some administrative and "technical" decision making. Analytical method: Synoptic	Revolutionary and Utopian decision making. Analytical method: None

Incremental change ←————————————————→ Large change

4	3
Incremental politics Analytical method: Disjointed Incrementalism (among others)	Wars, Revolutions Crises and Grand Opportunities. Analytical method: Not formalized or well understood.

low
understanding

Formulation by Stufflebeam *et al.*

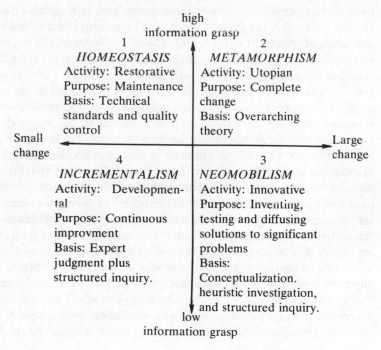

high
information grasp

1	2
HOMEOSTASIS Activity: Restorative Purpose: Maintenance Basis: Technical standards and quality control	*METAMORPHISM* Activity: Utopian Purpose: Complete change Basis: Overarching theory

Small change ←————————————————→ Large change

4	3
INCREMENTALISM Activity: Developmental Purpose: Continuous improvment Basis: Expert judgment plus structured inquiry.	*NEOMOBILISM* Activity: Innovative Purpose: Inventing, testing and diffusing solutions to significant problems Basis: Conceptualization. heuristic investigation, and structured inquiry.

low
information grasp

cal system, or it could be a quasi-scientific objectivist-rationalist calculus of p and v factors, as suggested by Tribe in his work on policy science (1972) or implied as the basis for 'neomobilism' by Stufflebeam *et al.* 'Scientific' aspirations notwithstanding, the administrator who would fashion his organization's future in the grand manner must move beyond the bounds of ordinary rationality into regions which are characterized by the phenomena of faith, belief, value and will—all difficult terms for the organizational theorist and anathema for administrative science.

Disjointed Incrementalism: We are left with Quadrant 4 (Figure 9). This is perhaps the most important policy realm to consider, for it is the one which seems to be most widespread and most grounded in the reality of practical affairs. Here, small decisions are made at the margin of action and the analytic method is based on expert judgment, the grounds of expertise being administrative skill and organizational experience. In this domain of policy means and ends, values and facts, are not rigorously distinguished but are treated as being 'intertwined'. The policy makers seek to avoid radical alternatives and any conflict of large values. Lindblom, in a classic article (1959) called this the *branch* method, contrasting it with the *root* approach of Quadrant 1 (Figure 9). The metaphor refers to organic development after the pattern of a tree. It recognizes that at the policy level there may be no agreement on values (the typical political situation) but calls instead only for a limited agreement on an immediate path of action. Such action may be experimental or tentative, and the method is alternatively called the method of successive limited comparisons. Lindblom himself described it as the 'Science of "Muddling Through" ' (*ibid.*), while Boulding has criticized it as the philosophy of 'Lead Kindly Light' (1964). Policy making decisions under this conception would be fundamentally cautious, conservative, pragmatic, tradition- and experience-based; its informing spirit is non-doctrinaire, oriented to maintenance of the status quo and to growth which is sure and slow rather than fast and furious. The method may appeal with equal force to all three kinds of administrator described above. It is said, for example, to be the basic technique for U.S. budget making (Bailey and O'Connor, 1975) and the way in which society makes most of its decisions. (Arrow, 1964) Any philosophy of administration must take cognizance of its status.[1] These, then, are the broad general strategies available if the attention is directed solely to the factors of grasp and change.

This type of analysis by decision setting, while important in showing the limitations of administrative rationality, does not of itself explain the way in which personality and motivational factors would intrude into the policy making process. Let us use the term interest to refer to this additional complexity. We can then speak logically of three kinds of interest: (1) *self-interest*, the interest of the individual policy maker; (2) *organization interest*, the interest of the collectivity as structured into the organization or the interest of the policy maker *qua* organization member; (3) *extra-organization* interest, the 'larger' interest of the environment and policy extraneous to the organization or the interest of the policy maker as citizen. These levels of interest parallel the motivational syndromes of Figures 5–7 in Chapter II above.

Granted at once that these forms of interest are not mutually exclusive, it is tempting to speculate on which is most logically characteristic of each type of administrator. Is it that extra-organization interest would be most characteristic of and best represented by the political administrator? Perhaps this idea might go to explain the Anglo-Saxon canon of amateur supremacy in organizational affairs. Or would organizational interest be most embodied in the professional category of administrator? And where then would the collegial administrators fit? These questions are enticing but perhaps distracting. What can be acknowledged is that interest is intimate and fundamental to policy formulation and, therefore, some degree of correlation can reasonably be expected to exist between dominant interest patterns and policy strategies. This reasoning suggests certain basic or classical patterns.

The logical possibilities for basic modes of policy formulation are not unlimited, and certain well-determined patterns clearly stand out. Three modes which to some extent parallel the preceding analysis of interest are (1) the *opportunistic* (2) the *rationalistic* and (3) the *doctrinaire*.

An opportunistic strategy would resolve policy on the basis of what would appear to be in the best self-interest of the decider. The policy maker under this scheme would be rational and logical to the extent that he could clearly perceive the ramifications of interest which would result from policy. Simon's comment in this regard is quite fascinating (1965, 149). He asserts that propositions about rational human behaviour (individual or organizational) would not ordinarily be psychological. His reasoning is that *rational* behaviour would be completely determined by values (individual or organizational) and the only role of psychology would then be to explain aberrations or *irrational* behaviour. An administrator pursuing this strategy consistently would of course find many occasions in which self-interest was merged with or subsumed under the two larger varieties of interest. It can also be safely imagined that where conflict existed he would couch his public and organizational utterances in such a way as to disguise or conceal the underlying policy. Simon, Smithburg, and Thompson (1950, 392–3) tend to view opportunism as being congruent with organizational maintenance in that the administrative self-seeker will also seek to preserve the organization as a means of goal accomplishment or as an object of pride of membership or as a source of personal power, position, and income. That this is not entirely the case and that ruthless opportunism can be organizationally dysfunctional ought not to be overlooked, however. Ambitious and mobile interorganizational careerists can trail a wake of organizational distress behind them, the end product of opportunistic policy strategies.

The form of policy orientation that I have labelled rationalistic deserves some special attention. Its dominant thrust is the organizational interest and there are the consequent presumptions that what is good for the organization is good for the individual and good for the larger society. It connotes an orientation which is positivistic, 'objective', primarily focused on means rather than ends, the latter often being assumed as given and obvious (e.g. making a profit, winning the war) and therefore justifying the deployment of whatever ends technology can serve and resources can fund. There is the risk of fallacy, however, of two kinds: first, from the ubiquitous naturalistic error which supposes that ends (and therefore policy) can be logically derived from the study of facts and second, from the identification with scientific norms of factual objectivity and rationality. Norms appropriate for the natural or 'hard' sciences may be quite inadequate for the humanities.

The ancestry of objective policy making can probably be traced to the powerful influences of classical economics and the simplifying assumptions and presuppositions which attend that theory. Working from the standpoints of philosophy and sociology of knowledge, Tribe has sought to criticize this type of policy science orientation and certainly he has shown that

> 'the policy sciences tend to partition and warp reality in certain patterned ways, generating a fairly understandable, and sometimes quite unfortunate, system of blind spots and distortions' (Tribe, 1972, 106).

This is putting it very mildly and modestly; the sweep of his attack is much more devastating. But in the search for a logic of administration, let us be content to note that the logical-rational approach to policy can itself prove contra-functional and thereby in the end illogical. The same critique can of course be levelled against the opportunistic and the doctrinaire approaches. Policy transcends logic.

Finally, let us consider the corresponding form for extra-organizational interest. Typically, this may appear in the form of a more or less articulated doctrine or set of guiding principles such as those espoused by hedonistic utilitarianism, or (say) the platform of the Socialist Party.[2] As a doctrine it may be well-formed or malformed, inchoate or embryonic. Even the vague sense of being an exponent of a cultural movement, for example, women's liberation or the 'now generation', may suffice to inform policy. In general, any patterned persuasion, if clear enough to the holder of it, can be used as a determinant of policy, whether or not it aspires to the status of a philosophy or ideology. When the complex organization assumes the magnitude of a nation or state, the doctrine is of course usually expressed as a political statement—a set of political propositions.

Lastly, there are the anti-strategies of *laissez faire* and negativism. The former can achieve the level of doctrine, as in the economics and politics of classical liberalism, but is used here in the different sense of reacting to circumstance in non-patterned or inconsistent ways. Such drifting with history would be evidence of a lack of organizational policy or leadership and organizations in this condition are reactive, not proactive; they are formed by, rather than formative of, the quality of extra-organizational life. Negativism, on the other hand, refers to the situation where the policy makers are quite clear about what they do *not* want but not at all clear about their positive objectives. There is a pattern but it is a negative one. A school trustee may want to reduce expenditures, and not much else. Ehrlichman as an administrator in the Nixon White House would be criticized for his lack of positive public policy initiatives (Rather and Gates, 1975, 270–272). Negativism and *laissez faire* are not necessarily illogical, but organizationally and administratively, they may contravene the metavalues (Chapter 11) and violate the canons of organizational interest.

From all this it is apparent that policy making can become almost literally a translation of philosophy. More or less articulated bodies of doctrine and belief become action. Organizational action. This, together with the attaching complexities and the lack of understanding of analytic method, take this area of administrative competence beyond the reach of logic *simpliciter*.

THE PROBLEM OF LEVELS

Policy making has been described as a high level function. Conventionally it is formed in the armchair or around the table in a deliberative ambience removed from the actual realm of action. Between any policy and its translation into factual reality extends a longer and shorter chain of 'sordid managerial detail'. The chain is a matter of logical necessity given the structure of complex organizations. But it entails psychological consequences which cannot be ignored in the philosophy of administration. The break in continuity between board room and assembly line or between G.H.Q. and battlefront is not merely quantitative, a matter of physical distance, but qualitative, a matter of intellectual perspective.[3]

'. . . Persons in administrative positions, particularly when they are several layers removed from the employees whose behaviour they are planning, are especially likely to treat the men and material in their organizations as neutral means to be used 'for accomplishing the purposes of the state' (or the purposes that the administrators consider important and desirable).' (Simon *et al.*, 1950, 496)

This psychological distancing can be, to say the least, *dangerous*.

Katz and Kahn give the illustration of the United States policy decision to aid Chiang Kai Shek on the doctrinaire premiss that China should be saved from the Communists (280). The fault, defective information grasp, could here be attributed to distancing and levels. On the other hand, Katz and Kahn stress that the logical paradigm of decision making is also frequently short-circuited on managerial grounds. That is to say, creative policy alternatives do not come up for consideration because they are aborted *ab initio*; they are held to be 'impractical' and the organization is already tooled up and committed in a contrary direction, the managerial difficulties are insuperable, or 'the eggs are already scrambled'. In such circumstances the policy or administrative level can be subverted by managerial and lower levels. There is a kind of Juggernaut phenomenon where the inertial forces of the organization prevent its being halted or changed in direction. This may be bad enough, the administrative dog wagged by the managerial tail, but it is in the reverse situation, when there is no impediment to the flow of policy from centre to periphery that the severest dangers, from a humanistic standpoint, can occur. Indeed, the constraints placed upon administration by management may be beneficial to the extent that they carry with them an increase of information grasp and energy flow in the organizational circuitry.

Looked at in another way, this problem of levels and distancing can also be seen as the problem of the separation of ends and means. Insofar as they can be separated at all we have the logical difference between policy and execution; between values informing policy makers and their actualization in the world. This gap or hiatus can result in a breakdown of the humane situation-comprehension of the decision maker and the logical can become the *pathological*. The perspective in the cool of the chancellery may be such that a 'final solution of the Jewish question' or a 'preemptive incursion into Cambodia' might seem reasonable policy in a way which could not be contemplated were the actual resultant human agonies of the holocaust or the Cambodian people *really* entered into the decisional calculus. Distancing is also reflected in language. Tribe gives the examples of 'body count', 'Phillips curve trade-off' and 'collapse mode in a world resource model' for 'killings', 'forced unemployment' and 'global starvation' respectively (1972, 97).

But perhaps it will be countered that such emotive factors *cannot* be taken into consideration. The administrator cannot indulge the luxury of imaginative comparison any more than the surgeon can contemplate with sentiment the person or the body to whom (or to which) he is applying the knife. It would be an impediment to his rational objectivity and his proper professional detachment. But the analogy is false. The surgeon, like the scientist, is a manager concerned with means, the ends of which have been determined elsewhere. And for that matter, the ends are rational and justifiable and may well have taken into their calculus all or any of the agonizing consequences. The surgeon's detachment is a technically justified attitude, but the policy maker's detachment is of a different logical order. At this level of administrative action philosophy and psychology interact, and if the emphasis upon ends as *logical* leads to the exclusion from consideration of ends as *realized*, that is, as projected forth in imagination with the full colouring of humane consequences, a gap can open up. The bridging of this kind of gap would call for qualities of compassion, empathy, and imagination which are rarely dealt with seriously in the administrative literature and which would be antagonistic to a *Zeitgeist* of scientific objectivity. Much less is cultivation of these qualities a recognized part of administrative preparation. On the contrary, we more usually find dispassion and objectivity being counselled, in line with Weberian prescription, along with a corresponding ethos of admiration for the 'hard-nosed', tough-minded administrator capable of making the 'tough decisions'.

To recapitulate: Administrators come to their policy making function with three kinds of interest—self, organizational, and extra-organizational. These interests overlap, though any one may become salient. Likewise, policy itself may be opportunistic, rationalistic, or doctrinaire. The policy process itself is such that, while it enlarges the philosophical scope of decision, it at the same time tends to attenuate or atrophy the factors of psychological insight. The body of knowledge on decision and policy making further indicates a limited possibility of any wide application of rational-synoptic methods. All of which implies that administrators, however they might come to their role, have need of competencies beyond those of merely rational analysis. These can be simply described as the philosophical skills of logical and value analysis. Yet still more is needed, however, and this would seem to embrace the 'human' qualities of empathy, compassion, and sympathetic imagination. In the formulation of policy, administrative behaviour must reach beyond the grasp of logic. This is well expressed in the following quotation:

> The decision-making of organizations may be highly rational within the frame of reference of the objectives of the particular organization, but these objectives may be so irrational in larger terms that the net result is systemic and human destruction. As individuals, some people like alcohol enough to make health problems for themselves; others are not affected by their casual drinking, and still others do not drink. If we organized ourselves into a group dedicated to the pursuit and use of alcohol, we could bring about a greater amount of physical and personality deterioration in a shorter space of time. Organizations are more efficient than individuals, whether concerned with good or evil, sense or nonsense. (Katz and Kahn, 1966, 298)

This indicates the capacity of organizations for good *or* evil, and I do not yet wish to assert that they lean in the one direction or the other. Logically they may be considered neutral *a priori*. Yet sociopsychological distancing and structural levels do suggest at least a propensity beyond amorality and towards immorality.

The working administrator who allows his moral sense to atrophy or who retreats to managerialism by one device or another is abdicating his philosophical responsibility. And this holds whether he is political, professional, or collegial, and whether his competence in policy making is claimed or unclaimed, overt, or covert, a product of formalized training or the happenstance of experience.

5
Power, Authority, and Leadership

In the preceding pages administration has been treated in a general way as a differentiated class of human behaviour within fields of action called organizations. We have been guided by the question, 'What are the special competencies of administration?' The idea that there might be an underlying logic or form to this activity, though vague and obscure, has also been part of our inquiry. So far it would seem that a serious administrative aspirant, whether amateur or professional, would be moved to gain familiarity with whatever body of knowledge or principle the social sciences could present, in the general form of organization theory, and to deepen his insight and his practical skills in the arts of decision making and policy formulation. As to logical form we have been able to discern only the faint delineaments of design in the conception of purposive systems with feedback mechanisms. The sharp edges of logic, the nice frontiers of conjunction and disjunction, and the straightforward exercise of calculative rationality continue to elude us in the face of complexity, uncertainty, and the ubiquity of the value factor. Moreover, we have not yet touched upon certain aspects of administration which are obviously intrinsic to its performance and about which claims would certainly be laid by administrators, claims of proprietory right and claims of special competence. These are the domains of power, authority and leadership.

One has to remember that administration is a primal human activity. Its origins predate the historical record. It has inspired great classics of literature, amongst which we must particularly note the works of Machiavelli and Plato's treatise, *The Republic*. A central concern of these works and one which must certainly go to the root of any theory or philosophy of administration is the concept of power. All the knowledge and skills mentioned to this point and all the discussion about them would be vain did the practising administrator not possess a lively and sufficient measure of power.

POWER

Administration seeks the accomplishment of collective ends. It is the shaping of these ends through the formulation of policy and the deployment of means through the technology of management. The achievement of ends requires power. Simply defined, power is the ability to gain ends. This is done physically through the expenditure of energy and psychologically through the application of will. Administrative power can be further defined as the ability to achieve ends through others. Ostensibly the ends are *organizational* ends, and of course it would be a mistake to equate power in the field of human action with simple physical power or force. Power over men is logically different from power over nature. Let us say, then, that administrative power is the ability of the administrator to have his will and get his way. It is important to agree on this point, for it means that the distribution of power within an organizational field is not simply a matter of organizational structure and game rules, that is, a matter of logic, but more complex, and carrying with it psychological connotations of conation, desire, and ego definition.

The power of men over men is fundamental to administration. That there is something dark and primitive about it has commanded the attention of depth psychology. Adler in particular treated it as an instinct for dominance and ranked it (*pace* Freud) with sex itself as a grand motivational reductionism. It is said, if we are to believe Lord Acton, to be corrupting; absolute power corrupting absolutely. The term has dyslogistic connotations: 'power-seeking' and 'power-hungry' are negative epithets. The administrator, even if he candidly admits publicly or privately to the pursuit of power, will not usually wish to have these terms ascribed to his behaviour, preferring instead such eulogisms as 'ambitious', 'driving', or 'dynamic'. The distasteful aspect of power might well arise, however, regardless of the truth or falsity of Adlerian theories, from the logical fact that its exercise implies a suspension, diminution, or subversion of the power of the person upon whom it is being exercised. One man's power is another man's impotence if the latter must forgo his will on behalf of the former. As we have all from infancy experienced this impotence, this frustration of our autonomy, we tend to approach the subject of political power or administrative power with some deep-seated unease. After all, the whole of human history *can* be explained under this term. So perhaps it is not surprising that Simon and Barnard, while they expatiate at length and with great insight on the topic of *authority*, are silent on the more basic and primitive notion of power.

I do not think, however, that the concept can be at all disregarded by the administrative philosopher. Power is the lifeblood of administration, and whether or not it is treated as a terminal value, an end intrinsically desirable in and of itself, it is a necessary instrumentality for the accomplishment or realization of any value. The systems theorists Ackoff and Emery (1972) take this reasoning to its extremity and acclaim power as the ultimate value, the *summum bonum*. We can therefore postulate a natural tendency for administrators to seek to increase their quantum of power. The individual administrator can question himself about the *interest* associated with his desire for power. Is that interest personal or organizational? But if the psychoanalytic theorists are correct, then even the posing of this question would be futile, for the deeper motivations might be inaccessible to conscious introspection. Yet such questions are never vain from the viewpoint of administrative philosophy. We would like to know the psycho-mechanics of power as an integral part of the pattern of organizational motivations. And we cannot desist from pressing for ever more penetrating explanations.

Looking at power from the perspective of sociology, Goldhammer and Shils (1939) were led to a threefold analysis. Having first defined power as the extent that a person holding it could

'influence the behaviour of others in accordance with his own intentions', they then show how it can be exhibited as *force, domination*, or *manipulation*. 'The power-holder exercises *force* when he influences behaviour by a physical manipulation of the subordinated individual (assault, confinement, etc.); *domination* when he influences behaviour by making explicit to others what he wants them to do (command, requests, etc.); and *manipulation* when he influences the behaviour of others without making explicit the behaviour which he thereby wants them to perform'. (*ibid*., 172)

The operative idea here is the 'influencing of behaviour' and it is instructive to note the role of language in power and persuasion.

Bertrand Russell has made clear (1973, 25–6, 49–51) that language is almost always an attempt to influence an audience. Even the propositions of symbolic logic and mathematics, if uttered, are uttered to the end of creating an effect. '1 + 1 = 2' has an intention. At its barest it means: (*Know that*) '1 + 1 = 2'. Or, (Know that I am aware that) '1 + 1 = 2'. So language itself is power-based. It follows that not just the administrative philosopher but also the practising administrator will have an interest in language; the former with the analysis of administrative terms, the latter with the use of language as a tool of persuasion. Both dialectic and rhetoric are crucial to the administrative enterprise. The more so as force and domination yield to manipulation in the exercise of power.

The need for power is bedded in the *Realpolitik* of organizational life. The more power an administrator has, the greater the ends that can be shaped, and the greater the range of administrative possibility. Power is the primitive term of the administrative lexicon, but its naked essence can rarely be exposed. Ethos and mores dictate that its starker reality be veiled in appearance and its usage concealed in elaborate language games; it must be re*dressed* and re*presented*.

AUTHORITY

Power can be legitimate or not so. Whether its presence and exercise is perceived as legitimate depends upon the organizational language game. (Wittgenstein, 1953, 23; 1969, 65) Authority is the term for legitimate or legitimized[1] power and the principle of legitimacy rests upon interest. The purpose of the organization determines the distribution of authority among the actors within it. If the organization is (say) a nation then it might be consistent with the interests of *that* organization to wage war and hence, its administration as agents (see Chapter 10) would have the authority (legitimized power) to conscript citizens and bring on harm and destruction to other humans defined as enemies. We can push the analysis one step further yet. Organizational interest and organizational purpose may be expressed in words, but the interpretation of these words, their meanings, and their intention is a matter of *perception*. At the level of the national organization this perception is dependent upon social ethos and mores. (Cf. Figure 7, p. 44) The citizens of Athens and of Sparta will see things differently. So it is

conceivable that the membership of the national organization might
not endorse (make legitimate) the national purpose as declared by
its administration of waging war. They might be *willing* (the term is
significant) to wage only certain kinds of war or even, in an admit-
tedly very hypothetical instance, not to wage war at all. This line of
reasoning places the source of legitimacy in the mass or the whole of
the membership, and this is congruent with Barnard's contention
that the ultimate authority rests with the commanded rather than
the commanders. The view is reinforced by Michels,

> Whether authority is of personal or institutional origin it is created and
> maintained by public opinion, which in its turn is conditioned by senti-
> ment, affection, reverence or fatalism. Even when authority rests on
> mere physical coercion it is accepted by those ruled, although the accep-
> tance may be due to a fear of force. (Barnard, 164)

A number of points could be made about this thesis—that membership ethos is fairly stable and inelastic in reaction, that it is susceptible to manipulation through control of the media of communication, that skilled administrators are well aware of this legitimizing
source of their authority and know how to use it and how to by-pass
it, that there is in any event a wide *a priori* zone of acceptance or
indifference with respect to commands, and so on—but the essential
thing for us to note is that authority derives its legitimacy in this
understanding from a perceived connection with the organizational
purpose and interest. The member, or even the stranger, who takes
command in a moment of organizational emergency can be vested
for the duration of the emergency with the full force, power, and
authority of the organization if it is perceived by those responding to
his will that he is acting in the organizational interest. It would be, in
contemporary jargon, entirely a matter of 'credibility'.

Authority, then, is legitimized power. In the cooperative myth of
origin put forward by Barnard, Katz and Kahn, and others, organization comes about in the first place because of the need to achieve
a common goal through collective effort—two men can move the
stone that one cannot. As the benefit of collective endeavour is
perceived, organizations of increasing complexity develop and the
initial productive 'system' is elaborated by devices or practices for
making and enforcing rules. These practices generate the authority

structure of the organization. We cannot return, however, to pristine beginnings. Even the new organizations which come into existence daily fall heir to an increasingly complex superstructure of already existing organizations and attendant authority systems into which they must fit and an increasingly complex technology of means which carries with it its own structure of authority. They also inherit a cultural ethos which, as even Simon admits, (1965, 133–146) is the real determinant of authority and its sanctions. In the real situation, then, the clear perception of either organizational purpose or of the source of authority is not a simple matter. Both indeed may have to be taken 'on faith'. The skilled administrator can take advantage of this state of affairs and even the unskilled or inept is upon taking office endowed, as it were, with a natural residuum of organizational authority and credibility.

Authority manifests itself in a special form of action, the communication of decisions through orders. (At the nation-state level of complexity these orders can take the form of statutes, decrees, or written *law*.[2] Barnard bases his definition on this *active* aspect of authority:

> 'Authority is the character of a communication (order) in a formal organization by virtue of which it is accepted by a contributor to or 'member' of the organization as governing the action he contributes; that is, as governing or determining what he does or is or is not to do so far as the organization is concerned' (163).

So it comes about that in the last analysis authority lies with the recipient of the communication. Barnard, however, is making a presumption of free will and this is philosophically important; I must be *able* and *willing* to apply his test if I am to have the authority to accept or reject formal communications, but with this proviso final authority does *not* reside with those who issue orders, that is, in the ordinary case with the administrative-managerial line.

The operative word is final. Presumably a final judgment would only be made *outside* the ordinary realm of acquiesence. Intrinsic to the Simon-Barnard view of authority is the idea of a zone of indifference (Barnard, 167–170) or acceptance (Simon, 1965, 12, 131). Within this region of complicity subordinates align themselves unreflectively with their superordinate's will. The zone defines the frontiers of administrative power. What determines its boundaries? On this Barnard is quite precise. If a subordinate can comprehend and perform an order then his concurrence with it depends on (1) his belief that the order is not inconsistent with the purposes of the organization and (2) his belief that it is compatible with his personal interest as a whole. (165) Such an analysis goes far to explain (if not to *justify*) some of the illicit actions of the Watergate administrators for example. It is also instructive to observe the shift which has subtly occurred into *a*-logical realms of belief and value in the discussion of a concept which is at the heart of administrative action and administrative theory.

These views can be said to constitute the current orthodoxy in administrative thought. If they are correct it follows that administrators will always be interested in legitimation, that is, in maintaining the *perception* in the organizational ranks of an *identification* of the administration with the organizational purpose. This can be done symbolically, through language games and the trappings of rank and status. Royalty, through a public display, can be used to legitimize the authority of their supposed ministers in whom the real power resides. Cosmonauts or astronauts (if successful) can be used by political administrators in a similar fashion. It may be (see Chapter 8) that the more general and diffuse the organizational purpose, the easier it becomes to achieve identification and manipulate legitimacy and authority. It may be, too, that the more purpose is hidden—deep in the secret labyrinths of the Kafkaesque Castle—the more administration can assume the attributes of priestly authority, sacrosanct and beyond question. If complexity of organization, society, culture, and technology combine to obscure and mystify purpose (as they do, for example, in the institution of public education) then the only challenge to administrative authority may come from the prevailing system of understanding and beliefs about self interest on the one hand and extra-organizational interest on the other.

INFLUENCE

Although all power is influential and all influence expresses power, it is useful to discriminate between the two terms on the basis of formality. Concomitant and coexistent with the formal structures of authority there are to be found shifting patterns of informal authority or influence. The patterns depend on the organization game and the game players. These in turn are difficult to classify or define because their origin is typically idiosyncratic and their existence transitory against the longer perspective of the organizational life. For example, individuals may have specific attributes of personal charm or may hold a special relationship with formal authority figures, or they may have specific skills uniquely in demand at some special juncture in the organizational history. Individuals may have the much touted 'political skills', or, generally speaking, the ability to get their way without interpersonal conflict. Again, the parties bringing influence to bear may be technically outside the organization altogether. In this way wives become authority figures and the maxim *cherchez la femme* is well-coined. Or the pattern of influence may be negative, born of interpersonal animosities, leading to feuding, sabotage, and the undermining of authority. In these and incommensurable other ways the formal *logical* structure of authority and responsibility in the organization is continuously modulated. The workings and influence of informal authority cannot be predicted in advance nor indeed fully explained even after the fact. Case studies have repeatedly shown how difficult, hypothetical, and tenuous it is to isolate and identify the subcutaneous workings of individual influence.

The phenomenon of influence is unquestionably important, and it can assume pathological proportions, but the body of empirical research on informal organization presents us with very thin gruel. The logic of administration links power and authority to formal organization by way of the concept of responsibility and the characteristic of influence is that it is a form of power which evades responsibility in the sense of being formally accountable to the organization and its purpose. There is a sort of logic of administration which is expressed in the construction of more or less elaborate organization charts. These logical endeavours are perfectly legitimate. They may even, at best, be highly functional. They represent the *nomothetic* dimension of administrative rationality. Yet we must at once concede that the fabric of reality which they seek to structure and reduce has a compresent *idiographic* character which is never entirely negligible and which is fundamentally irreducible.

THOMPSON'S THESIS

According to Thompson (1961), modern organizations are increasingly dependent for the exercise of their functions upon the services of technical experts or specialists. Such specialists (e.g. engineers, accountants, faculty, skilled tradesmen, lawyers) individually represent large-scale, long-term career investments in professional or vocational training and as investors they may have extra-organizational loyalties, interests, and status satisfactions (Gouldner, 1957). Moreover, they embody an *authority of expertise* distinct from the *authority of position* represented by the hierarchy of the administration-management line. Furthermore, their specialist form of authority can often be directly identified with the organization mission in a way which is distinct from that of the hierarchy. Thus there is, for example, a sense in which schools exist to provide teaching-learning situations in which the central *authority* figure is the *teacher*. Likewise, hospitals provide healing situations in which the crucial authority figures are *doctors* and *nurses*. By contrast, the traditional theory of authority identifies the administrative *line* with the organizational purpose and hence endows the orthodox hierarchy with rights, status, and privileges distributed in the classical pyramidal manner. The growth of expertise authority can lead to intraorganizational conflict upon a number of grounds. The experts may claim to have a clearer vision and sense of the organizational purpose; they may challenge the legitimacy of line authority because of the disparity between perceived rights and abilities; and, idiographically, they may resent taking 'orders' from a 'superior' who is incapable of performing their technologically vital function, who is incompetent in their own terms. Conversely, the administration threatened in its credibility may seek to enlarge and enforce hierarchical privileges or resort to a variety of bureaupathological reactions such as dramaturgy and withdrawal (*ibid*. 138–78). In any event the potential will exist for contest about the organizational reward system, and the handling of any ensuing conflict will engage the administration as a self-interested party.

It is not that a power struggle is inevitable; there may not be disagreement about the role structure of the organization with its mutual interdependencies of role, but the seeds of conflict are present and the increasing possibility of conflict of authority paral-

lels the growth of technology. It is probably because of this administrative reality that the classical paradigm of hierarchy, the military
organization, is in modern times much less pyramidal. Air crew, for
example, usually hold commissioned rank and in contrast to less
technological times, there are relatively fewer unranked non-
specialists and relatively more chiefs. With sufficient increase of
technical specialization one might imagine the utlimate disappear-
ance of the generalized private soldier as such. And to some extent
this has already happened in industry with respect to the common
labourer.

What is at issue in Thompson-type challenges to authority is the
distinction, once again, between means and ends. I have argued that
in the last analysis authority is grounded in purpose—the ends of the
organization. If these ends are sharply focussed and clearly dependent for their achievement upon the co-operative articulation of
expertise-based means, and if the expertise is inaccessible or
inscrutable to those responsible for the articulation, that is, the
administration, then the organization pursuing such ends must have
a dualistic structure of authority. The threat of withdrawal of services, the power to strike, is consequently enlarged as technology in
effect increases both intra-organizational and inter-organizational
interdependence. The Barnardian view of authority is reinforced
and the need for philosophical, political, and diplomatic skills in
administration intensified.

Modern complexity suggests—if it does not demand—that
administrative competence should represent an expertise in its own
right. Administrators must be 'specialists in generalism' if they are
to reconcile the twin authorities of line and staff, hierarchy and
expert, under the aegis of organizational unity. Thompson's
analysis would lead us to predict an increasing dialectical tension
within organizational ranks. It also substantiates the trend towards
collegial administration for the collegial administrator has a foot in
both worlds. Yet the converse view should be taken into account
and this is that logically speaking, technical competence does not
argue for its possessor a corresponding administrative competence
any more than does administrative expertise presuppose technical
competence. What tends to be overlooked in discussions about the
Thompson thesis is the possibility, if not the actuality, of an *administrative* profession, replete in its own expertise and legitimized by its

own investment in professional training. As we have said before, however, administration is a putative profession and administrators are of three kinds (P2.42, 2.421 Chapter 13).

ANTI-AUTHORITARIANISM

The rational professional concept of authority at the heart of Weberian theory, and general bureaucratic practice is further undermined when the extra-organizational ethos is markedly anti-authoritarian or radically democratic in nature. The description and explanation of such climates of opinion is a matter for social historians. On the face of it causation is multiple: growth in formal and informal education, technical advances in communication, decline in the perceived quality of life; a sharpening perception that most of the gods (authority figures) made ever more familiar (and open to contempt) through improved techniques of communication are indeed made of mortal clay. Whatever the causes any anti-authoritarian mood is bound to affect administrative action. (If it is more than a mood or vogue, if it assumes the proportions of an ideology then it becomes a direct concern of administrative philosophy.[3]) Administrative reaction may take the form of modified *style*; administrators may become more overtly conciliatory, more persuasive in communication, more accepting of input, more anxious to maintain a 'low-profile,' and so on. There may be structural changes also, more co-optation and participation in decision making processes, more concessions (up to a point) in the reward system. It might appear indeed that the non-administrative member of the organization has much to gain and the administration much to lose by a whole-hearted and full-blown bout of anti-authoritarianism.

Yet the fact is that the logic of legitimate authority is unassailable if the premiss is accepted that authority stems from purpose. Purpose-formulation is a special kind of philosophic act. It refers back to the complex of interest composed of, first, the individual organization member, second, the organizational collectivity, and third, the extra-organizational polity. That these several interests should at times conflict is not only possible but likely; their analysis and reconciliation is the basic task of administrative philosophy, only when this task is defaulted can anti-authoritarianism be logically consistent.

LEADERSHIP

Power and authority merge in the concept of leadership. They also cease to be abstractions in that they become personified and *embodied*. Leadership is an abstraction but leaders are persons, fleshy creatures. Though an abstraction the term is in much currency in organizational life. It is a convenient slogan word, eulogistic, blurring many levels of meaning but also connoting many things which in an administrative sense are value-laden and significant. Its ambiguities make it a useful rhetorical instrument and the claimants to administrative office will also seek to appropriate many of the meanings inherent in the term, the more so as the word can serve as a semantic utterance which *eo ipso* legitimizes power, authority and rank. This usage is facilitated by the fact that the term 'leadership' is often, indeed usually, accepted uncritically and without analysis. It is almost unthinkingly attached as a sort of implicit function to the administrative-managerial subsystem of the organization and its slogan usage often passes unchallenged. It would be considered somewhat improper, if not plain insubordinate, for a subordinate to question his superior's use of the term by the request: 'Yes, but what do you *mean* by leadership. . .?'

Yet there is also a common understanding that leadership is not a mere attribute or concomitant of a formal authority role. Men seek administrative office on the grounds and with the claim that they, to a degree greater than their competitors, possess the qualities of leadership. There is thus a sort of established mythology about leadership which upon analysis seems to involve the assumptions that (1) it is a very good thing, (2) its qualities or components are known, (3) these qualities, components, traits, or attributes can be identified or associated with individuals, especially the individual laying claim to them, and (4) the natural home or resting place of this assemblage of virtues is with the administrative personnel of the organization. The empirical evidence does not entirely substantiate these assumptions. On the contrary the concept itself is obscure. We are not quite sure what we are talking about (hence the shift into rhetoric and the great *political* advantage of the term). 'There go the mob,' said the revolutionary Comte de Mirabeau, 'and I must follow them for I am their leader.'

At least three streams of thought can be brought to bear on this topic: the contributions of empirical social science, the speculative opinions of social scientists, and the general observations of orthodox administrative thought. Let us consider, briefly, each in turn.

It would require a large volume to present, even in digest form, the findings of studies which have been conducted on or about the phenomenon of leadership. Certainly we would have to include under this head the massive Hawthorne investigations (Roethlisberger and Dickson, 1939), as well as the classic Ohio Leadership Studies (Stogdill, 1948) and the extensive labours of individuals among whom the names of Bates, Fiedler, Stogdill, Selznick, and Lewin are by no means exhaustive. Large sums of money[4] and much intellectual effort have been expended and we have surely, as a result, come to appreciate the complexities of the leadership concept. A few generalizations can also be made. First, the trait theory of leadership has been exploded. This maintained that there were specific personal attributes or characteristics which could be shown to be highly correlated with leadership performance. Leaders exhibit an infinite variety of traits and attributes and though the belief in commonalities and generalities persists, and the search goes on (Reddin, 1970) the data have so far proved to be unyielding and the general notion has been set aside if not entirely discounted.

Second, factor analytic studies (Stogdill and Coons, 1957; Halpin, 1966, Chapter 3) concur in the isolation of two orthogonal dimensions which are variously described in the literature but which can be most easily thought of as referring to (1) the *task* of the led group; (2) the membership *morale* of the led group. Putting it oversimply, the effective leader is the one who can simultaneously score high on both of these dimensions. He sees that the assigned job is done *and* that the men doing it are not unhappy in the doing of it.

Third, leadership is a complex dynamic function which has at least the following analytic dimensions: the nature of the task; the psychological relationships between leader and led; the power and authority (formal and informal) of the leader; the informal organization in the followership, the favourableness of the situation (Fiedler, 1967); the characteristics and the character of the leader, and of the led; the general organizational structure, history and context.

Weber's analysis of leadership (Parsons, 1947) is a classification into the categories of traditional, rational, and charismatic. Traditional leaders come to their role through social conventions (monarchy, primogeniture, nepotism, oligarchical privilege) and rational leaders are appointed on the basis of expertise (bureaucratic professionals) but it is the charismatic category which intrigues. There is a general recognition, the defective trait theory notwithstanding, that there are forceful or magnetic personalities (Napoleon and Hitler are historical archetypes) who possess the elusive quality of charisma. This quality is not properly understood; it is mysterious, but its possessors seem capable of inducing extraordinary fealty on the part of their followers, and also seem able to exert their will in an extraordinary way upon the led. Though the concept is unpleasantly vague the phenomenon itself is sometimes disturbingly real. The gamut of its organizational manifestations is another problem for administrative philosophy, though not under the subdivision of logic. I am inclined to the suspicion that the charismatic leader has a special gift of being able to verbalize the wishes (conscious or unconscious) of the followership; to voice the desires that they cannot properly express, and to give them thereby a sense of meaning or purpose. In the search for purpose, meaning, vocation, man will reach beyond life itself. And certainly beyond logic.

Lastly, there is the view, not unconnected with what has just been said, of the leader as moral exemplar. This notion tends to receive short shift in the administrative literature, with the notable exception of the work of Barnard. Orthodoxy and conventional administrative thought does link the difficult concept of leadership to the equally difficult concept of responsibility but seems to assume straightforward and automatic connection. Simon's logical positivist leader simply effects the values of the organization, and there is no need for psychological propositions about him (see above, p. 20). Barnard's ideas are more Platonic and unique. We shall discuss them in the next section. For now it remains to be noted that leadership can be formal as designated by the organization role structure and this a *prerogative* of administration; or informal, appearing anywhere within the ranks of the organization. Enough has been said to show that the concept of leadership is complex indeed and that its facile usage among the naïve must be discriminated from its sense, reference, and intent in administrative philosophy.

LEADERSHIP AS EXCELLENCE

In a democratic ethos there is an emotional attachment to, and consequent confusion about, the concept of equality and, concomitantly, a tendency to be ambivalent about superiority. I have gone into this elsewhere (Hodgkinson, 1973) and am somewhat persuaded to the view that meritocracy, *could* it be defined and translated into actuality, would be *logically* preferable to democracy. Such a logical preference for aristocratic elitism can also be discerned in the writings of Barnard, paradoxically one of the foremost exponents of the doctrine that power and authority are essentially seated in the lower levels of the organizational hierarchy. The argument depends upon what is meant by superiority. Superiority in the sense of technical excellence or superior competence is that which is logically desirable in the technologies, sciences, and arts. This reasoning should also logically apply to administration, management, and leadership. But when superiority is conjoined with formal role authority, this is in turn with a hierarchy of privilege, status, responsibility, and power; and, further, when this superiority extends to the determination of the quality of a subordinate's organizational life, then suddenly there is cause for caution. Mere technical superiority is somehow not quite enough; save perhaps in a world inhibited by logical positivists. Outside of such a Wonderland more is demanded, but it is difficult to specify with precision just what this more may be. Barnard seems to insist that it is a capacity of *moral* excellence, a capacity for 'moral complexity'.

What is it that endows a leader with the quality of leadership? First, it would not seem to be something which can be constructed—formal authority may be designed, legislated, structured, but leadership authority is different in that it appears to be something which is *conceded from the followership*. Though it tends to be claimed by most administrators as a specific and transferable competence, it is organization-bound to the extent that it is dependent upon follower perceptions, upon the operative context of phenomenologically conceived and invented social reality within an organization. To that extent it cannot just be traded in the market-place of unemployed executives. Yet is there a personal leadership quality or attribute?

Barnard's explanation is this: There are two dimensions to leadership, and both represent a kind of superiority. The first kind results in technical proficiency and is a superiority 'in physique, in skill, in technology, in perception, in knowledge, in memory, in imagination.' (260) The second is

> the more general; the more constant; the least subject to specific development; the more absolute; the subjective; that which reflects the attitudes and ideals of society and its general institutions. It is the aspect of individual superiority in determination, persistence, endurance, courage; that which determines the *quality* of action; which often is most inferred from what is *not* done, from abstention; which commands respect, reverence. It is the aspect of leadership we commonly imply in the word 'responsibility,' the quality which gives dependability and determination to human conduct, and foresight and ideality to purpose. (*ibid.*)

This passage approaches the rhapsodic and it seems to suggest that the proper leader is a kind of paragon. We must note not merely the conventional 'bag of virtues' but also Barnard's unique stress on a quality of restraint, removal, abstinence, or aloofness . . . it is deciding when *not* to decide, *not* deciding what should be decided by others, that which is *not* done, that which is *abstained from* which is important. And there is an almost 'religious' overtone. A little earlier he has described leadership in these words:

> '. . . the power of individuals to inspire cooperative personal decision by creating faith: faith in common understanding, faith in probability of success, faith in the ultimate satisfaction of personal motives, faith in the integrity of objective authority, faith in the superiority of common purpose as a personal aim of those who partake in it.' (259)

Faith. Integrity. Inspiration! And later, having characterized leadership as the strategic factor in achieving cooperation he reiterates that its components are (1) technical competence (2) moral 'complexity' and (3) a 'propensity for consistency in conformance to moral factors of the individual.' (288)

This language is quite different from the sterilized terminology of administrative science and empiricism: 'initiating-structure-in-interaction' (Halpin); 'least preferred coworker correlations' (Fiedler) and 'cognitive-affective two-way subsystem orientation' (Katz and Kahn). Still, it cannot escape the scrutiny of the administrative philosopher. Barnard is speaking from a background of executive experience and reflection. His ideas demand attention not so much on the ground of their empirical truth—they are generated after all from intuition and a case study sample of one—but because his concern with the *moral* component of leadership has been ignored or elided, despite its resonance with Plato's work in the *Republic*, by most of the contemporary theory and research.[5] The distinction here seems to be what was referred to previously (pp. 15–21) as the distinction between character and characteristics. Whatever moral superiority may be, whatever its subtle components, the ordinary usage is pragmatically understood, as is evidenced from the claims of persons seeking political leadership offices. It has a well established rhetorical function and even the most modest and retiring of administrators, by the very fact of holding administrative office, is laying some sort of organizational claim to this special competence, a competence which takes us, however, across the frontier of logic into the discourse about value.

PROBLEMS

The problems which our observations have so far raised are manifold. There is, of course, the unpleasant logical imprecision of the concepts discussed in these pages, concepts fundamental to the field of administration. To the extent that these problems are merely logical, having to do with the consistency of a language and its propositions, the difficulty can be overcome through agreement upon working definitions and syntax. Or, psychologically, they can be ignored by a means of a tacit agreement to live with ambiguity and vagueness, leaving any worrying or fretting to scholars and men of inaction. The latter seems to be the solution most practised in the field. But there are problems which go beyond mere disorder and untidiness in the body of knowledge, and though these are for the most part valuational, we have already seen that few administrative utterances can be made before implications of value are raised.

Consider, for example, the proposition that organizations are interest composites (P3).* As benefit devices they embody an internal reward system (P3.6112). This system distributes quantified rewards in the form of monetary emoluments and qualitative rewards in the form of psychological gratifications, rank, status, prestige, opportunities for intrinsic work satisfactions, a fireplace in one's office, the use of the company limousine, and so on. Who carves and distributes this pie? In the conventional orthodoxy it is a function and prerogative of the administration. Upon what logic? Upon the grounds that the administrative subsystem has the responsibility for formulating and achieving the organizational ends, and because it has the system perspective and overview and is thus best located within the organizational space to assess and determine the contributions of members. Eminently reasonable. But we have seen already that there is a challenge to this argument from the direction of specialist competence and the authority of expertise. We have also seen that if this challenge is rebutted on the grounds of the specialist expertise of administration there is then (as there has been for that matter all along) the further presumption of leadership. And this can imply paragon qualities—the moral leadership of Barnard and Plato.

Even more eminently reasonable, then, that superior rewards should flow to superior contributors. (We shall ignore for the moment that this contradicts Plato, whose Guardians would have an austere lot indeed.) There is now the problem, however, as to how administrators prove these special competencies. Are they a result of their background and training? Is there some form of professional investment which endows them with these attributes? Or are they God-given, innate, haphazard, or perhaps a by-product of (say) legal training?

Again, much of the argument hinges upon the notion of *responsibility*, a concept which we have yet to examine but which an established authority defines as 'responsiveness to values' (Simon *et al.*, 1950, 548). Does the distribution of responsibility parallel the organizational distributions of power, authority, status, and reward? Who is capable of the greater *irresponsibility*; the workman

---

* The numbers in parentheses refer to the propositions listed in the concluding chapter.

or the vice-president? These problems would lead us at once beyond the frontiers of administrative and organizational logic into an exploration of the constituents of those regions depicted as dotted circles in Figures 5 and 6 above (pp. 41, 43). That is, into personality and value theory.

Throughout this initial survey of the logic of administration we have been seeking those special competencies which would distinguish an administrative profession. These would now seem to include at least the following: Some special understanding of organizations and the body of theory accumulated on this subject to date. Some special understanding and knowledge of the theory and practice of decision making, especially of that class of decisions subsumed in the concept of policy. This in turn implies some special competence in the domains of (1) logical analysis, (2) value analysis. It also suggests psychological attributes (imagination, will, empathy, etc.) which, though part of the human endowment, may be especially called upon in the exercise of administration. Finally, there is the elusive concept of leadership with all that it entails by way of moral components and interpersonal skills.

I would be the first to concede that these competencies are not well comprehended and are vague in conception and definition. Obscure or not, however, an administrative profession would have to engage itself in their mastery. The alternatives are dilettantism, amateur incompetence, and compounded corruption of both amateur and professional. At stake is the quality of organizational life, the ratio of harmony to conflict within and without organizations. More than this. We all by virtue of our interdependence share in the consequences of organizational harmony or disharmony; we all live in and by organizations, directly as members or indirectly as associates or clientele. We are all, therefore, administered or administering. Human worth, human dignity, the meaning of human life is involved in this. And already we have gone beyond logic, into value.

SUMMARY: PART ONE

The first part of this book has tried to show that, while administration is a rational pursuit, its rational boundaries are heavily circumscribed. This is so because of the intensely human character of this activity, one which depends for its accomplishments entirely upon the cooperative endeavours of men assembled in purposive organizations. The activity of administration is of increasing significance as society becomes increasingly complex, differentiated, organized, and administered. If a distinctive administrative profession exists, or is coming to be, the fact is noteworthy from a social standpoint. If it does not exist and our collective lives are dependent on amateurs then this fact is also important.

This survey of the putative profession of administration and the general search for a logic of administration leads us towards certain propositions. Chief among these are the beliefs that administration can be construed as philosophy in action; that we are all either administered or administering; that organizations are purposive collectivities; that man finds a large part of his life-meaning in organizations; that administration is a moral activity; and that power is the central term of administrative discourse.

Professions seek bodies of rational principles and specialist knowledge or logic. Their claim upon the social reward system must be grounded in some form of expertise that is in social demand. The ideal is often indicated by the eulogistic term, science. But administration cannot qualify as a science despite some pretensions to the contrary. There is, it is true, a body of knowledge, a subset of social science, which can be put forward as organization theory and which can serve partly as a basis for a claim to some special administrative competence. The main administrative acts, however, are decisional and the quintessential form of administration is the making of policy. These imply philosophical skills and entail the exercise of power, influence, authority, and leadership.

Administrators, however they may come to their role, and they may come in three logically distinct ways, are identified with a hierarchy within the organization which includes among its functions the control of the organizational reward system. There is increasingly the problem of organizational authority, that which is based on specialist expertise and that which is hierarchical. The problem at the heart of administration has to do with the question: who is to rule? Much orthodoxy and much conventional wisdom argues that amateur administrators should rule professional managers. Yet the logic of contemporary administration may already be such that the amateur is rendered if not impotent then at least illogical.

It would be reasonable to presume that administrators are, on the average, ordinary men rather than supermen. Some of the mythology and popular belief nevertheless attributes extraordinary qualities to administrative leaders. Plato in antiquity and Barnard in modern times add substance to these conceptions. Even more remarkable is the logical positivist idea that the executive can approximate to a robot-like personification of his organization's values.

Problems about the characteristics of administration and the character of administrators inevitably lead us into the realm of discourse dealing with values. Administration is not a pseudo-science, and, while it has at its disposal a managerial quasi-technology, it is essentially a philosophical endeavour, a kind of humanism. Its overriding mission is the civilization of power.

II
VALUE

If the unexamined life is not worth living the unexamined value is not worth holding.

6
The Nature of Value

The first part of this book has made the argument that a knowledge of value somewhat beyond that of the ordinary man is a desirable professional attribute in administration. Such an argument may be persuasive without being conclusive. One may still maintain that the instinctive or unsophisticated value knowledge of the man in the street is adequate for the practical pursuits of management and administration. Why should administrators be any more value-knowledgeable than their fellows? Is this not somehow pretentious and unnecessary? After all, values are everywhere and their con-flicts are daily resolved; let philosophers and political scientists worry over the formulation and resolution of such problems while administrators concentrate on the running of their organizations.

I shall seek to answer these questions and contest the underlying attitude of *laissez faire* as we progress in our inquiry, but for now perhaps we can at least agree that there is a large component of value judgment in the practice of administration and that adminis-trative action affects the quality of organizational and extra-organizational life. This should be incentive enough. Before pro-ceeding to a closer scrutiny of the value problem it is first necessary to define some terms and reach some common understandings. What follows may become technical and apparently removed from ordinary administrative discourse, but it is essential to any deeper understanding of values in administration.

THE BASIC DUALISM

Administration is characterized by a number of dualisms as has been shown in Part One (P1.1231; 1.3212; 1.34; 2; 3.2; 4.2) but the dualism of most direct interest here is that between fact and value. The distinction is most important philosophically and easily grasped by common sense but it is not quite as facile as Simon, writing from a

positivistic standpoint, might lead us to believe. 'Factual propositions,' he says, 'are statements about the observable world and
the way in which it operates' (1965, p. 45). Presumably he means by
'world' the region of publicly verifiable experience where
measurements can be taken and agreed upon and colours, sights,
and sounds labelled and identified in the proper names of ordinary
language. But surely some private unverifiable statements are also
facts. The pain in my tooth can never be experienced by anyone but
myself, yet it is a factual proposition in the observable world of my
dentist and affects the way in which he operates.

The problem is that we live simultaneously in two worlds, the
worlds of overlapping value and fact. It is also not quite right to
define facts in terms of the propositions of physics, for the latter are
conceptual hypotheses forever inaccessible to direct sensory
experience. My pencil may be a transient compresence of molecular
particles (or atomic wavicles in a space-time flux) but it is a relatively tangible, relatively persistent, and distinctive *fact* within my
sphere of action. And it already has *value* in that it is useful to me, it
works, it is made of gold, it was given to me by a lady-love, it has
been around in my life a long time . . . and so on and on until the
factual object which *in essence is valueless* is imbued with any
amount of value or worth. So value, fact, and the hypotheses of
scientific conception cohere and are simultaneously compresent.
How to differentiate?

It might not be precisely true but perhaps we can adopt the
convention that one of our two worlds, the world of fact, is *given* and
the other, the world of value, is *made*. The former is objective; we
had little or no hand in it. The latter is subjective; we can have as
much of a hand in it as we wish. The characteristic of the given
factual world is that it is publicly verifiable and logically consistent.
Given the axioms and presuppositions of arithmetic 'one and one
make two' and this proposition is a conceptual or intellectual fact.
The world of facts is also, and preeminently, before us in the stuff
and furniture of the observable world. This world is an object of
perception, and science is the discrimination, analysis, and comprehensive synthesis which follows upon acts of perception. Perception stimulates conception, and conversely. They interact. As per-
cepts and concepts become increasingly sophisticated and refined
the sub-languages or jargons of scientific discourse proliferate and

the world can be, depending upon choice or preference, reduced to biology or chemistry or physics or even the strange transcendences and dissolutions of sub-atomic energy fields. At this level the hard corners and sharp edges of the universe of fact vanish altogether into infinities, improbabilities, and indeterminacies. Energy is the last bastion of materialism.

All this is quite beyond the normal range of administrative factual discourse, at least until it is brutally brought back into focus by discernible events such as a nuclear fusion explosion or the negotiation for the funding to bring about such an explosion. It is also the case that shifts in level of discourse reflect shifts in values, for the values of the physicist are not necessarily or likely those of the administrator who employs him. Let us agree, however, that facts, no matter how difficult they may be to define,[1] refer to propositions which are ostensible, publicly verifiable, and in some way possessing the quality of being *true*.

It is this last attribute, the quality of truth, which most clearly distinguishes values from facts for value can *never* be true or false. Values are facts of a kind. They are concepts. They are subjective. They occur only in the head. They can be defined in a preliminary way as 'concepts of the desirable with motivating force.'

There is an important point to be made here; it is that while values *can* be thought of as special kinds of facts, they are logically distinct. More, the world of value is *altogether* different from the world of fact though it be compresent with and superimposed upon it. Let me explain. A value can exist only in the mind of the value-holder and it refers to some notion of the desirable, or preferred state of affairs, or to a condition which *ought* to be. It becomes 'factual' once it is expressed in language or made the object of observation. But to move from the 'is' of fact or the 'is' of logic to the 'ought' of value one must make a quantum leap. The world of factual existence is valueless! Mass-energy displacements in a space-time continuum utterly void of value.

The objective terminology of science and logic deals with the true and the false. The subjective terms of value are 'good' and 'bad', 'right' and 'wrong'. What administrators, philosophers, and men in the street would wish to know, and what science can never tell them, is how to 'know' the good and the bad, the right and the wrong. It is a very special concern of administrative philosophy. Science answers no value questions, but rather creates them as it enlarges the field of factual sophistication.

To confuse value with fact or to presume that the former can somehow be derived from the latter is to commit what Moore called the naturalistic fallacy (1903, 10, 18–20). Moore was particularly concerned with the value term 'good' which he declared could not be defined or analyzed because it was a primitive term in language. It was essentially private.

I would concur that the experience of the good is thoroughly subjective and that it is a superimposition upon an objective ground. Value is a function of individual mind, sentience, consciousness. Facts can subsist (if only as expectations) independently of individual consciousnesses. The tree I am observing and the world of which it is a natural part will persist as continuing events for other observers after this I-now observer, the assemblage of events known as 'I', has disintegrated and ceased to be part of the here-now for postulated future observers. But what I cannot legitimately do is find value 'out there' in the present scenario of events. There is no 'object' in the world which *is good*. There is no goodness in the world as there is blackness or heaviness or roughness to the touch. There may be many things which are valu*able* but nothing which is *of* value. Exactly likewise there is nothing that is beautiful. The ground of perception is a bare canvas upon which we project goodness and beauty and all the palette of values. We do not value anything because it *has* value but because we *give* it value. To do the former (as administrators are often tempted to do) is to commit the naturalistic fallacy.

Let us recapitulate. Apart from human perception the world is valueless. Human interaction with the world *discovers* facts and imposes values. Although these two activities are conjoined, the discovery of facts may induce men to vary their imposition of values and the pattern of values may determine the facts which are discovered; no amount of empirical knowledge or logic can prove, justify, or legitimate value in any objective sense. To think that we can find the rightness of value from a study of nature is to commit the naturalistic fallacy.

VALUE TERMINOLOGY

To disentangle, so far as we can, value from fact is a step forward in our understanding, but we must now cope with another order of linguistic confusion. This stems both from common sense and from the facts and theories of psychology. An example is provided by the term 'needs'. Maslow, the great psychological value theorist, rarely wrote of values as such, but preferred instead to talk about needs. What are needs and how are they to be distinguished from (say) wants or desires?

The idea behind need is that of a discrepancy or undesirable imbalance in a state of affairs. Needs imply tension and disequilibrium and provide a dynamic for rectifying action. We shall take needs and the cognate terms 'desires' or 'wants' as being indicators of some state of individual or group deficiency or shortfall with a consequent potential or propensity for remedial action. As such they are *sources* of value.

Needs, wants, and desires are also related to the concept of motive. The idea behind motivated behaviour is usually that there is for the motivated actor some kind of end-in-view. The trouble with this interpretation is that the end may not be 'in view'. It may be semiconscious or even unconscious. The impulse to action may be subliminal; psychological language contains such concepts as 'drives' and 'drive states' about which there is much contention and inconclusive experimentation. For our purposes, let us accept motives as either conscious reasons or unconscious drives, or some combination of both, which are a *source* of value. I may be fully aware, partially aware, or totally unaware of my motives for action, but the fact that I myself or other observers can pass value judgments upon those motives is sufficient to show that value is something other than motives, desires, wants, or needs.

Motives then have this push-pull correlation with consciousness and the faculty of reason. To be completely unmotivated is not to exist as a sentient being. To be fully aware of all our motives would be to be supersentient. And to approve of them all would be superhuman. Motives existing in the depths of the psyche as dark forces of the id or fully exposed in the light of day as validated and justified *reasons* are also correlated with the phenomena of *attitude*.

I wish to define attitudes as surface phenomena, predispositions to act or respond to stimuli in relatively stable or persistent ways.[2] As motives provide a source of value, so value is a source of attitudes. Attitudes are manifestations of values at the interface of skin and world. The world demands attention in a great variety of ways. How we attend is a function of our attitudes. And attitudes are measurable facts in the world. If we take the simplest biological organism we may by observation reduce and classify the number of attitudes to two or three: fight, flight, or freeze. For the complex human organism the attitudes may be legion because this level of organic complexity is linguistic, engages continuously in language games (one of which is called administration) and *expresses* its attitudes in language categories, some of which are referred to as opinions. Thus, polls assess collective attitudes and individuals are categorized as open-minded or close-minded, conservative, radical, authoritarian, permissive, innovative, and so *ad psychologium nauseamque infinitum*.

Let us note, however, the arithmetic of this line of reasoning. First, there is the unitary self (we avoid the complexity of split and multiple personalities described in psychoanalytic literature). Next, a very few basic motives: perhaps a bare will to survive or the Freudian dualism of Eros and Thanatos, an urge to life counterbalanced by a wish for surcease. At a more surface level, but still interior and closely related to the integration of the self the deepseated motives are manifested in a system of *values*. These value complexes or value orientations depend upon their holder's circumstances, biography, and culture. They may be unconscious and in logical contradiction as, for example, when kindness and honesty are openly (consciously) expressed, but the ruthless and dishonest acquisition of wealth and success secretly or subliminally admired. The values are more in number than the motives[3] but less than the attitudes. Both, however, are organized more or less cohesively into systems. Emergent at the interface of psyche and world, at skin-level as it were, are the attitudes, expressions of preference and predispositions to act in response to the countless issues of living and life style. They are commensurable in so far as they can be observed, classified, and organized so as to make conceptual sense. In number they logically exceed the underlying values which they represent. Lastly, there is the realm of behaviour and action with its incommensurable infinity of possibilities. Behaviours manifest as observable facts connected by inference through chains of cause and effect to the psychological phenomena of attitudes, value orientations, values, motives, and self-concept. The scheme described above is shown diagrammatically in Figure 10. The figure is not intended to be dogmatic or definitive. It does not specify, for example, the locus or function of *will*, about which much more will have to be said later, nor does it explain how the several components are articulated. But it is pragmatically useful as a descriptive and explicatory device for the argument which follows. It postulates a continuum at one end of which are private (but culturally conditioned) value phenomena, perhaps intensely private and inaccessible to public verification. At the other end of the continuum are purposive behaviours and strivings taking place in an observable,

Figure 10: Schema of Value-related Terms

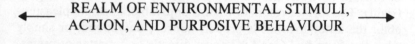

REALM OF ENVIRONMENTAL STIMULI,
ACTION, AND PURPOSIVE BEHAVIOUR

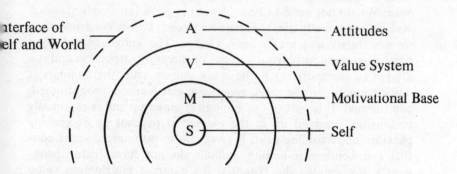

Interface of
Self and World

A ——— Attitudes
V ——— Value System
M ——— Motivational Base
S ——— Self

public, collective realm in which motives can be spelled out linguistically as goals and collective purposes and in which values can be expressed verbally as ideals, *summa boni*, social norms, and cultural standards. Such values may occasionally be objectified into systems of law, codes of ethics, systematized philosophies and ideologies. Between these extremes lie the gamut of attitudes, opinions, preferences. The continuum is dynamic through the action of modulating feedbacks and feedforwards. From its ground in individual consciousness to its relevation in the public play of sensory data, the universe is intentional and teleological.

A VALUE MODEL

I now wish to present an analytical model of the value concept which I believe has some merit in helping us to chart our way across the seas of value confusion. It will also enable us to classify values and establish eventually some bases for the resolution of value conflicts, but its present use will be in developing a common understanding and terminology for the remainder of this inquiry. The model is given in Figure 11 opposite.

The first distinction drawn in the model is to break apart the basic concept of value into its two components of the 'right' and the 'good'. This is the difference between the 'desirable' and the 'desired' (cf. Kant, 1909, 285) and is technically known as the distinction between the axiological (good) and the deontological (right). The former refers to what is enjoyable, likeable, pleasureable; the latter to what is proper, 'moral', dutybound, or simply what *'ought* to be.' *Good* is known directly as a matter of preference. We do not need to be told what is good (although Madison Avenue continually tries) because we already *know*. We drink when we are thirsty and prefer beer. Or tea. The knowledge of good comes spontaneously from impulse or direct introspection and is a kind of value experience we have in common with other animals. It may be innate, biochemical, genetic, or else learned, programmed, conditioned. It is part of our biological make-up and is essentially hedonistic, summed up in the elemental psychology of seeking pleasure and avoiding pain. It gives rise to no internal value conflict (an hence non-human animals do not have 'value problems'), but creates the potential for external interhuman value conflict in the general competition for satisfaction from limited resources.

The other dimension of value is the one, we are tempted to say, which really causes the trouble, and it is logically different. We have (although it will be denied by some philosophers) a moral sense, or sense of collective responsibility, a conscience, or perhaps, psychologically speaking, a 'superego'. At the personal level this gives rise to a kind of internal conflict—two desirables warring within the bosom of a single self—as we feel on the one side the pull of affect and on the other the demands of the situation and what ought to be done. It is the common experience of daily discipline in

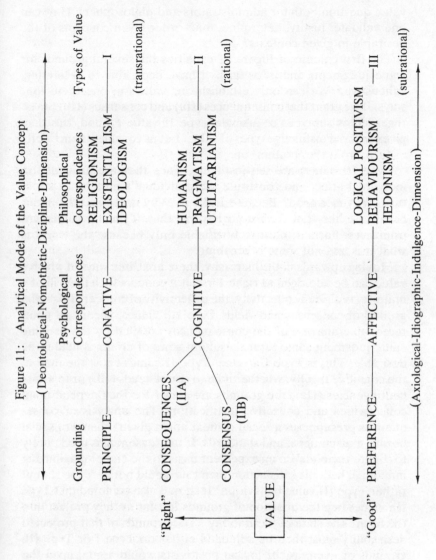

Figure 11: Analytical Model of the Value Concept

(Deontological-Nomothetic-Dicipline-Dimension)

Grounding	Psychological Correspondences	Philosophical Correspondences	Types of Value
PRINCIPLE——CONATIVE		RELIGIONISM	
		EXISTENTIALISM——I	(transrational)
		IDEOLOGISM	
	COGNITIVE	HUMANISM	
		PRAGMATISM——II	(rational)
		UTILITARIANISM	
CONSEQUENCES (IIA)			
CONSENSUS (IIB)			
"Right"		LOGICAL POSITIVISM	
VALUE	AFFECTIVE	BEHAVIOURISM——III	(subrational)
"Good"——PREFERENCE		HEDONISM	

(Axiological-Idiographic-Indulgence-Dimension)

foregoing our self-indulgent desires in favour of other more nomothetic demands.

But how are these demands to be justified? Upon what grounds do we override our emotive claims and impulses? This is the basic value question both for administrators and philosophers. How can one validate, justify, determine, rank-order given concepts of the desirable in given contexts?

The first column of Figure 11 classifies the several grounds for value judgments and is, as far as I have been able to determine, exhaustive.[4] We can only establish our values in one these four ways. If we grant that consequences (IIa) and consensus (IIb) can be regarded as subtypes of a single Type II value ground, this then gives us three distinctive types of value. Let us consider them briefly in turn, from the 'bottom' up.

Type III values are self-justifying, since they are grounded in individual affect and constitute the individual's preference structure. Why is x good? Because I like it. Why do I like it? I like it because I like it. I cannot go beyond that. Type III values are primitives. Facts of nature. Justifiable only because the world is what it is and not some other thing.

Moving upwards in the hierarchy, there are three ways in which a value can be adjudged as right. First, if it concurs with the will of a majority in a given collectivity, the collectivity of context. This is the ground of consensus and yields Type IIb values. Second, if upon reasonable analysis of the consequences entailed by the pending value judgment some future resultant state of affairs is held to be desirable. This is Type IIa value. Type II values enlist the reason, the cognitive faculty, whether it be to count heads (IIb) or to assess contingencies (IIa); the grounds are *social* for they depend upon collectivities and collective justification. The analysis of consequences presupposes a social context and a given scheme of social norms, expectations, and standards. If the reasoning is used purely to 'figure the odds' on an expedient basis to the end of maximizing individual hedonic satisfaction then this would not be Type IIa but rather Type III value behaviour.[5] It should also be noted that Type IIa values beg the question of grounds insofar as they project into the future the state of 'desirability'. The grounds of that projected desirability must then be adjudged either on Type I or Type IIb grounds or even, as the logical positivists would argue, upon the collective preferential grounds of Type III.

Lastly, there are Type I values. The grounding of Type I values is metaphysical. We can concede this without apology. I have called such grounds grounds of principle. The principles take the form of ethical codes, injunctions, or commandments, such as the Kantian categorical imperative or the Mosaic 'Thou shalt not kill', but whether they derive from a postulated moral insight, an asserted religious revelation, or an aesthetic sense of individual drama, their common feature is that they are unverifiable by the techniques of science and cannot be justified by merely logical argument. The farthest that argument can lead is to an ethic of enlightened self-interest. But this is essentially Type IIa in grounding, a sort of game theory solution to the problem of maximizing hedonic (Type III) satisfactions. Type I values have, moreover, a quality of absoluteness which distinguishes them from the more relative Type II values and the entirely relative Type III values. Principles are also *transrational* in that, while they *need* not conflict with rationality, they may equally well do so and may be, from a Type II standpoint, perverse, irrational, absurd as (say) when human sacrifice of the Kamikaze variety is grounded in extreme patriotism or when one finds murder desirable on existential grounds (Camus, Dostoievsky). The characteristic of Type I values is that they are based on the will rather than upon the reasoning faculty; their adoption implies some kind of act of faith, belief, commitment.

The second column of Figure 11 shows the psychological correspondences for each of the three types of value. Type III values are rooted in the emotional structure; they are affective, idiosyncratic, idiographic, and direct. They are basically a-social and hedonistic. Type II values engage the reasoning faculty; they are preeminently rational, cognitive, collective and social. To the extent that they conflict with and override tendencies to individual indulgence, they are disciplinary and nomothetic. They tend to lead to an ethic of enlightened self-interest or some form of humanistic liberalism, this being as far as logic and the cognitive faculty can go in the determination of an ethic or system of cohesive moral imperatives. Type I values invoke the will. An act of faith or commitment is necessary. This act can only be done on an individual basis, and so in a sense Type I values are highly idiographic, although they may be nomothetically endorsed. Let me illustrate.

A ballet company endorses artistic merit, a military organization subscribes to the value of patriotism, a football team is dedicated to winning. In each case Type I values are set up which must be individually adopted by the sweating dancer, the bleeding soldier, and the bruised player. Dancer, soldier, and player must each at some point have made some act of personal commitment to the respective value. If they have not, they may still accept the degraded Type I value at the level of consensus, Type IIb, that is, as a norm or level of expectation peculiar to that collectivity. Needless to say, there is a change in the quality of commitment if this is the case and administrators would generally prefer to induce the higher level type of engagement in subordinates. More than the member's reason must have been involved where Type I values are operative, and this *more* is not a simple matter of emotive preference. Because of this more, because of the deontological or duty aspect of value, any discussion of the value concept leads easily into questions about the phenomena of loyalty, commitment, guilt, conscience, and responsibility. These concepts are difficult at both the philosophical and the psychological levels of analysis but they refer generally to those personal experiences of internal states of tension between the types of value portrayed in the two arms of the model.

The figure also shows in column 3 some of the main philosophical correspondences. Type III values are those which lend themselves to the reductions of logical positivism and behaviourism. In the extreme case we can argue that *all* values are mere expressions of emotive preference. To declare 'murder is wrong' or 'one should not kill' is only to say 'Murder, ugh!' or 'I do not *like* killing.' (Ayer, 1946, 103–110) One may counter that this position simultaneously commits the naturalistic fallacy and unjustifiably elevates logic and science above ethics and values (itself an emotive preference), but the strength of the arguments underlying it are not to be underestimated and, in administrative philosophy, the position is exemplified by Simon. Again, at the sociological level, the so-called playboy and hippie philosophies of self-indulgence are by no means inconsistent with the positivist position.

Type II values, as already indicated, correspond to the philosophical positions of humanism, utilitarianism and pragmatism. They are buttressed by the social status quo, and the ethos, mores, laws, customs and traditions of a given culture. This may be attributable to the postulate of degeneration, as explained below. In general, reason and compromise are venerated, and the subscription to prudence and expediency makes such philosophical orientations particularly attractive to administrators.

Type I values have metaphysical or transrational grounds. In consequence, they are often codified in religious systems. Such systems can, of course, be quite atheistic, as in Communism and in some forms of Buddhism. They can also be deliberately irrational, or perhaps anti-rational, as where the Nazi recruit swears a blood oath in the forest or the French existentialist, convinced that the universe is alien and absurd, yet seeks 'authenticity' by 'becoming engaged' to a code of values. Once again, to the logical positivist such values are either literally non-sense or else they, like Type II values, are disguised expressions of affect—emotive preference at one or two removes. We need not enter the arguments between philosophical schools at this point—our object is only to comprehend the model—but we may note that while the positivists reject the upper dimension altogether the adherents of Type II values must walk a razor's edge between the chasms of positivistic nihilism on the one side and metaphysical commitment on the other.

POSTULATES

The model of value expounded above carries with it some far-reaching implications. These extend both to the problem of resolution of value conflicts and to the formulation of a value theory or philosophy. For example, the model implies that the value problem is a universal feature of the human condition and is defined by the tension which exists between the lower dimension of indulgence and the upper dimension of denial. Everyone, with the possible exceptions of saints, supermen, and psychopaths, experiences this dialectical tension. For the saint it disappears because he *wishes* to do what *ought* to be done; affect and will are unified. And for the Nietzschean Superman there is again no ambivalence, for what he wishes *is* what is right: he is *jenseits Güte und Böse*, beyond Good and Evil. But ordinary men lead lives of inner conflict; they are exposed to the warring clash of moral codes without and to the internal stress between the value dimensions within. The conflict is not simply a matter of the desirable versus the desired, it is as likely to be one between two or more desirables or between two or more desireds. We have to choose between rights and between goods as well as between right and good. Taken together with the continuous interplay of interest which is intrinsic to organizational behaviour this value complexity substantiates Barnard's claim (272–278) that the critical contribution of administrative leadership is a capacity for the creative resolution of moral conflicts.

The model also suggests three postulates:

Postulate 1: Hierarchy. Implicit in the model is the idea that Type I values are superior, more authentic, better justified, of more defensible grounding than Type II.[6] Likewise, Type II superior to Type III; and the nomothetic or moral dimension to the idiographic or indulgent dimension. There is a hierarchy of rank.

Postulate 2: Degeneration. Values tend to lower their level of grounding over time. There is a natural tendency for values to lose their authenticity or force. The force of moral insight attenuates.

Postulate 3: Avoidance. There will be a natural tendency to resolve value conflicts at the lowest level of hierarchy possible in a given situation. We seek to avoid moral issues. This applies particularly in administration.

Let me illustrate these postulates by examples from ethics, aesthetics, and administration.

The notion of adultery as a wrong (and conversely of marital fidelity as a positive good) may originally have been instituted by a creative moral thinker or moral leader on bases of moral insight, intuition, and conviction. In the course of time and with public acceptance this institution might degenerate, its original moral force might be weakened, but the value can still be justified on prudential, expedient, pragmatic grounds such as enlightened self-interest; it being argued at the cognitive level, for example, that a society in which adultery is disapproved may be on the whole more functional or beneficent than one in which it is not. Again, the force of this cognitive moral reasoning may weaken and degenerate until fidelity or non-adultery becomes a mere norm or social expectation, that which is right because it is the conventional expectation of the majority. Finally, all moral force may be spent and the value becomes merely a matter of individual preference. One does one's own thing, subject only to the reality constraints provided by the moral vestiges of marital law and societal norms.[7]

From aesthetics let us take the example of (say) Turner's paintings. These may have been conceived by the artist on the basis of deep insight into nature, profound conceptions which he then strove to render in his work. Initially they were not understood or appreciated by critics lacking these insights, but with the passage of time, they were defended at the cognitive or intellectual level by, in this instance, the critic Ruskin. Eventually, larger numbers of aesthetes were persuaded of their value and in time the appreciation of Turner became an aesthetic norm, or social convention. Finally this level of justification could also pass and it would be argued that the works have value over other works only in accord with individual preference; beauty is entirely subjective and in the end, nihilistically, everything (or nothing) is beautiful. The original vision is no longer transmitted even dimly through the intellect or the lenses of social convention but, if at all, darkly through idle and fleeting preference.

The postulate of avoidance has been called by Broudy the 'principle of least principle' (1965, 42–58) and he gives as example the case where Negroes marching against housing discrimination (a moral issue) are arrested on the count of traffic obstruction (a relatively trivial norm). Again, a student guilty of cheating is expelled on the grounds non-payment of fees and the conflict is avoided at the moral level by being resolved at the normative level.

More generally, we can state that it is an aim of bureaucracy to rationalize and routinize procedures for the resolution of value issues at the level of least organizational cost. The administrative-managerial preference for the avoidance of 'moral issues' or contests of principle can also be explained by the fact that lower-level resolutions may be amenable to compromise and persuasion, whereas higher-level conflicts may be irreconcilable, not only moral but also mortal.

ALTERNATIVE CONCEPTIONS

The concept of value can be approached quite differently and with the advantages of specialist disciplinary insights. In a social context of cultural pluralism and moral relativism, the context prevalent in contemporary, technologically advanced, Western democracies, there may well be a rational tendency to prefer a psychological over a philosophical treatment of value issues. This perhaps explains the popularity with administrative theorists of the work of Abraham Maslow (1943, 1954, 1965, 1968). His work has been influential.

Many organizations, for example, now seek to elucidate their purposes not in terms of the old-fashioned profit motive but in Maslovian terms of self-actualization opportunities for their membership. The system of public education has been greatly affected, and many schools, programmes, and curricula now claim to be designed to afford growth possibilities and opportunities for maximizing the growth and self-realization potentialities of their clientele. Maslow himself addressed administrators in his book *Eupsychian Management* (1965), proselytizing for 'self-fulfilment' in the oftentimes inimical world of industry and commerce.

Maslow's model-of-man is essentially optimistic. It gives rise to a motivational scheme of needs which are prepotent and hierarchically arranged as in Figure 12 (Maslow, 1943, 370–396). The lower

Figure 12:   Maslow's Hierarchy of Needs

needs are essential, primary, prerequisite, or 'deficiency' needs which must be to some extent satisfied before the higher level needs can emerge. One cannot be a philosopher with the toothache. And one must have a measure of oxygen, warmth, food, clothing, and shelter before seeking social satisfactions and affective relations with fellow beings. Given adequate satisfactions of lower-level needs, the higher-level needs can become activated. Man develops his social propensities, fulfils himself in social and collective endeavour, finds satisfactions (i.e. values, concepts of the desirable) in mature love relationships and, if he proceeds to the apex of the hierarchy, develops his fullest potential (seeks to realize his highest values) in self-actualization. He becomes what he is potentially, what he is capable of becoming. Maslow was a clinical psychologist, and he based his theories on his observations of healthy people. This is in deliberate contrast to Freud whose patients were, by definition, sick. Very healthy people, according to Maslow, tend towards the self-actualizing level of the hierarchy. They seek growth or *being* values as opposed to deficiency or maintenance values. In their search for the satisfaction of the highest level of needs they may have 'peak experiences', quasi-mystical states of well-being in which they feel themselves in a unitive harmony with a benevolent universe (1964).

Let us reserve any critical commentary for the moment. It can be conceded that the schema has an initial persuasiveness and when translated from the individual to the collectivity there is some cogency and appeal in the idea of organization for purposes which extend the possibilities of satisfaction of higher-level individual needs.

Maslow's theory of motivation is paralleled in many respects by the work of the industrial psychologist Herzberg (1964, 1966). Herzberg's research, conducted mainly through interviews of middle-management, enabled him to identify factors such as salary, status, job security, responsibility and promotion which formed the bases for work attitudes. On further analysis these yielded a dualistic scheme of 'satisfiers' and 'dissatisfiers' which he called respectively motivational and hygienic factors. These sources of value correspond to Maslow's growth and deficiency need clusters. The motivators are essentially achievement, recognition, intrinsic satisfaction in the work, responsibility, promotion, and salary, while the hygienic factors (which also include salary) are more numerous, more extrinsic to the job, more prerequiste. Very simply one works in the first instance to overcome the dissatisfactions of being unemployed and then, secondly, to attain as much motivational satisfaction (self-fulfilment) as the job will allow subject to the constraints imposed by administrative, managerial, and reality factors.

The significance of Maslow and Herzberg for administrative philosophy lies in their presumptions of optimism. Maslow's theory presupposes the intrinsic worth of *man*; the self which is to be actualized is worth actualizing. The potential for man-in-organizations may be unlimited, for man is basically *good*. Criminals and psychopaths are presumably also good in essence, their evil manifestations being attributable to defective growth patterns due in turn to frustration of deficiency and growth needs. (This doctrine of social responsibility is, of course, contentious, and though it is apparently shared by Professor Skinner (1971) I must disassociate myself from it in this work.)

Likewise, Herzberg's theory seems to suggest the intrinsic worth of *work*. Work can be the means whereby the self-actualizing end can be accomplished. Work has, at least in potential, unlimited possibilities if rightly organized and designed. Work is *good*.

While highly suggestive philosophically, both of these theories have encountered difficulties at the empirical level. The former is difficult to operationalize and test, and research has so far failed to validate it empirically or at least been frustrated in that attempt (Alderfer, 1969; Schneider and Alderfer, 1973). Herzberg's work has likewise engendered misgivings at the level of empirical investigation (House and Wigder, 1967; Schneider and Locke, 1971). On the other hand the case is not proven either way, and until this occurs they remain as reasonable bases upon which an administrator can build towards his personal philosophy. We must acknowledge Maslow's work at least as providing a logically defensible model-of-man and neither Maslow's theory of needs nor Herzberg's theory of work motivation are inconsistent with the typology of value expounded in this chapter. Their psychological orientation, however, deflects attention from the dialectical tension inherent in the nature of value itself.

Psychological theories of moral development such as Piaget's formulation of stages (1932) and its sophistication in the theories of Kohlberg (1963) are consistent with the model of Figure 12, but, being developmental, again share the presumptions of optimism characteristic of Maslow and seem to be prejudiced towards democratic institutions. Moreover, unlike Maslow and Herzberg, their work has not been influential in administrative circles.

TOWARDS UNDERSTANDING

Values were defined above (p. 105) as concepts of the desirable with motivating force. This is, of course, tautological if it be assumed that all human action is motivated by desire. It is easier to define than to understand but, for our purposes, we can adopt, without contest or argument, the more elaborate definition first framed by Kluckhohn:

A value is a conception, explicit or implicit, distinctive of an individual or characteristic of a group, of the desirable which influences the selection from available modes, means, and ends of action. (Parsons and Shils, 1962, 395)

Such values may be characterized in various ways as (say) political, moral, religious, aesthetic, economic, but as I have sought to explain them they are phenomenological entities intermediate between motives (which may or may not be accessible to inspection) and attitudes. Values may be organized into clusters which reflect in attitudinal orientations and general predispositions to act. They are of three types with respective psychological and philosophical correspondences and give rise to the postulates of hierarchy, degeneration, and avoidance. Some degree of value conflict is the normal human condition. Even more so is it the administrative condition. Values have special relevance for administrative behaviour and this will be discussed in the next two chapters. Our ultimate goal is to explore the possibilities of an administrative philosophy which will provide techniques and justification for the right resolution of conflicts of value and interest. Sophistication about the nature of value is a necessary prerequisite to this end.

7
Values in Administration

It may already be conceded from our search for an administrative logic in Part 1 that administration is a value-laden, even value-saturated enterprise. The conventional wisdom would sustain this. No practical administrator would reasonably deny it. Why, then, can we not rest our case and move at once to enunciations of moral philosophy which would bear directly on the field of administration? Because, I think, of the tendency to simultaneously concede and beg the value question. Having agreed to being beset by value problems, it is not uncommon for executives to exemplify in practice the postulate of avoidance or to retreat into managerialism. This may be excusable; it often is, but what is of deeper concern is the not unencountered reluctance or inability of administrators to provide details of any philosophical commitment (or understanding). An abhorrence is sometimes apparent for any value proposition which could be supposed to be in some way absolute or, at least, in contravention of the cultural absolute that 'all values are relative'. A retreat to positivism is another way in which the value problem can be begged. A hesitancy about coming to grips with the value question in administration is quite understandable, if not quite forgivable. The complexity alone is a disincentive; the contemplative aspect is a deterrent to the man of action. But the problem must be faced, and explored.

In Part 1 we were concerned with showing implicitly where values intruded into administrative behaviour; now we can make that concern more explicit.

POSITIVISM

It can be argued that *all* human behaviour is value-laden simply by virtue of the fact that, random activity excluded, it is motivated. Administration can therefore claim no particular distinction. The rebuttal to this argument lies in the special collective characteristic of administration. Values in administration refer not simply to the individual person of the administrator, nor even to his extended ego in the form of family, clan, or interest clique, but to the nomothetic collectivity of the organization. They are ostensibly of Type II. Nevertheless, it would be quite unrealistic to suppose that the administrator is a mere value functionary of the organization, as Simon at times seems to maintain, nor must we ever lose sight of the idiographic interest complex represented by the administrator himself. His commitment to Type I and Type III values could be crucial.

The problem is difficult. Fields of value interlace and overlap. The temptation to avoid it altogether is powerful. One technique of avoidance is the retreat to managerialism: separate ends from means and apportion the latter to management whereby the only value test need then be the criterion of goal accomplishment. Simon, as mentioned, sometimes beats this retreat, but in his philosophical posture he goes further and explicitly espouses the doctrine of logical positivism (1965, 45). He attempts to separate means from ends and facts from values so as to make the former of these pairs the special province of a practical administrative science (1965, 45–60; 248–53).

> 'It is sometimes thought that, since the words 'good' and 'bad' often occur in sentences written by students of administration, the science of administration contains an essential ethical element. If this were true, a science of administration would be impossible, for it is impossible to choose, on an empirical basis, between ethical alternatives. Fortunately, *it is not true*. The terms 'good' and 'bad' when they occur in a study on administration are *seldom* employed in a purely ethical sense. Procedures are termed 'good' when they are conducive to the attainment of *specified objectives*, 'bad' when they are not conducive to such attainment. That they are, or are not, so conducive is purely a matter of *fact*, and it is this factual element which makes up the real substance of an administrative science. To illustrate: In the realm of economics, the proposition 'alternative A is good' may be translated into two propositions, one of them ethical, the other factual.
>
> 'Alternative A will lead to maximum profit.'
> 'To maximize profit is good.'
> The first of these two sentences has no ethical content, and is a

sentence of the practical science of business. The second sentence is an ethical imperative, and has no place in any science.' (1965, 249–50, my italics)

Of course we cannot agree. Either in fact or in philosophy. The terms 'good' and 'bad' are, as shown in the previous chapter, often inextricably confused with 'right' and 'wrong'. It is not correct to say that they are seldom used in a purely ethical sense in administrative studies, nor, to put it the other way round, that when commonly used they are void of ethical content. The ubiquity of value terminology in administrative literature only goes to show the difficulty of attaining to any administrative *science*. Simon is indirectly asserting that the end justifies the means and, while his position might conceivably have reference to some hypothetical managerial 'technology', it does not sensibly apply to the activity of administration. The terms 'good' and 'bad' may indeed at times be specified by some 'objective' and this may reduce the element of value judgment to 'near-fact', but reduction is not elimination and even here the value terms would be materially affected by the larger value culture of the organization. It would depend, for example, on sub-cultural notions about the desirability of efficiency, workmanship, excellence, responsibility, and *how* process-means were related to product-ends. The situation is value-infused, subtle and subject to continuous modulation. 'Standards', for example, change over time and place and person. On the other hand, we must agree with Simon that ethical imperatives are non-scientific but this is only to reiterate what we have been saying all along, that administration is philosophical.

Simon's treatment of the value issue could also appear suspiciously like Type IIa pragmatism—values are assessed in terms of consequences as related to 'specified objectives'—but this only begs the question as to how, in turn, the specified objectives are to be determined and value-judged and this, in the logical positivist mode, returns us to essentially Type III positivism. The values are there because they're there because and any one set is as ethically valid as any other.

If, then, the philosophical position of logical positivism is adopted, ethical statements tend to vanish by way of the reduction of value judgments to emotive preference. The administrator can deny 'ethical imperatives' by talking only of preferences. The pursuit of his own interest to the exclusion of that of others would be (subject to games rules or organizational constraints) as valid as any other position. This nihilistic view lends a pseudo-scientific atmosphere to the discussion of values in administration, and is one of the ways in which serious value debate can be avoided. Let us defer its refutation, however, to another place while we now consider the actual modes in which values function in administrative behaviour. In doing so we may also take some account of any possibilities of defectiveness or ailment in the value behaviour of administrators.

MONITORING

Administration is a perpetual becoming, a journey in which the destination is never reached. The end of a war is the beginning of a peace; one problem situation dissolves into another. In a sense for the man of policy the future is always more real than the present. It is the impending which presses on the mind.

To an extent this is so even at the level of Simon's divorce between factual means and valuational ends because organizations always represent states of inadequacy. The inadequacy is the gap between the way things are—the factual state of affairs at a given instant—and the way things ought to be at some future instant, that of the consummation of the specified objective. Since the present is always distinct from the future and can at most be only a kind of 'straining towards' some future condition, a state of inadequacy is defined by the mere act of establishing a future goal or target; it is a price which must be paid by any purposive entity. The price of intention.

But the 'ought to be', the desirable future state, affects the present in another and more immediate or practical way through the imperative to check that the best means are being employed in the best way at any given instant so as to achieve the best progression of means to ends and the best conversion of present into future. I have used the term 'best' four times in the last sentence and the terms 'ought', 'desirable', and 'imperative' once. The value language is inescapable, and points in this instance to the omnipresence of what we shall later call the metavalues: concepts of the desirable such as efficiency and effectiveness, growth and productivity which guide administrative value judgments at the nomothetic (Type II) level.

Administrators, through the agency of management, have a continuous onus (a duty or responsibility) to monitor their organizations in this way, to seek best means for given ends and best conduct for given means, even without entering into the determination of the ends which are here given or specified. This is traditionally regarded as the supervisory function. But it too has ethical, imperative elements.

In his supervisory or monitoring behaviour the administrator will, consciously or unconsciously, engage his own interests and pattern of motivation. This is one part of his idiographic aspect. Another is his 'model-of-man', the structure of his world-view as it applies to his organizational life. This idiographic structure is compromised by, and compresent with, his nomothetic commitment to the collective values of the organization. There are, moreover, extra-organizational values which can serve either as constraints or temptations. (Pollution, crime, confusion, war *could* be good for the organization.) The degree of awareness with which an administrator is able to enter all of these elements into his decisional calculus and into his monitoring function is the measure of his sophistication, of his capacity for Barnard's moral complexity.

Still, this is not all. Each organization member is a value actor though each need not have the formal allegiance to the nomothetic realm which is imposed upon the administrator. But if the members are not monitoring, they are being monitored, and it is here where the administrator's knowledge of the informal organization and his perception of shifts in values within the complex of subsystems is called upon. How is this value information to be gathered? If Mintzberg is correct the administrator will rely upon a private intelligence network and the flow of 'gossip' (1973, 45, 71–74, 97), and this in turn raises the political question as to who is controlling the flow of information. Obviously there is at least some scope for power play, intrigue, and subversion.

Monitoring not only engages the administrator's philosophy in the performance of his nomothetic role, it also raises the problem of his organizational speciality. He has an onus to keep himself informed (in a general way) of advances in technology which bear upon his organization's life, both with respect to ends and to means.

Technological advance, better means, can have value implications. Failure to adopt them, their rapid adoption, or their too rapid adoption may affect the organization in its competition for resources, and determine its growth or survival prospects. A change such as automation may have radical effects on organization membership. Quite apart, then, from his idiographic value orientation, the administrator must be engaged in a continuous *nomothetic* value monitoring which is difficult, subtle, protean, and taxing.

MODELS OF MAN

Miles, in his work on theories of management, maintains that there is essentially a triad of positions which can be held about man in organizations (1975, 32–46). He further maintains that managers[1] do hold one or the other of these positions and that they have important implications for organizational design. The positions, which are clusters of attitudes and assumptions about organizational man, he calls the traditional model, the human relations model, and the human resources model. It is clearly suggested that the human resources model is more synthetic and desirable than either of its dialectical precursors. These precursors, the traditional and human relations models, are restatements of McGregor's Theory X and Theory Y (1960, 33–57). They also reflect the early endeavours in scientific management and the later influence of the human relations movement. The human resources model, on the other hand, seems to derive from the speculative theories of Maslow and like-minded psychologists. The models are more properly descriptive stereotypes than theories, but since they are influential in practice we can note their essential features.

The basic assumption in the traditional model is that work is inherently distasteful for most people. But even more distasteful yet is responsibility. Work must therefore be extrinsically motivated, chiefly through the means of pay and security measures. Herzberg's and Maslow's lower-level needs dominate. It follows that monitoring must be rigorous. Workers should not be left unsupervised nor should subordinates be left to their own devices. Caution should prevail over trust. In general, people are above all self-seeking, they will take advantage if they can, and they are notoriously incompetent. They adulate power and despise weakness. Therefore work should be designed to stress simplification of tasks, routinization of decisions and clear lines of authority and command. The time clock and the punch card are essential. Hierarchy is the natural order. Fear is the prime mover.

The logic extends to management as well as workers. It is a safe assumption that managers too are selfish and greedy, but in contrast to workers they may *not* be lazy, and instead may be power-hungry and ambitious. These features can be capitalized upon, as for example by designing hierarchical ladders for the upwardly mobile underlings to climb.

In general, the meta-assumption behind the postulated assumptions of the traditional model seems to be the notion that it is safest in collective enterprise to assume the worst of the collective constituents. In that way one can only be happily surprised. The same principle underlies conservative accounting practice, conservative economics and, generally, wherever men talk of 'keeping each other honest'.

The human relations model rejects simple self-centredness and stresses instead the social aspect of human nature. Man seeks social gratifications, acceptance and recognition by his fellows, group satisfactions, some sense of belongingness. We move into the upper reaches of Maslow's and Herzberg's schemes. Type III values yield to Type II. Status is important. Men, as Napoleon said, are led by baubles. They can be manipulated. Money is only one mark of status, one of the motivators. Subordinates like to be considered and should be treated considerately, informed of organizational affairs, catered to in their informal groupings. The reach of the organization should extend into the extra-organizational life of its members. Happy cows yield more milk. It is better to persuade than to command. The techniques of group dynamics and the manipulative findings of social psychology afford ways in which the harsher truths of Theory X and the traditional model can be glossed over. Administration must be concerned about morale, organizational climate, *esprit de corps*. Political skill is the prime mover. The modal value is Type IIb.

All these principles apply with even extended force to management personnel. The shape of Whyte's 'Organization Man' begins to appear; conformist, other-directed, a creature of his organization. The human relations manager is genial, smooth, suave, highly manipulative, spiritually empty, unauthentic to the core. Machiavelli knew him well and it is to be carefully noted that Machiavelli would have endorsed *both* the traditional model and the human relations model.

The human resources model rejects manipulation, denies the distastefulness of work, and bases its presuppositions on Maslow's highest levels of needs. Democratic biases are also evident. People like to work if it be fulfilling, especially if they have had some say in the determination of the work and in shaping the organization's objectives. They can be creative and can enjoy responsibility. Each individual represents a wealth of 'resources' which can be 'tapped' by right administration. The field of organizational life can be structured so as to provide occasions for self-fulfilment. Even discovery of purpose and life-meaning can come from work. Democracy is the natural order. Love is the prime mover. Authenticity and Type I values are to triumph over and synthesize those of Type II and III.

Again the stereotypic human resources view of man can be applied to executives as well as to subordinates. Indeed with even more force because it is likely in the hierarchical nature of things that the opportunities for the creative exercise of inner resources, for authentic responsibility and moral complexity, will be greatest of all in the administrative-managerial ranks. However, that administrator X wishes the human resources model to be applied to him by *his* superiors does not necessarily entail that he will apply it to his subordinates in turn.

These three orientations are not necessarily mutually exclusive. They are model stereotypes which are held, purely or in combination, by administrators, and which carry implications for administrative style and practice. It would follow that, within the limits of technological and economic constraint, work can and should be designed so as to best exemplify the particular model adopted. I do not wish to contest at this point either the veracity of these models or the empirical support for their adoption in the field. It will suffice at present to concede that the administrator's view of man becomes an effective part of organizational life; one of the ways in which values intrude into administrative practice; and a facet of administrative philosophy. Later I shall attempt to argue for a position which opts for no particular convention but seeks an inclusive synthesis embracing all three of these models of man.

It is true that each administrator has his own idiographic scheme of values and his own unique value biography. This has to be reconciled with his special nomothetic commitment to the organizational values. This reconciliation is facilitated in a number of ways, the most significant of which, perhaps, stems from the fact that administrators control the organizational reward system. They are thus on the face of it more identified with the organizational interest; organizational success is more proportionately meaningful to them than to other classes of member. What is good for the organization is good for them, although, as is often overlooked, what is bad for the organization is often *less* bad for them, especially if they have *de facto* or *de jure* tenure. (That the captain is the last to leave the sinking ship may mean in the real world of administration that he is the *only* survivor.)

Again, because of greater relative rewards, and usually greater status, administrators are prepared to work harder and longer than other classes of member. The empirical evidence for this is strong (Dubin and Spray, 1964, 100–108; Mintzberg, 1973, 28–29) and supports the literary stereotype of the tireless executive. All of this dynamism and the visible attachment to his role tends to identify the administrator with nomothetic values.

It is not uncommon to ascribe to successful administrators at least a sympathy for the variously called 'Puritan', 'Prussian', 'Protestant', or 'Work' ethics. This general value orientation, made much of by Weber in *The Protestant Ethic and the Spirit of Capitalism* (1930) is typified by self-denial, hard work, deferred gratifications, future-time orientation and a general belief that industry, discipline, authority, and productivity are good. It would be a distortion to assert that administrators as a class subscribe to this ethic on a Type I basis, but it is legitimate to draw attention to a natural affinity for it which might exist as an administrative value bias. Work must tend to rank highly as a value for executive personnel because it provides self-fulfilling opportunities and because of its structured liaison to the hierarchical reward system.

SOCIETAL BIAS

Extra-organizational cultural values impinge in many ways upon the organization. Where the administrator is of the amateur type, it could perhaps be argued that, because of the tenuous nature of his organizational membership compared to his professional counterparts, he may be more sensitive to extra-organizational interests. On the other hand, it is certain that the professional administrator cannot afford to be unaware of the context of social motivation. There has been, for example, a contemporary shift to an emergent cultural value orientation which is more permissive and consummatory in character than the traditional pattern. There are also various causes or movements: towards greater power-sharing on behalf of minorities, women, the environment and so forth. In the interests of his organization the administrator will be monitoring these movements and any Type IIb shifts of consensus. Where conflict exists between societal and organizational values, the possibility will also exist for a failure of authenticity, and the conditions for an administrative ethical decision will be established.

In general we can conceive of a progression of interest from (1) the administrator's idiographic value orientation to (2) his nomothetic value orientation to (3) the societal value orientation and its consensus in the conventional morality. At each 'break' in this progression, opportunities for value conflict will be maximized and so, concomitantly, will opportunities for failure of authenticity. By failure of authenticity we mean not so much a fault in valuation, such as incorrect reasoning, but the deliberate concealment of the operative value (as where self-interest is pursued but group interest professed). It would be unreasonable to expect, in anything short of totalitarian fantasy, a unification of value along the line of progression from individual to community. The natural condition is one of continuous conflict continuously modulated. A pluralistic society will multiply and intensify the breaks in the value progression, it will also intensify the demand for administrative moral complexity. Obviously an instrument or technique for resolving value issues would be desirable.

The model expounded in the previous chapter can be used as such a tool, but its use will always be relative to the social context of its employment, and it implies that the value actor who is disposed to resolve issues at the Type II level—the typical administrative mode —may be at a situational disadvantage in a pluralistic society to those whose value positions are extreme. The religious, the ideologically committed, as well as those in passionate pursuit of self-interest, have as it were a methodology of decision at their disposal which permits them to see quickly and easily where value conflict can be resolved, where their interests lie, and which concept of the desirable should be allowed to prevail. By contrast, the rational administrator seeking consensus, compromise, and consideration of consequences may be less able to perceive any easy or right answer. The issue is 'sicklied o'er with the pale cast of thought' and 'the native hue of resolution' is lost. The dogmatic, the committed, the aggressive, the self-seekers can often carry the day. And this potential 'weakness of the centre' will be the more likely in a societal context of cultural pluralism and moral relativism.[2]

PRELIMINARY PATHOLOGY

If there were no endemic ailments in administrative-organizational practice we might be able to conceive of a descriptive, non-normative value theory. But it is a canon of this book that organizational life, at any level, is presently short of the ideals which can be discerned for it. I would go further and declare that many aspects of administrative practice and organizational life do not merely fall short of the ideal but are positively sick. A philosopher of administration will be a physician of organizational culture and his constant task will be to diagnose the presence of disease. In our investigation so far we have already palpated several soft spots in the body administrative, and in Part III we shall undertake a more thorough examination. Before then, however, let us consider some particular ways in which the value problem in administration can be compounded.

We have already touched upon the fact that administrators have egos, vanities; their hierarchical career pattern implies a need for achievement in the sense of McClelland's N-*ach* (1961, 1953). They will often be in competition with each other for promotion and recognition and, while this motivational thrust can provide a dynamic for effort, it can on occasion conflict with the organizational good and can push the administrator's value orientation towards dysfunctional Type I commitments (the drive to personal success outranking considerations of organizational welfare). This is the affliction, ever prevalent, of opportunism, and in its more virulent forms is characterized by single-minded pursuit of self-interest.

While opportunism is a commitment of sorts, a commitment to the ego, there are also types of group commitment of the factional or clique variety which can be inimical to the organizational good. This is touched upon by Kipling in his words:

'How smoothly and how swiftly they have
sidled back to power
By the favour and contrivance of their kind'.

This malady is established in the organizational literature as the phenomenon of executive succession. It occurs where the tendency for like to approve of like is combined with the control of promotional channels and appointment procedures, this leading to the self-perpetuation of an administrative in-group with mutually gratifying patterns of value orientation. Here again, the commitment may not be to the good of the collectivity but instead to the differential good and advantage of the in-group or old-guard dominating the organization's power-structure. This is not to say that executive-succession is necessarily evil; indeed, in its forms as nepotism, senatorial oligarchy, and monarchy it is often revered, but its presence in organizations is more pervasive than commonly supposed; appointments to administrative offices are often made (whatever outward procedures may be adopted) through some version of informal selection which assures continuity of vested value interests. At the very least the potential for a bias of value orientation is present.

The logic of opportunism and executive-succession can be extended to the value pathology where commitment to the organization outweighs more universal interests yet; where what is good for General Motors (or the C.I.A.) is considered to be good for the nation. This form of value myopia is, of course, well-recognized and endemic. It is a form of organizational feudalism.

The purpose of this chapter has been to show that values, concepts of the desirable organized about foci of interest, are omnipresent in administrative action. The problems associated with value cannot easily be disposed of, certainly not by arbitrary adoption of a positivistic position or by abandonment to psychologism or moral relativism. Although the temptation is great to give up in the face of complexity, we can distinguish the natural trends of bias and the broad schemes of value presumption which differentiate between models of man and their attendant administrative philosophies. We are also able to discern the first faint delineaments of disease.

8
Organizations and Goals

Organizations have already been described as goal-seeking entities (P3). Indeed, their entire rationale must lie in their capacity to serve collective ends. However, as the size and complexity of an organization increases until it reaches institutional dimensions (the military, the police) so must statements of purpose become increasingly general, unspecified, or, as March and Simon (1958) would put it, *nonoperational*. The broad purpose can be operationalized or specified into objectives when means can be discerned for the accomplishment of the subgoals and criteria such as efficiency and effectiveness exist for comparing alternative means. Yet the deductive path from general to specific is treacherous and difficult. Consider, say, the goals of 'education' or 'national interest'. They are vague and general and their specification is complicated by ambivalence and ambiguity.

The broadest goal which can be ascribed to any organization is that of the welfare of its members. It is only, however, in the case of the largest and most complex of organizations, the mega-organization of the national state, that this collective selfishness can be expressly avowed and, even here, it is conventionally couched in appropriate rhetoric. Statesmen and politicians talk of the 'common weal', 'public interest', 'preservation of freedom', 'manifest destiny' and use similar eulogistic devices to refer to the pursuit of the collective goal. Even at the national level some restraint is exerted by the overriding welfare interest of the international comity, an interest which at this level of generality is utterly diffuse. Restraint may be informal, inchoate moral suasion, as in the universal condemnation of 'crimes against humanity', or it can be formalized into international superstructures such as the European Economic Community and the United Nations Organization. Nevertheless, it remains true that violence and warfare of one sort or another are the ultimate value arbiters in international (megaorganizational) affairs.

At lower levels of organizational complexity than the national, the open declaration of organizational purpose must be tempered and constrained by whatever higher levels of interest are considered to be applicable. Thus, the public school system enunciates goals such as self-actualization, social skills, and character development, which, though vague, are stated in terms of the larger clientele of pupils and parents which makes up the supportive environment for the school system. The unenunciated goals would have to do with the pay and perquisites of the system employees, that is, the welfare of the organization's members. Likewise, workers seek to justify claims on the organization in the rhetoric of organizational purpose (increased productivity) or extra-organizational pressures (cost-of-living). A claim in the simple valuational terms of self-interest would be considered inadequate. And an individual member making claims on his organization will do so on some grounds of organizational attachment such as long service, or increased sales, or greater work-load.

The chain of ostensive purpose extends from the individual with his particular values and goals through the subsystems of his organization with their subpurposes to the organizational entity and its purpose. The end of the chain merges into the community of context made up of those individuals and groups who interact with the organization and this in turn merges imperceptibly into the social whole and the cultural community defined by some national boundary. Even this last distinction may be transcended or superseded, as is the case with international corporations and multi-national conglomerates. At each stage in this progression of purpose, statements about goals can be made which are capable of a double formulation: that which is expressed in the rhetoric appropriate to the next and higher levels of value, and that which is indeed the case but which for political reasons cannot be publicly expressed. The language of purpose conceals more than it reveals; it is untrustworthy. The administrator has the task of reconciling rhetoric and fact, of monitoring and shaping the flow of purpose, the task of integrating organizational value. In this it is likely that the amateur administrator will work more at the rhetorical Type I level while the professional administrator will be working more at the level of Type II dialectic.

RATIONALITY

The logic of a line of purpose from broadly diffused general purposes to narrowly defined, specific task objectives has endowed organizations with a deceptive if not spurious appearance of rationality. This is epitomized in such variations on the administrative theme as MBO: management by objectives, PPBS: planning, programming, budgeting, systems and PERT: program evaluation review technique. The success of these methods depends upon the specification of material objectives. If the cause-effect connections necessary to achieve these objectives can be perceived, then it becomes a merely technical problem of planning to connect means and ends, a positivistic calculus of resources and time lines. Modern technology combined with computers and automation greatly facilitates the resort to this kind of method and its associated devolution from administration to management. Values need hardly enter into it; the problem of values can be made to appear to disappear. Rationality is triumphant.

At least two kinds of difficulty interfere with this appearance of rationality. The first has already been referred to above as covert interest. Such unenunciated interest may subvert or deflect the attainment of stages in the purposive chain. The second has to do with the type of objective. While the rational techniques may work well for clear end items such as building a submarine or placing a man on the moon, they may work poorly, if at all, where the end item is conceptionally diffuse such as 'good education' or 'the public interest' or even, covertly and unenunciated, 'maintaining the organization'. It is not always possible to specify with clarity the means-end chain if the end item is vague. Moreover, vague end items will connote different values for different people. They may be both ambiguous and ambivalent. A newly formed film making organization may be differentially seen as having the major purpose of (1) making as large a profit as possible (2) making an artistic reputation (3) providing the service of entertainment (with profit as a subsidiary means to the end) (4) providing career opportunities for specific members of the organization (5) providing a tax write-off for investors or a parent corporation.

Organizational goals may be, and usually are, pluralistic rather than monolithic. Trade unions, for example, may have political and welfare ends. Education may be comprised of the competing purposes of literacy attainment, socialization, vocational preparation, and character development, yet no one of the subgoals can be excised without damage to the overall integrity of purpose. And, to make matters worse, some of the integral components of the overriding purpose may be quantifiable (in the instance given, reading and mathematical skills) while others may be qualitative (literary appreciation, moral development). In this event a rational bias towards the quantitative may depreciate or discount the qualitative elements of purpose.

Lastly, the *real* purposes may be misperceived. A university department may in all good faith (let us make the best assumptions) define its chief priority as teaching, but in fact its function may be more properly described as research and scholarly production. And some of its members will use it chiefly as an avenue of career advancement or promotion. In these and other ways organizational rationality may be much more apparent than real and values may percolate into even the most sterile interstices of technology.

CLASSICAL DOCTRINE

Barnard devotes much of his book to discussion of purpose. His general position can be gauged from the following quotation.

> The formulation and definition of purpose is then a widely distributed function, only the more general part of which is executive. In this fact lies the most important inherent difficulty in the operation of cooperative systems—the necessity for indoctrinating those at the lower levels with general purposes, the major decisions, so that they remain cohesive and able to make the ultimate detailed decisions coherent; and the necessity, for those at higher levels, of constantly understanding the concrete conditions and the specific decisions of the 'ultimate' contributors from which and from whom executives are often insulated. Without that up-and-down-the-line coordination of purposeful decisions, general decisions and general purposes are mere intellectual processes in an organization vacuum, insulated from realities by layers of misunder-

standing. The function of formulating grand purposes and providing for their redefinition is one which needs sensitive systems of communication, experience in interpretation, imagination, and delegation of responsibility. (233)

This both acknowledges pervasion of purpose and the special philosophical demands upon administrators, while at the same time maintaining the characteristic Barnardian recognition of the individual as the 'ultimate' contributor to the organization. Elsewhere, however, he points out that intellectual understanding of purpose is unevenly distributed, at least at the general level of organization goals.

'But in general complex organizations are characterized by obvious lack of complete understanding and acceptance of *general* purposes or aims. . . . It is belief in the cause rather than intellectual understanding of the objective which is of chief importance. Understanding by itself is rather a paralyzing and divisive element.' (137/8)

This suggests that, while knowledge of subgoals is essential, the larger purpose is relegated either to the realm of Type III affect or Type I moral commitment. Presumably it is an executive function to treat of general purposes at the synthesizing or integrating Type II level.

Barnard's recognition of value conflict and of the possibilities for its resolution is clear from the following:

Individual motive is necessarily an internal, personal, subjective thing; common purpose is necessarily an external, impersonal, objective thing even though the individual interpretation of it is subjective. The one exception to this general rule, an important one, is that the accomplishment of an organization purpose becomes itself a source of personal satisfaction and a motive for many individuals in many organizations. It is rare, however, if ever, and then I think only in connection with family, patriotic, and religious organizations under special conditions, that organization purpose becomes or can become the *only* or even the major individual motive. (89)

(One could take issue with Barnard's assertion about the rarity of organizational purpose as a major individual motive—not so much on the possibility of conscious subscription to this motive, but on the practical grounds that most people's *livelihoods* depend on their organizational connection, their lowest security level of needs are engaged, a major portion of their life *is* organizational life—and the rest of it is *affected* by organizational life, so the impress of organizational purpose is of no mean motivational significance.)

Simon's position on organizational purpose has already been mentioned (p. 27 above). Ideally, organizations are rational goal accomplishment devices and 'the content decisions of the higher administrator deal with more ultimate purposes and more general processes than the decisions of the lower administrator. We might say that the lower administrator's purposes are the upper administrator's processes.' (1965, 246) This puts it nicely. And again,

> We see, then, that the work of the administrator, as organizations are now constituted, involves (1) decisions about the organization structure, and (2) the broader decisions as to the content of the organization's work. Decisions of neither type can rest entirely, or even primarily, upon a knowledge of or facility with administrative theory. The former must be firmly grounded in the organization's technology. The latter must be grounded in the organization's technology and requires in addition (a) a thorough appreciation of the theory of efficiency, and (b) a knowledge of those aspects of the social sciences which are relevant to the broader purposes of the organization. (246)

But one will ask, what is the *theory of efficiency?* Does it have value implications? And what are those aspects of the social sciences which tell us about the broader purposes of the organization? What, indeed, is meant by broader purposes?

Classical doctrine tells us only that the formulation of the general organizational purpose is an administrative prerogative. It tells us nothing about how this should be done, what principles should be engaged, what analysis employed. And so far as it assumes nomothetic purity of administrative intent, it compounds vacuity with naïvete.

THE GOAL PARADIGM

It may be, as Georgiu (1973, 291) has suggested, that we have left unexamined, through a sort of intellectual myopia, the concept of organizations as goal attainment devices simply because this concept seems so patently obvious. But, he would claim, this notion of an organization as a distinct social unit based on the pursuit of its goals does not give a satisfactory explanation of what actually takes place when men get together in goal-seeking collectivities. Rather, it is more accurate to describe an organization as an arbitrary focus of interest, a sort of market place of values, where accommodating structures and functions are developed as the members pursue a wide diversity of goals. Georgiu looks for a 'counter paradigm' by drawing upon the insights of Barnard. For Barnard 'the individual is always the basic strategic factor in organization' (139). The individual contributes to the organization in return for incentives, and over the middle and long terms some kind of favourable balance of trade must be maintained. This emphasis on the maintenance and extension of individual interest is related to Barnard's central theme, that of the informal organization. By contrast, Simon tends to see individual interest as subordinate to the rational purpose of the organization, and Katz and Kahn would make organizational purposes, not the individual, the 'basic strategic factor' (1973, 300). The counter-paradigm view of organizations would see them as co-operative incentive-distributing devices where contributions are obtained in return for participation in the organizational reward system. A wide variety of personal goals are satisfied through trade in this organizational 'market place'.

While it is certainly true that there must be a favourable individual balance of trade in value if services are to be properly forthcoming this truth must be quite radically adjusted for the various inelasticities in the organizational market place. The intransient contributor to organizational purpose has a limited number of organizations accessible to him. Perhaps only one organization is desirous of his services; certainly his mobility is limited, and he is constrained by a formidable array of disincentives in the form of vested interest, natural inertia, structured retention devices in the form of seniority increments, pension schemes and the like. Moreover, individuals' capacity to bargain in their own interests and to take risks in the pursuit of their career goals can vary greatly. As Hook once said, "Any change, even if it be for the better, is accompanied by inconvenience.' Again, there is an override to the organization's purpose in that once a member is accepted into the system, he becomes subject to a continuous process of identification with the organizational interest. The shifts of alignment which occur may rarely be sufficient to fuse individual and collective purposes, but the processes of integration are unremitting and remain a key function of the executive. One may conclude that the interorganizational market is far from free and that individual values, if they are to be traded successfully, must carry on this exchange largely within the intraorganizational forum.

It does not seem to be fruitful to try to resolve the empirical issue as to which of the two value elements, organizational or individual goals, is the basic 'strategic factor.' It is clear that there will be a dialectic between them, and varying degrees of harmony and conflict from the extreme of the dedicated organization man to that of the individual saboteur. What is to be noted about organizational nomothetic purpose, however, is its tendency to apparent simplicity, rationality, and logicality, as contrasted with the richness, complexity, intensity, and variety of idiographic needs and values. This difference parallels that between the divergent emphases of the personality school and the general systems school of organization theory. The former exhibits Types I and III value biases, while the latter has a Type II proclivity. Again, the social science approach to the study of organizations tends to a nomothetic bias—it is believed that there are discoverable laws of society and human conduct and that organizations are autonomous means of pursuing social order in accordance with uniform sets of values and goals. In contrast, the phenomenologists would stress idiographic interpretation. Organizations depend on their *members'* goals and are fields for manipulation of power.

Notwithstanding the strength of idiographic factors, I would concede an overriding quality to organizational goals, particularly for those members in the administrative-managerial hierarchy. But one must avoid the biological fallacy. This would occur if we were to confuse organizations with organisms (see Chapter 2). Organizations do not *live*; they are contrived social entities which find their reality in the *power* which they can exercise in the affairs of nature and of man. In general, this power will rest with the administration, although other organization members may contend from time to time for participation in its deployment. The administrator's philosophical task is to establish the value base for control of this power. He must be able to articulate the justification for it, to himself at least, whether or not he then considers it politically expedient to make the true justification overt. In doing so the administration may be led to change the organizational goals or to change their own goals to align with those of the organization. The organization's goals can be viewed neither as autonomous (the biological fallacy) nor dictated by either environment or the membership. The basic difficulty with the problem of organizational goals seems to be that of reconciling scientific rational Type II explanations of human behaviour in organizations with the larger view which would embrace the transrational and subrational elements of value. The *meaning* of an organization is twofold: that growing out of the phenomenology of its members; that capable of logical reduction through a rational or sociological perspective. The administrator is positioned at the interface between these two realms of value, and must reconcile both.

DUALISM

Administration is schizoid. The dualism of our value model (pp. 110–117) rested on the distinction between the hedonic values of personal indulgence (which might well include such desirables as power, social approval, reputation and prestige) and the obligation values of collective morality, duty, and transpersonal commitment. As has been said in another context,

> In any system short of the Absolute, men are torn between the incompatible motives of self-assertion and self-sacrifice and infected by the self-contradictions of 'desire', which can satisfy itself only by utterly destroying itself. (Passmore, 1968, 67)

Discipline forever wars with indulgence.

Two different kinds of sanction operate to ensure at least partial hegemony of discipline over indulgence. First, there are the collective sanctions of organizations and society as expressed in conventional morality, consensus, and the constraints of all enforceable rules and laws. The pay cheque, the time clock, the executive diary, and the workings of the informal organization all illustrate this Type II kind of pressure. The second kind of sanction to discipline is that provided where there is self-commitment, that is, the attachment of the will to an obligation-value by way of ideology, religion, or philosophical reflection. The latter is a transrational act and can lead, of course, to excesses when assessed from a lower level of value analysis. Nevertheless, organizations will usually seek through their administrations for some measure of this Type I value infusion into their ranks, it being commonly recognized that self-discipline is better (more efficient and effective) than imposed discipline. Failing this, and in the ordinary course of events, administration will be prepared to settle for the lesser Type II suasion and, where necessary, Type III coercion through control of economic and security systems.

This goes to explain why Japanese employees assemble in the morning to sing their corporation's song, why British soldiers are deliberately steeped in regimental history and traditions, and why ceremonies of all kinds, the American highschool pep rally, the solemnities of Soviet awards of red scarves to Young Pioneers, are part of institutional and organizational life. It is an attempt, as Selznick said, to 'infuse with value' beyond the rational needs of the occasion, beyond the technical requirements of the task at hand (1957, 17). At best this may engender Type I zealotry, but in any event it will serve to buttress the Type II sanctions of discipline and maintain the hegemony of the nomothetic dimension.

Katz and Kahn (1966, 341) have analyzed the motivational patterns of organization members into four logical sets. There is, first, legal compliance where contributions are compelled and a machine theory of organizational labour would be applicable. This is the realm of naked power and Theory X. Next, there is inducement to contribute through a system of rewards and incentives. A modified machine theory and a behaviourist S-R type psychology would be here appropriate. Next, men seek organizations as fields in which to exercise their special talents and skills, they seek professional self-fulfillment; and, lastly, men come to identify themselves with an organization's goals and so seek self-actualization in their work, in the attainment of organizational purposes. Clearly, this is a Maslovian type of analysis, there is a hierarchy from lower-level to higher-level needs, and one can make the fair assumption that administrators and executives will be operating in the self-fulfillment/self-actualization range of motives. Ideally, under this scheme, the administrator would have a Type I attachment to the goals of his organization combined, of course, with the motivational satisfactions deriving from the exercise of his special administrative-managerial talents in the organizational context. But to declaim the ideal is far from describing the actual. Lest we commit the naturalistic fallacy in reverse, let us hasten to acknowledge that the divergence between organizational goals and administrator's private purposes may be deeply schismatic, and necessitate much in the arts of concealment and unauthenticity. Nevertheless, it is again a fair assumption that the modal range of purposive behaviour will be somewhere between the extremes of cynical opportunism and organizational fanaticism.

The problem of organizational value conflict resolution is one of alignment of idiographic and nomothetic values. For the ordinary man this means some accommodation and compromise, but for the administrator it is a matter properly calling for careful analysis of his own values and those of the organization as expressed both in its formal goals and policies and in its informal workings. They do not have to be entirely reconciled; it is improbable that they ever are, but there is a point of discrepancy beyond which the administrator cannot go without either dissociation or war. The burden of change in this value complex is an administrative onus. It is a heavy onus and presents the administrator with a philosophical challenge. To answer this challenge successfully may well call for some degree of withdrawal and reflection, both behaviours which do not particularly commend themselves to action-oriented administrators.

SUMMARY: PART TWO

The object of this Part has been to explain the value concept and to show how values pervade organizations at the idiographic and nomothetic levels. Values can be analysed into dimensions which are analogous to these levels and into three classes of engagement. The highest and most powerful of these classes is that invoking individual commitment through an act of faith or will. The lowest is that of the self-indulgent search for sensory gratification. Between lie the realms of value associated with custom and reason. Value tends to seek its lowest level over time, and administrators in their work will generally prefer to settle value conflicts at the lowest level of resolution available. There is, however, a natural affinity or bias in administrative practice for the pragmatic or reasoned level of value dialectic.

A continuum runs from the individual, with his specific needs, to the organizational collectivity with its goals, and thence to the community and society at large. If we agree with Socrates that the unexamined life is not worth living we can also assert that the unexamined value is not worth holding. It then follows that the chain of interest from individual through organization to society implies that administration is rooted in philosophy, ends in philosophy, and throughout translates philosophy into action. But this is not to say that administrators as a professional group are either particularly sensitive to their philosophical obligations or particularly desirous of them if they were. Indeed, many executives might prefer to avoid complete value analysis and reflection altogether. Many avoidance or retreat mechanisms are readily available. These include the retreat to managerialism, the resort to bureaucratic rationality and impersonality, and the relapse into scepticism or positivism. Moreover, administrators have natural value biases which can become what Veblen called 'trained incapacities' or, as Burke would have it, 'unfittedness through being fit in an unfit fitness.' Also, more subtly, philosophy can be abjured in favour of social science. This preference would run the risk of the naturalistic fallacy, however, for no science, social or physical, can tell us what is right or wrong.

Administrators need a technique for resolving value conflicts which is superior to the methods of avoidance, least resistance, or lowest principle. To gain such a technique they must do some philosophy. A first step is a foundational understanding of the concept of value and the model expounded can be used later for conflict resultion.

However, even if sophisticated in value theory, it is not to be assumed that administrators will necessarily pursue the highest level of interest in any situation. The opportunities presented by organizational life for various forms of value sickness or pathology are manifold. This subject demands more exploration, but already it is clear that because of his power position the administrator faces uncommon demands of a value nature. Many of these value problems will not yield to purely cognitive or rational treatment. The administrator himself may have to overcome strenuous temptations if he is to integrate his own values with those of his organization and the extra-organizational context. More than other organization members he has to cope with several sets of value bias and, wittingly or not, he will personify a view-of-man which will encompass many philosophical assumptions and which will affect the quality of organizational life. The exposure of these assumptions and their reconstruction into a philosophy is a not unperilous task which can make of the administrator who undertakes it a one-eyed man in the kingdom of the blind.

III
PHILOSOPHY

With everyone sold on the good how does all the evil get done?

Saul Bellow

9
The Pathology of Administration

I SURFACE PATHOLOGIES

THE PLATONIC DILEMMA

One of the difficulties of discussing administration with sympathy and understanding lies in the fact that a gulf exists between the unreal value sterility of the textbooks and the knowing world of 'hard-nosed' practice, a world of cut and thrust which has converted more than one political scientist to doctrines of cynicism and despair. The sterilized extreme would be epitomized by Weber's ideal-type bureaucrat, an organizational tool or agent who has divested essential elements of his humanity before the altar of rationality; the 'real world' extreme by *homo politicus*, the political animal, who would sacrifice his own integral humanity in the over-worship of success. The dichotomy appears in a different guise in Plato. In the *Republic* it takes the form of a dilemma. Trying to answer the question of why men should do right rather than follow the apparently more rewarded practice of injustice, Plato has to develop a whole theory of the ideal State and its rulers or administrators or 'Guardians'. The Guardians are peculiar in that they are philosophers who have had some insight into the nature of truth, the 'Form of the Good'. Such an experience is mystical or quasi-mystical, and because of it and the personality reformation it entails, they then have no wish to engage in administration, much less enjoy the perquisites of that activity. They would rather withdraw, *pour cultiver ses jardins*, than engage in the hurly-burly, and can only be obliged to administer out of a sense of duty, moral obligation, or responsibility. Russell has postulated a three-way classification of men into aggressives who seek to dominate (the commanders), submissives who seek to be dominated (the obeyers), and those who would rather withdraw. The last represent, presumably, the philosophical type, and it is more than subtly indicated that they are in some sense *superior* (1975, 19). The Guardians, then, would have to be compelled (or impelled) to do that which they do not like, that which at the same time is the most competed for and desirable end of those who are most unworthy for it. The dilemma thus is that the right men will have to be obliged to undertake the necessary administrative training while the wrong, the unjust and self-seeking, will avidly pursue the administrative career. This accounts perhaps for the rather despairing note sounded by Plato when he says, 'I was forced, in fact, to the belief that the only hope of finding justice for society or for the individual lay in true philosophy, and that mankind will have no respite from trouble until either real philosophers gain political power or politicians become by some miracle true philosophers.'[1] (Plato, 1975, 16)

It is not that Plato is wrong, but that it is both impracticable and unreasonable to expect either his miracle or his other alternative. Administrators will continue to be ordinary and defective men. Yet they will have to deal with power, their basic coinage, and all its corrupting influence. To counteract that influence they need the aid of philosophy, not to make them into Guardians so much as to inoculate them against the other extreme.

In value terms the problem is one of interest conflict. If we assume without cynicism that self-interest is prime, then the dilemma comes about because the ambitious man's *concept* of self is different from that of the Guardian. The former has the imperfect vision of the ego, however much this ego may be rationalized or enlarged so as to include kin, clan, and organization. This imperfect vision often fathers its own private sense of *Realpolitik*, one in which the strong hand and the quick wit triumphs and the weak and the benevolent go to the wall. In the patois of the American success-wisdom: 'Nice guys finish last' or 'Show me a good loser and I'll show you a loser'. Even Fromm, a firm believer in the benevolence of human nature, in commenting on Milgram's aggression experiments concedes that realistically life teaches people to seek their own advantage even if others are harmed. (Fromm, 1975, 75) The Guardian's concept of self presumably reaches beyond this to a vision, however dimly perceived, in which the ego is either transcended or in some sort of union or harmony with the whole order of things. His viewpoint would not deny the lower perspective but would exceed it. He would have in fact that vision of self-interest and reality which could somehow reconcile and sublate Type III and Type I value commitments. Such a natural persuasion would not necessarily be tantamount to a sort of Hegelian, Marxian, or totalitarian 'ethics of the hive'. The latter ethic, where it exists at all, would be explicable as a reconciliation of Type III and Type *II* value orientations. The Guardian would see beyond mere order and harmony in the organization and the State, beyond social welfare as commonly understood.

In describing dilemmas one must be careful to avoid the errors of extremes; few men will be of finest Guardian material and few (we trust) of purest Machiavellian stuff. Psychopaths and saints carry us beyond the reaches of our value model at the same time as they illuminate it. The mass of men and the majority of administrators can be expected to be normally distributed between these extremes. Nevertheless, in the ordinary practice of administrative affairs the comfortable but dangerous assumption can be too easily made that all are honourable men. While Theory X is often rigorously applied to the non-administrative ranks, it is often overlooked and given insufficient weight when applied, if at all, to executives. Without gainsaying the normality of character distribution, in view of the fact that control of the organizational reward system is a prerogative of administration and in view of the presumptive bias of honour attaching to leadership roles in our organizational society, it might be only conservative to make the worst assumptions: that those in office and seeking office are motivated in addition to any higher motives by vanity, greed, and egotism rather by any spirit of service. Further, being professionally sophisticated, they are the better able to disguise, conceal, and re-present their basal motivations. Perhaps in denying the realistic possibility of finding philosopher kings we may have thrown out the baby with the platonic bathwater. But it would be safer to assume some bias in the unworthy direction and some use for philosophy as a therapeutic against pathology. And let the Guardians if ever and wherever they appear take care of themselves.

THE HIERARCHIC DILEMMA

The difficulty of matching right motivation with administrative role is compounded in modern complex organizations by what can be called the hierarchic dilemma. This has been discussed above in the context of power, authority, and leadership (pp. 88–90). What occurs is that the distribution of power becomes out of phase with the distribution of organizational rewards. In the pathological version monetary and status returns accrue disproportionately to the administrative-managerial line, while staff and workers become increasingly self-conscious of the power implications of their own technological expertise. This leads to conflict with the non-specialist hierarchy, and insecure or incompetent administrators may exacerbate the rift by resorting in reaction to dramaturgy, Thompson's term for an unauthentic reliance on symbology and role-playing. The executive tries to 'act' his role, maintain an 'image' of authority, give a good leadership 'performance', and seeks support from his management 'troupe'. In interviews and meetings he interposes his desk as a reminder of his nomothetic status or, worse, comes out from behind it to emphasize his 'democratic' pretensions. Throughout, his major effort is to conceal his incapacity or inability to grasp or cope with the technical dimensions of the situation.

There are variants. Bureaucratic roles are used so as to settle value conflicts arbitrarily and at the lowest level of resolution. (pp. 116–17) Devices such as formalistic delaying routines, executive inaccessibility behind ranks of subordinates and protective secretarial cover, inaccessibility by travel, by conference, by convention, or by being 'tied up'—all are used to decelerate or retard conflict resolution. In short, the hierarchy, essential to every organization, is subverted and becomes dysfunctional to the collective pursuit.

Although this particular kind of organizational ill can be expected to grow with technology and professionalism, it is important to note that, of all the value illnesses besetting organizations, this may be the easiest to treat. It occurs primarily because administrators fail to make a profession of their own specialty of generalism, a fault which can to a large extent be remedied by training and education. This profession must have credibility for the other ranks and specialists; it must be comprehended and communicated and this, of course, cannot happen properly without at least a modicum of authenticity. Such authenticity would imply an ethical commitment to the nomothetic value aims of the organization. When administration is recognized as a profession with its own domains of competence and expertise, this pathology will be attenuated.

There is a difficulty here. It is that while this argument holds true for our type of professional administrator, it is unlikely to be so easily fitted to the important type of the amateur administrator who is, by definition as it were, *non*-professional. The powers of any elected official can be expected to generate conflict with subordinate and co-ordinate levels of expertise-power when respective interests are perceived to be divergent. And in the class of the collegial administrator, there is the further pathological potential of compensating for an inadequate performance (or inadequate satisfactions) in one field by a reversion to the other alternative; as where an academic failing to succeed in his discipline gradually develops administrative ambitions or, conversely, a frustrated academic administrator expresses the fond wish to return to his first love, scholarship.

SUPERFICIALITY

Another increasingly recognized fault in administration arises from the interaction of work-load, time, and information flow. Managers notoriously, and administrators rather less so, tend to dispose of their time resource through diaries and structured appointment routines. They are often ostensibly very busy men who appear to work longer, if not harder, than their fellow organization members. Mintzberg has shown, however, that much of their busy-ness is characterized by superficiality. It is not uncommon for serious reports on controversial organization issues to go unread, or for them to be merely scanned, despite the labour that may have gone into their production. (Indeed the report or consultant study may often be used not to solve a problem but to defer it or 'buy time'.) Problems demanding action may be repeatedly deferred through other executive engagements and priorities until the decision point is forced. It is then found, not unnaturally, that only the briefest time is available for any kind of serious value-fact-probability analysis and none at all for any philosophical reflection. (Simon *et al.*, 1950, 533) Specialist literature, trade and professional journals, books, are simply not read; there is no time after all, and reliance for critical intelligence is placed on informal contacts with peers inside and outside the organization, or with cultivated points in the informal organization network. Problems are not dealt with in their policy implications but on an *ad hoc* basis. Impending confrontations are deferred. Committees are used as deflective devices or to delay the resolution point which, when it does occur, then arrives without any commensurate time for reflection.

All of this creates an appearance of busy-ness, and an air of pseudo-efficiency; yet it is a side-effect of the quite necessary practice of 'compartmentalization'. It has been said apocryphally that Hitler could interrupt a temper tantrum when the bell went for lunch to resume it in mid-scream when lunch was over. The practice of structuring agendas, of 'keeping to the point', of dealing with one thing at a time and one thing only is technically admirable but it can lead to strategic error, to superficiality, and to affective psychopathy when the membranes between compartments become too impervious and opaque. Reduction of time for reflection through busy-ness techniques reduces the probability that all points of view will be entered into the decision account and increases the likelihood of minority positions being suppressed, forgotten, or lost on the agenda through pressure of time. More ominous yet from the metavalue standpoint, the new imaginative idea, the breakthrough, will simply not be conceived or if conceived then stillborn. V-factors in decision making will be affected by the given situational bias. And attitudes, howsoever disguised by miens of gravity or levity, will be pressed to the shallower rather than the deeper limits of their range. The scope for unauthenticity is increased, while the opportunities for the exercise of true consideration and principle may wither under the steady impress of *ad hocism*. Meanwhile, however, the errant administrators will find in this superficiality, neither guilt nor concern, but rather comfort, for their very busy-ness serves to persuade them of their worth to the organization (are their diaries not crammed to capacity? their appointments bottlenecked?) which the organization should reward by providing them with still more support staff and assistance. When this state becomes chronic the work ethic itself subserves and reinforces value pathology.

MISCELLANEOUS ILLS

Administration can go wrong in an infinite number of ways. I can but sketch some of the main scenarios. Lack of theory is itself an ill. Even management, which makes the strongest bid towards scientific status, is hampered by the absence of any substantive or overall theory. This is a weakness shared by other great occupations (education for example) and it undermines growth towards any fully professional status. Despite the plethora of texts on administration, there is, at this stage of evolution, no universally accepted theory which is substantiated by a body of tested behavioural hypotheses. And despite the busy intrusions of social science we have not progressed far beyond the mutually contradictory sets of proverbs that Simon castigated. Yet this is not a value defect so much as a corollary of complexity. Human organisms and their organizations are notoriously perverse in refusing to sit still under scrutiny or submitting to the quantitative reductions and simplicities demanded by the scientific approach.

This complexity breeds its own version of error, as is illustrated in what I shall call the paragon fallacy. Because administration is so unscientific and yet so obviously vital to so many interests, it can lead to the attribution of superlative characters and qualities to its role incumbents. Add in the facts that reward systems are commanded by administrators, that a long conditioning to authority, though it varies from culture to culture, is a universal facet of human socialization, and that the executive competencies are supposed to be those of decision making and leadership. It then becomes easy, partly out of sloppy thinking (we have seen how vague are the concepts of leadership and decision making) and partly out of a perception or intuition of the magnitude of organizational problems, to impute paragon proportions to the administrator. Job descriptions for administrative positions bear out this assertion. The sought leader is not only to be wise and virtuous, but is to be extensively and intensively experienced, and must have this, that and the other qualification, from academic credentials to subcultural and political acceptability. In the end the executive searchers fill the role with a mere mortal, often promoted from within—a mortal draped, however, with an authoritative mantle as a result of the paragon fallacy. The organizational world is very familiar with the phenomenon of the presidential 'honeymoon'; and the fairy tale of the Emperor's new clothes should be required reading for any administrative aspirant, indeed for all who would understand organizational behaviour.

Among practising administrators, though the evidence for this would be harder to collect, there is often a certain spirit of anti-intellectualism. This grows perhaps out of the pseudo-machismo commonly affected by men of action. Administration and management are seen as practical affairs: the former a subset of politics, the latter a non-reflective set of skills, and each misperceived as simply pragmatic. Though it would be improper to make any sweeping accusation of administrative anti-intellectualism, administrators as a caste are not renowned for their contributions to scholarship. Barnard is a singular exception. More usually, when they write at all, they tend to add substance to the paragon fallacy by means of their additions to the autobiographical literature of 'great men'.

In modern times certain rather startling evidences of administrative pathology, traceable to the value domain, have thrust themselves upon the public consciousness. I have the cases of Watergate, Adolf Eichmann, and Lieutenant Calley in mind. In Watergate a unique and freakish set of circumstances; the recording by an American president of his administrative intimacies and their subsequent forced exposure, provides some remarkable empirical data. However idiosyncratic these data may be, they do reveal the subsurface, covert depths of action, and give some supportive evidence of the machismo and anti-intellectualism mentioned above. The case study from the standpoint of serious administrative research has not yet been undertaken, but it would seem especially worthy of the attention of scholars, if only because the principal actors in this executive drama were ideologically committed to success, to the work ethic, and to a tightly run 'zero defect' managerial system. That they failed and *'alles in Scherben fällt'* seems to be not so much because of any managerial fault or administrative incompetence, but rather because of a value pathology which infected the moral climate of the organization. Authentic Type I value commitment was continuously discounted by Type II pragmatism and the Machiavellian mode. Cunning was more valued than candour, power than propriety. The pathologies of disengagement, superficiality, and compartmentalization all seem to be strikingly revealed.

The cases of Eichmann and Calley, though military-bureaucratic rather than politico-bureaucratic, are equally disturbing in their administrative implications. Here the problem is posed by the putative Type I value of loyalty and by the general value-attitudinal orientation of willingness to obey authorities and to accept orders.

Deeper examination would reveal the possibility of success-values (Type III) ranking high in the protagonist's value schemas.

It is a characteristic of military organizations to over-infuse the values of loyalty and hierarchical authority in their functionaries. The problem of value conflict in these organizations (consider, for example, the military displacement of the cultural-traditional values of human life and dignity) is compounded by the factors of agency and collective responsibility, factors to be discussed more fully in the following chapter. Let us ask this question now, however: To what extent can any collectivity be held responsible in any way commensurate with individual responsibility? Eichmann can be hanged, Calley can be discharged from the Army, a terrorist can be put behind bars; but one cannot execute the Gestapo, rap the knuckles of an army, or jail the I.R.A. Collectivities are intangible, and 'one cannot hang a common seal'. Such notions are punitive or retributive aspects of the concept of responsibility, and imply the attempt to force the resolution of a value conflict through the imposition of Type II sanctions. While individuals can be coerced or persuaded by such sanctions, it is difficult to extend the logic to organizations. Organizations can be broken up, disbanded, destroyed, but it is hard to conceive of their being rehabilitated in any sense other than the reformation of their principles, that is, of their original stock and fund of value. And if that is changed, they are no longer what they were but something else. We shall return to this problem of organizational morality again below.

Since military organizations are the agencies of naked power for the higher organization of the national state, they provide especially clear instances of value conflict; insofar as they manifest the lowest levels of national value and interest they may be authentically despicable, and so, by way of psychological countervalence, much susceptible to the rhetoric of honour, duty, patriotism, pomp and circumstance. Thus, brutality and death-dealing may be genuinely repugnant (at any level of value) and therefore would necessitate redress (re-dress) through such means as uniforms, decorations, parades, and the enlisted subservience of the arts in creating a theatre and literature of supportive glamour. Medicine, on the other hand, dealing intimately with the realities of death, disease, and the infinite manifestations of physical decay, enlists a dramaturgy of antisepsis and professional detachment, gives rise to a minor industry of melodramatic literature and art and, latterly, through guild action extracts enhanced material rewards and status from its supportive and dependent environment. By a similar process, administration, value-contaminated through its association with power, is amenable to glorification through the leadership and paragon fallacies.

Let us now turn to those value pathologies, which, though they may be merely reflections of the sorry human condition, yet must be an essential part of the fabric of any realistic administrative philosophy.

II DEPTH PATHOLOGIES

EGOTISM AND MACHIAVELLI

Machiavelli is famous in Western culture for his analysis of the realities of intrigue and politics. The term Machiavellian has come to connote slyness, trickery, socio-psychological clevernesses, and scheming manipulation, all attributes and skills which are denounced at one level of propriety but often admired and practised at another level of action. Implicit is the notion that men, though interdependent, are essentially self-seeking. The seeker of success, the man ambitious for power, though self-seeking to excess, can make efficacious use of the same motivation in others. The power-seeker postulated in Machiavelli's version of Theory X is, however, distinctive in having an especially clear vision of his own ends. These ends have a Type I quality for him and the means of their accomplishment derive their justification from an overall commitment to the values of power and success. Thus, a thoroughgoing Machiavellianist will righteously scheme for the betrayal and downfall of his superiors and will use his peers and subordinates as means. Not, as Kant would have it, as ends in themselves. And he will do so unhesitatingly, ruthlessly, without remorse or compunction. Yet withal he will not let this be *seen*; it must not be perceived or at all obvious in any way that this is going on: quite the opposite, especially in a culture which elevates the values of sociability, co-operation, and conformity. It must be well-concealed and disguised. So such a value protagonist will present himself as especially charming, likeable, candid, persuasive, without guile . . . perhaps even diffident, outwardly professing denial of any power ambitions and avowing all the collegial values.

He will necessarily become adept in all the arts of human relations manipulation and acquire the full panoply of political skills, arts and skills which in the world of the twentieth century Renaissance can be reinforced by the findings of social science. He may even succeed in deceiving himself by resort to several species of rationalization: he is doing it for the family, his dependents or, even, for his organization, his country or, pseudo-philosophically, because if he doesn't somebody else (much worse) will.

This value orientation may be defended on the grounds of providing a necessary organizational energy dynamic. Lord Thomson, for example, is quoted in the *Times* (Jan. 2, 1976) as having castigated British administrators for their lack of ambitious drive. In his native Canada they would be motivated by the principle expressed, in his words, as 'I want that bastard's job'. Not that Lord Thomson was going to let them get his job, but he thought that it was good that his subordinates should want it in this valuational way. But such a value commitment can be criticized on both philosophical and psychological grounds. It contradicts those who would subscribe to the humanistic (and Kantian) ethical principle that human beings are ends-in-themselves and it is philosophically dubious if defended as a disguised version of utilitarianism, the most skilled rising in this manner to occupy the leadership roles and (*pace* Adam Smith) each pursuing his selfish ends to accomplish the benevolent whole and the collective good. A divine hand in human affairs, even if that hand is wearing both chain mail and velvet glove.

Psychologically it is wrong also, to the point of pathology, if its practice reduces value sensitivity. Where rationalization has occurred the administrator has lost sight of his own motivations and may similarly misperceive those of others. His competence is reduced. The practice of ruthlessness and deceit breeds fear of counter-ruthlessness and counter-treachery leading to an excessively defensive posture and an uneconomic and organizationally dysfunctional expenditure of energy and effort. It is inefficient. More speculatively it has from ancient times been suggested (cf. Satprakashananda, 1965, 208) that the practice of virtue heightens intellectual clarity while its converse tends to dull the mental capacities; virtue here being defined in its conventional and rather universal form as subscription to the values of honesty, unselfishness, kindness and the like.

The basic question, let me stress, is not whether egotistical ambition and power-seeking are evils which can be abjured; most certainly they are empirical certainties ever-present and ever-characteristic of administration, but whether in their excessive Machiavellian manifestations they can be detected and deterred. It is only the pathological variants which demand philosophical surgery; doctoring will suffice for the rest.

AGGRESSION AND COMPLIANCE

The question as to whether human aggressiveness is innate, destructive, and evil (Lorenz, 1966) or constructive, learned, benign (Fromm, 1973) appears to be in contention. Certainly the argument from history can be made to weigh rather heavily in the negative side of the balance, but regardless of whether aggression be malevolent either in essence or in outcome, it can be fairly assumed that this psychological attribute is distributed amongst administrators in average to above-average proportions. One is unlikely to climb far in the organizational hierarchy without it. A concern with its pathological manifestations comes about because opportunities occur within the administrative role which can magnify or exacerbate the malevolent effects of aggression. Administrative roles are authoritative ones and are functionally dependent upon the attitudes of compliance and the zones of acceptance or indifference. Experimental work in social psychology has recently revealed the potential which exists for moral or valuational abuse of this authority.

Milgram's work is especially illustrative in that it dealt directly with the phenomena of authority and obedience (1963, 1974). In an experimental simulated situation his subjects displayed a remarkable willingness to obey orders even when those orders contravened the value requirements of conventional Type II morality. The findings in these experiments and the experimental procedures are of course susceptible to various interpretations and criticisms, but they are sufficiently cogent and impressive to take on an especially sinister force when assessed in the light of modern experience in large bureaucratic organizations. Eichmann and Calley again come to mind as notorious examples.

Obedience or compliance can be construed as a way of abdicating responsibility (see Chapter 10). Conscience can be suspended. Milgram does not deny the concept of conscience; on the contrary, he uses his findings as evidence for the existence of some such moral faculty, but he does suggest that it can be attenuated or lost in certain organizational environments and that conventional value inhibitions can disappear under certain structural conditions, perhaps giving socially approved release to aggressions which may have been hitherto socially inhibited.

> Any competent manager of a destructive bureaucratic system can arrange his personnel so that only the most callous and obtuse are directly involved in violence. The greater part of the personnel can consist of men and women who, by virtue of their distance from the actual acts of brutality, will feel little strain in their performance of supportive functions. They will feel doubly absolved from responsibility. First, legitimate authority has given full warrant for their actions. Second, they have not themselves committed brutal physical acts. (Milgram, 1974, 122)

The sinister implication here, of course, is that aggressive outlets can be systematically designed. Evil in this sense would be within the conscious scope of administrators; not merely unconscious or epiphenomenal as in the phenomenon of psychological distancing discussed above (Chapter 4).

A reservation must be entered. Two difficulties always beset the philosopher of administration as he studies any organization. He has first to discover the true allocation of power (necessitating an intimacy with the informal structure) and secondly to find the true allocation of value (necessitating an intimacy with the personality structure). When organization members are ready, for whatever reasons, to 'overaccept' authority, they yield power to the administrative hierarchy which permits the actualization of the administrator's values, both idiographic and nomothetic. When these in their turn are philosophically unsound—romantically evil ideology combined with anti-Semitic aggression (Eichmann); undermined pluralistic ideology combined with aggressive careerism (Calley)—the stage is set for tragic pathology. It is not simply liberty that has the price of eternal vigilance. The price of morality is continuous monitoring of the bases of authority.

CAREERISM

Executive aggression is harnessed to ambition. Both provide energetic drive for the purposes of getting the organization's or the administrator's way. When frustrated they may fuel ulcers and sour the executive soul, but dammed and channeled, they can subserve both the administrator and his organization. There are value difficulties, however. Career progress in an hierarchical arrangement is not oversimply viewed as ascent of the hierarchical ladder. Progress is made by moving on and moving up; not by staying stuck, and certainly not by moving down. And contrary to some liberal wishfulness there is *not* 'more room at the top'. That this need not result in naked competition or internecine warfare among administrators we have already seen in discussing the problems of executive succession and cliquism. The growth of some form of mutually regulated competition and reciprocal co-operation is more likely than any solitary savagery. In the large complex rational bureaucracies it is axiomatic that no one is indispensable, that parts are replaceable or substitutable. Checks and balances emerge at an informal level to restrain individualism as epitomized in the folk wisdom 'Be nice to people on your way up the ladder, you may meet them again on your way down'. And this in turn need not be pathological; it may assist the rhythms of organizational life and provide something of the often adulated quality of 'continuity'.

Continuity, of course, tends to mean continuity of value, and this may lead to dysfunctional organizational rigidity. The exigencies of extra-organizational history may demand changes to which the careerists as a group are antagonistic. Again, technological progress in the ranks from which the administrators themselves once emerged may have outstripped their experience. So the administrator may become, naturally, out of touch, with the outside and with the inside. Logically, this could be easily remedied by occasional recycling, by a return to the ranks, but the whole point of a career ladder is that it is made for ascent, not descent. The worker who becomes a manager will not wish to return to the bench nor does the politician willingly go back to the people unless it be to seek re-election. Even under the Maoist regime the 'intellectuals' have to be forcibly compelled to rejoin the ranks of workers and peasants.

There is more to it than this. Good teachers are promoted to the administrative ranks and cease to teach; good salesmen likewise become sales managers and cease to sell. If they are more organizationally effective in their former than in their latter roles, then the Peter principle, a sort of Gresham's law of administration, is operative. Fortunately, however, there is no law or principle which dictates that aggression, ambition, and competence cannot flow together nor even that adequate or perhaps even superior morality cannot be combined with the mix. Our concern here is to draw attention to the propensity for pathology. Careerism implies that successive organizational roles are left behind and that return to them is commonly viewed (though not necessarily overtly so) as a form of failure. There are structured exceptions to this, the return of an academic administrator to lecture hall or lab; the return of an amateur-type administrator to his former profession, but for the professional administrator these face-saving exits do not normally exist. There is only one road, and that is up. He must press for recognition and promotion or risk the stigma of being unsuccessful.

An overcommitment to careerism can also create its own special form of irresponsibility, particularly when the upward mobile executive advances by extra-organizational movement. He can then leave behind unfinished work, stalled decisions, unfulfilled obligations, and a host of moral or ethical responsibilities when his 'divorce' occurs and he 'remarries' into the new role. Even when career progress is intra-organizational, the climber can effect the same shucking of responsibility and the inheritor of his abandoned role is obliged to 'pick up the pieces'. A somewhat similar phenomenon occurs in political life when role-seekers and governments standing for re-election make decisions calculated more to win votes (i.e. advance their careers) than to advance the true collective interest.

It is plain that careerism poses ethical problems, but the view is sometimes maintained that ethical issues are irrelevant when organizational life is construed as a power game in which the object is to discover and develop a winning strategy. Under this view,

Promotion would involve individual officials making, for each situation which arises, a guess about various important aspects of conduct: Is persistence a virtue or a crime? Should one argue with one's superior or even one's Minister? Should one try to establish contacts relevant to one's work outside the department? The answers would depend on one's judgment of the state of play in the game: conduct would be good or bad according only to the situation.

and

Those who failed to get promotion would, almost by definition, be possessors of inferior strategies, who cannot find a way to match their personal qualities to the situation in which they found themselves. (Report of the FDA, 1972, 1974).

In the same report and context Sisson is quoted as saying that the administrator

'must always avoid all those questions of value to which a philosophic study of relationships is apt to lead. . . . If his most desperate concern is to thrust himself to the top . . . he will not be deflected by a temptation to examine values.' (*loc. cit.* and Sisson, 1959, 20)

That such views are tenable, even in a highly respected bureaucracy, endorse the identification of careerism as a putative source of pathology.

These are some of the dysfunctions of hierarchy. When careerism becomes pathological it can not only prevent any of the potential benefits of recycling but can generate an insecurity which can lead to self-perpetuating cliques with an elaborate control of the reward system and mutual reciprocities between in-group members, all of which can be organizationally dysfunctional. Or conversely, when the career system is manifestly competitive it can lead to personal problems by way of the phenomena of executive stress and insecurity. Finally, when tenure is assured and career progress is a function largely of seniority, as in public administration or Japanese industry, there are the further hazards of executive impotence, irresponsibility and anomie. In short, careerism and hierarchy, both essential and both in their non-pathological forms beneficent aspects of administration, can easily be subverted, leading to a rich assortment of value pathologies.

THE PHILOSOPHY OF SUCCESS

We have been looking so far at value pathologies which can be traced to defects of motivation or organizational structure, and which can in some way be considered as wrong or bad. But this wrongness or badness is only from the Type II standpoint of conventional morality or from Type I subscriptions to certain values and value orientations such as, say, Christian ethics. From the standpoint of the individual seeker after success who takes as his basic philosophical truth the overwhelming priority of self-interest, the limited supply of prizes, and the consequent clash and struggle for power, the singleminded pursuit of his goal may be not only logical but ethical in its own right. He may believe, for example, that he has had the vision of the world as it really is and the courage to face that vision. Let us try to suspend our individual value judgments for a little while and look, as clinically and objectively as possible, at this world view. It is sanctified by age and has been embodied in the Eastern wisdom from a period predating Machiavelli by many centuries. This secret doctrine was known to the Hindus as the *arthasastra*. In the following commentary I shall be deeply indebted to the work of the eminent Indologist, Professor Heinrich Zimmer (1951).

The *arthasastra* holds that there are four main ways in which a neighbour can be approached, that is, four principal strategies for dealing with people politically. The first applies when one is in an inferior power position to an opponent (and in the jungle savagery of the competition for success *everyone* is an opponent, including those whose passing role is that of friend or ally or political bedfellow). It can be called the technique of conciliation or negotiation. Here one seeks appeasement of the superior by whatever means; by personal charm, by rhetoric and flattery. He must be soothed, made to feel secure, unaware of any threat from his subordinate, confident in and dependent upon him if at all possible. It prevails among administrators when, for example, we courteously keep the lines of communication open, even with those whom we despise. Power must be constantly respected and the more powerful must be conciliated; one can only 'negotiate' with one in command, play upon his ego, insinuate oneself into his favour, indulge his vanities, be the courtier, the negotiator, the man of political skills and diplomacy.

But suppose one *is* in the superior power position. Then the correct, second approach is that of *force*. If one has power one will wield it, one will let it be known. As Napoleon would have it, one should hang a man from the ranks occasionally, *'pour encourager les autres'*. Chastisement and punishment should be visible and felt occasionally otherwise the superior's impotence will be revealed. In modern jargon it is advisable to 'lean' on subordinates from time to time, to pressure them, to make sure it is the lieutenants who have the ulcers and not the captain. The sudden firing, the swift execution, can be most salutary. The steel beneath the velvet must be delicately perceived from time to time or, in a different style and different situation the outright rage, fury, or tantrum can be displayed with great effect to strike terror into subordinates and rivals. The seeker of success will master all these techniques and use them ruthlessly in his pursuit of power. But whatever the power relationships, the remaining approaches—'donation' and 'division'—are always to be recommended.

Donation is well known to us today in its maximal extreme as bribery or graft and in its minimal commonplace form as the social exchange principle (Wright, 1973, 4). Indeed at times sociologists would seem to elevate the strategy to the status of a universal norm or metavalue of reciprocity. One advances one's social reciprocity index by buying a colleague a lunch or a drink. The underlying tacit force of *quid pro quo* is very pervasive and subtly powerful, whether it be the tip to a waitress or the lavish country weekend with sexual overtones planned and designed to suborn the recipients in the donator's interests. In parts of the Orient the practice is often semi-formalized but its usage is universal and its varieties infinite.

Donation seeks to bind by gift, interpreting gift in its widest sense. It is especially valuable to our hypothetical protagonist when it can be used to corrupt an opponent's agents or to undermine the opposition. The climber may seek to use it directly on his superior but perhaps more effectively on his superior's lieutenants and entourage, on those who have his ear. There is no more insinuating flattery than that which endears its author at one or two removes. On the other hand, constrained in his use of force, the modern administrator may seek to compensate by the judicious use of donation on his underlings.

There remains the classical principle of division, the Roman divide-and-rule. It comes as second nature to the true success-seeker. He will be skilled in splitting the ranks of any opposition, in spreading ambivalence, and playing upon it by sowing rumour and dissension if the resulting disruption can further his ends, in undermining competitors, rivals, colleagues by the wrong word in the right ear, in the generation and the manipulation of confusion. Towards these ends ambiguity is good and ambivalence better yet.

The four strategies described above are to be used in concert with the minor tactics of 'deceit', 'overlooking', and 'feint'. One must be as ready to resort to any trickery, treachery, or fraud which can advance one's ends as one is ready to assume the guise of moral indignation if these behaviours are perceived in others. One is most friendly to the intended victim and one should strike without warning. Nevertheless, despite all these manoeuvres, rivals will occasionally succeed and then the right attitude is that of 'overlooking'. One discounts the opponent's successes by ignoring them; or one feigns unconcern or at best damns with faint praise. The skilled administrator will contrive not to be at those meetings at which he knows he will lose his case (he can be out of town or send a deputy; more important matters are to hand). He will also carefully disparage or discount any promotion or organizational achievement on the part of his colleagues unless he can attach some or all of the credit to himself. It is important, too, to master the skills of false appearance, to 'feint' where necessary, or, as we would nowadays put it, to be able to present the correct image. Especially is it important to be able to give a convincing performance of honesty, conviction, and authenticity. Modern techniques in combination with modern gullibility can make the Satanic appear angelic and the demonic the epitome of social value.

Enough has perhaps been said to give the flavour of the *arthasastra*, but we may reinforce it with some quotations, from both East and West, which capture the perennial nature of this value orientation:

As clouds change from moment to moment, just so thine enemy of today becomes, even today, thy friend.

Power grows out of the barrel of a gun.

Might is above right; right proceeds from might; right has its support in might, as living beings in soil. As smoke the wind, so right must follow might. Right in itself is devoid of command, it leans on might as the creeper on the tree.

Macht macht Recht.

If men think thee soft, they will despise thee. When it is, therefore, time to be cruel, be cruel; and when it is time to be soft, be soft.

God is on the side of the big battalions.

Whoever desires success in this world must be prepared to make deep vows, swear love and friendship, speak humbly, and pretend to shed and wipe away tears.

My enemy's enemy is my friend.

The last word of social wisdom is never trust.

This doctrine, though ancient, is modern, classical, eternal; and it has its place in the field of administrative studies. It is not because I subscribe to it that I have dwelt upon it at such length, but because it is surely an essential ingredient in the values preparation of administrators, a possible starting point in the search for higher wisdoms. If administrative aspirants are not so sophisticated by exposure to it they can hardly be in a position to combat it, to contest it philosophically, or even to know that it is there and that they are, from time to time, themselves being manipulated and used. The *arthasastra* sensitizes us to the darker side of the moon, makes us aware of the administrative id, and serves as a point of initiation for higher aspirations. It can only fully succeed where there is a sort of liberal failure of nerve, a refusal to recognize its presence, a surrender to cynicism, or an abdication of value discussion through positivism. Yet both liberalism and positivistic influence are widespread in the literature, and cynicism is always present. Philosophy has to begin in the dirt. It has to deny the charges sometimes levelled against it of being sterile or irrelevant or trivial and it must do groundwork in sensitizing us to the perils and dangers which lurk within those ostensibly benevolent collectivities of purpose, organizations. Administrative pathology is the disease of which philosophy can be the cure.

10
Organizational Morality and Responsibility

In the previous chapter I have concentrated upon ways in which the administrator can by one vice or another contribute to organizational value pathology, and I have dwelt, in particular, upon the so-called philosophy of success. Why, in an age of supposed scientific enlightenment, of so much social welfare, progress, and concern, would an administrator consciously, as an act of individual morality, secretly subscribe to such philosophy? For several possible reasons and in several ways. First, he may come to believe from his private experience and personal phenomenology that this philosophy best reflects the truth about the world, a truth to be sure which most men would rather not face because of their tender-mindedness, or lack of courage and nerve in the face of an inimical reality. And so he adopts it as a reflective and reasoned response: to be evil in an evil world, to beat the world at its own game, and so on. Or he might suppose that, true or not, a differential advantage could be gained by its adoption. Most men are too socially conditioned to subscribe to such a philosophy; the comfortable half-truths of liberalism and the sentiments of the human relations and human resources views of man are more to their taste; and so they are likely dupes and proper victims for the ruthless spirit. This would be the wolf in the sheep pen theory. Again, he may not totally accept the secret doctine but acknowledge it as being partially and significantly true and therefore worthy of conditional acceptance. Pragmatically, then, he will embrace the philosophy from time to time as and where he judges it appropriate. This would be *ad hoc* commitment. Or he may succumb, as many have done, to the lure of the Grand Temptation; that the end, if it be righteous, justifies the means. So the philosophy can be used to achieve power so that, once achieved and secure, just rule and righteous administration can follow. Dostoievsky has enshrined this version of machination in his famous Grand Inquisitor dialogue.

In such ways, whatever the revulsion or offence to ordinary sensibilities that the doctrines of power and their associated value orientations may convey, it must be accepted that the administrative careerist can make this type of philosophical commitment. That he does so, however, is a matter of individual choice, individual morality, or, in our language, the translation of the values of power and success to the Type I range of valuation. It is, of course, subject to critique from other philosophical positions but all that the proponents of these contending positions can do is to seek to persuade their audience by reason and rhetoric and all the powers at their disposal, that they have the better values. In the end the act of choice is individual; and if free and conscious, then moral.

We must now consider morality from the standpoint of the organization, the collective, and ask whether organizations in and of themselves are in any way morally responsible or could in any way constitute a deterrent or impediment to moral action.

ORGANIZATIONAL MALEVOLENCE

In the matter of organizational morality the case for the prosecution has been put most cogently by Ladd (1970). He argues that formal organizations and bureaucracy are in certain critical aspects antagonistic to ordinary morality, that is, to Type II conventions and the Type I ethics summed up in the Kantian imperatives. This antagonism comes about because of the organizational value of rationality and the nomothetic principle of depersonalization. In the complex bureaucracy, individuals are not whole persons but role incumbents, partial sets of skills which are of utility to the organizational whole. They are *parts*, replaceable and substitutable parts at that. In the organization, rationally construed, no one is indispensable. Morality, in glaring contrast, is a function of total personality and this latter exceeds and overflows any role.[1]

In any event, it does not matter what such 'personalities' feel or think, for the organizational language game determines the values appropriate for the social or collective decisions which are made in its name. Organizational goals combined with rational procedures for their attainment (glossed and glazed where necessary by the refinements of the human relations movement) make organizational life analogous to chess. Within the game there are no 'right' or 'wrong' moves, only those of more or less efficacy given the set system of rules which cannot in itself be challenged. The ordinary member becomes a logical factotum, alienated or manipulated. Even that extraordinary member, the administrator, is not an author of acts but an *agent*, one who does things in the name of others.

There is a special way in which the administrator can be irresponsible. This would be by philosophical and psychological detachment—by the belief that the organization is bigger than any individual and possesses a destiny and logic of its own. He then commits the biological fallacy and worse; the organization is not only reified, but deified. And the agent is not personally or morally responsible for the acts which are under the authority or *authorship* of the collectivity. Bureaucrats and civil servants, administrators of industry and education, no less than Adolf Eichmann, must 'faithfully execute policies of which they personally disapprove' (Merton *et al.*, 1952, 132). And outwardly benevolent organizations can become latent collective forces for evil.

AGENCY AND RESPONSIBILITY

We are not concerned here with the legal aspects of agency, but rather with the socio-psychological ramifications of collective or social decision making where the administrator's decision is imputed to the organization. In the case of contracts, for example, the official concluding the agreement is neither personally bound nor personally responsible for the consequences of what becomes an organizational act. And we may all have felt a certain *frisson* of irresponsibility when the will of the group, or the leaders of the group, is allowed to sway and prevail over valid opposition.

The agent is conceived to act in the interest of his principal. Since organizations are ostensibly rational interest-pursuing collectivities, it follows that their acts may conflict with the interests of the next and higher orders of collectivity within their sphere of operation. The agent may thus find himself from time to time engaged in doing things of which he would not personally approve under the more liberal conditions of individual responsibility; in an extrapolation, as it were, from the lawyer who knows he is seeking the exculpation of a guilty client. Or the group ordained by the organization's structure may have arrived at a decision to which the administrator is opposed on idiographic value grounds, but which he feels on nomothetic value grounds must be advanced and executed. The organizational decision is made, according to Barnard, 'non-personally from the point of view of its organizational effect and its relation to the organization purpose' (203). Simon's corresponding positivistic text is 'decisions in private management must take as their ethical premises the objectives that have been set for the organization' (1965, 29). But this appearance of ethical neutrality can serve as a cover for Type III malice, spite, and animus, within and outside the organization, at the same time that positive morality of the Type I order can be made to seem irrelevant. And the appearance of rationality can serve to excuse most, if not all, of the well-documented record of personally felt injustices at the hands of bureaucracy. Not every anti-bureaucratic sentiment can be explained away under Thompson's term, bureauticism.[2] Organizational dehumanism or inhumanism extends even to those organizations which by definition are Type I collectivities: the Roman Catholic Church with its religious purpose, the Communist State with its ideological purpose. 'Apparat' stifles. Administration devalues value. All in the cold light of reason and the cool detachment of agency.

Ladd pursues this line of reasoning to the point where he concludes that social decisions cannot be moral:

> Thus, for logical reasons it is improper to expect organizational conduct to conform to the ordinary principles of morality. We cannot and must not expect formal organizations, or their representatives acting in their official capacities, to be honest, courageous, considerate, sympathetic, or to have any kind of moral integrity. Such concepts are not in the vocabulary, so to speak, of the organizational language-game. (We do not find them in the vocabulary of chess either!) Actions that are wrong by ordinary moral standards are not so for organizations; indeed, they may often be required. Secrecy, espionage and deception do not make organizational action wrong; rather they are right, proper and, indeed, rational, if they serve the objectives of the organization. They are no more or no less wrong than, say, bluffing is in poker. From the point of view of organizational decision-making they are "ethically neutral." (1970, 499–500)

This is a restatement from the perspective of moral philosophy of the constantly recurring dilemma in administrative studies which, following Getzels and Cuba, we have referred to above as the nomothetic-idiographic dialectic. It is paradoxical that though morality governs relations with *others* it is itself an *individual* matter.

In the analysis of value we have identified this dilemma as a contest between discipline and indulgence and, throughout, I have implied that the administrator should identify himself with the collective interest. This ethical implication now needs to be emended, sophisticated. It holds good only with qualifications. Here, for example, it is being suggested that organizations are not necessarily benevolent nor forces for social good but may be corrupters of their members and their agents, that 'actions that are wrong by ordinary moral standards are not so for organizations'.

The administrator's proclivity for the nomothetic must be morally grounded and have sophisticated justifiability. I do not contest Ladd's analysis of the moral problem; *per contra* I would lend some strength to his vision of organizations as morally stultifying and ethically dangerous entities, but I would take issue with any underestimation of the *administrator* as an agent incapable of altering the moral climate and moral destiny of his organization. His power to do this may not be what he (or I) would wish, but what he does have is his golden potentiality. If he denies that potential by adopting the *persona* of the agent, he offends as Pontius Pilate then and the positivistic bureaucrat now. He becomes his organization's faceless creature instead of its creator, a functionary in the lowest sense of the word. Yet, to fuse individual morality with social decision is difficult; it demands much, as Barnard constantly stressed, in the way of moral complexity. In comprehending this complexity it is necessary to cope with two difficult concepts: self-interest and responsibility. The first is only simple on the surface. The administrator has to get clear about his own deepest interests and where they ramify and lie. To do this calls for much insight, some intuition, and if not, Guardian-style, the vision of the form of the Good, then at least something of the Pauline vision through a glass darkly, of one's own true self.

The second concept, responsibility, is vexed and tortuous and must be unravelled. We have already raised the question, When *all* are responsible who *is* responsible? Let us try now to elucidate the notion of responsibility.

It is first necessary to distinguish between legal, formal, and moral responsibility. The concept is also vacuous without the connective linguistic particles, 'to' and 'for'. Responsibility is always *to* somebody *for* something. The subtlety is that the some*body* may be oneself and the some*thing* may be an internal phenomenological event.

We shall not be concerned with the causative sense of the term, e.g. when I accidently trip and in falling break the china vase. I am here the efficient material cause of a series of entailed consequences which are unhappy in their outcome. The owner may hold me 'responsible' for the damaged crockery, but the sense is trivial, and we shall interpret moral responsibility as requiring the condition of some element of voluntarism or free will.

To return to legal responsibility: in this sense both bodies human and bodies corporate are held accountable for their acts to a system of game rules as established by law or legal system; local, national, or international. My accidental breakage of your vase may, of course, oblige me to recompense you with damages, depending upon the circumstances and the legal game within which we are players. The only moral element here is any sense of obligation I may happen or choose to have. The law game rules will usually, however, trace their origin to and seek their foundation in Type II consensus values and Type I principles.

The difficulty in the present context of argument has to do with bodies corporate. That one cannot hang a common seal has already been stated. And it is clear that corporate acts cannot always be reduced to the acts of individuals. If I own ten shares in General Motors I am not responsible if it violates the anti-trust rules, or does those things which are not good for the nation. And if it goes bankrupt I am not financially responsible beyond the rules of legal limited liability, even if the greatest individual economic hardships are a consequence. On the other hand, accountability of a sort can be impressed upon the individual actors who are *agents* of a corporate body through such legal devices as fines, imprisonment, and loss of licence. Law has the sanctions of naked power. The force of legal responsibility is real enough, especially since the corporate agents are usually administrators, but it is distinctive from moral responsibility.

Formal responsibility can be considered as a subset of legal responsibility. It refers to the accountabilities sanctioned by the game rules of an organization. Acts are constrained by a potent system of rewards and punishments, including salaries, promotion, demotion and termination. The monitoring functions of administration and management are a part of this responsibility system. And, just as law seeks a ground in societal values, so the system of formal responsibility seeks its ground in the organizational values and policy. Again, the organizational parallel to corporate bodies would be found in those group acts (group decisions) stemming from group processes and structures (committees, boards, and *ad hoc* groups) established formally within the organization. So if a committee of peers decides by secret vote, or unrecorded consensus, that a colleague should be dismissed, against *whom* can the injured party point his finger? The popularity of committee action is understandable. It can be a way of responsibly avoiding responsibility. But the responsibility then avoided would be moral responsibility.

This last, moral responsiblity, can reduce to the individual only. It is uniquely phenomenological. It is the responsibility of a person to himself for his adherence to his entire range of values but especially to those Type I values with which he has become authentically engaged. It is the ultimate sense of responsibility.

MORALITY, MORAL COMPLEXITY, AND LEADERSHIP

The notion of morality described above is self-referent and psychologically complex. It suggests the presence of internal factors such as conscience and will, and internal dialectical tensions between principles and preferences. This self-centredness should not be allowed to obscure the fact that the *content* of moral discourse is outside the individual, and conventionally treats of relationship with others. The disciplines of ethics and moral philosophy are relevant to our understanding of responsibility in so far as they can clarify concepts, set out the arguments, and make the case for Type I and II value. Their function is also to persuade and conduce to moral behaviour. They are, as it were, ancillary to moral action.

They are not prerequisites of responsibility, but rather aids to moral navigation.

In the administrator's purlieu of the organization the moral actor finds his value difficulties magnified in a special way, for he is not, so to speak, entirely himself. Technically and officially he is a role incumbent. If we construe this fact as a reduction of personal responsibility it opens the way for the criticisms of agency and bureaucracy given above. But the administrator for one is not a faceless agent, a depersonalized role incumbent. At least four conditions amplify and compound the moral complexity of his task: (1) he designs and creates roles, for himself as well as for others; (2) he has the overall charge of reconciling the nomothetic and idiographic aspects of his organization; (3) he determines, in part or in whole, the organizational values, and; (4) he must do all this within the constraints imposed by the metavalues (Chapter 11). Consider, too, that his role embraces such activities as settling value disputes among organization members, determining the organizational language game, negotiating with levels of interest outside the organization; he is sometimes a leader, sometimes a statesman, sometimes a philosopher, sometimes a judge.

In the face of this, Barnard recognized and stressed the need for moral skills. His definition of morals is 'personal forces or propensities of a general and subtle character in individuals which tend to inhibit, control, or modify inconsistent immediate specific desires, impulses, or interests, and to intensify those which are consistent with such propensities'. When such morals were 'strong and stable' there would exist a 'condition of responsibility' (261). The translation of values into action, however, rather than their existence in the abstract, is his primary concern, and he illustrates:

> I know men whose morals as a whole I cannot help believe to be lower ethically than my own. But these men command my attention and sometimes my admiration because they adhere to their codes rigidly in the face of great difficulties; whereas I observe that many others who have a 'higher' morality do not adhere to their codes when it would apparently not be difficult to do so. Men of the first class have a higher sense of responsibility than those having, as I view them, the higher ethical standards. *The point is that responsibility is the property of an individual by which whatever morality exists in him becomes effective in conduct.* (266–7, Barnard's italics)

I would not wish to contest this, but would draw attention to the operative phrase *'whatever morality exists within him'*. The demands of administrative life can be responded to in different ways and the response will be a function of the moral substance of the actor. The administrator is also in a special position because he has more scope than the ordinary member for the creation and acceptance of his own role. This, too, will depend upon his moral complexity and sense of responsibility, upon the 'morality that exists within him'. To some extent the moral sights can be raised or lowered, but even if the value structure within is set, the moral act of consistency with that structure is in the last analysis private and personal.

I now wish to make a general hypothesis—one which would be difficult, though not impossible, to test. It is that the quality of leadership is functionally related to the moral climate of the organization and this, in turn, to the moral complexity and skills of the leader. Leadership as presently understood is commonly regarded as having three main dimensions: consideration, production emphasis, and situational factors (see Chapter 5 above). I would postulate a fourth dimension, the 'morality that exists within the leader'. This, I suggest, can become subtly externalized, contributing to the administrative phenomena of legitimacy, credibility, and even charisma (where Type I attachments are notably evident). It can on occasion infuse organizational life with a quality of meaning going beyond the nomothetic to the most human and the transrational; it can be, in plain language, inspiring. Yet this aspect of leadership goes unresearched and unexplored at the level of social science.

If this hypothesis were to be confirmed, then there would be an incentive to moral behaviour and an organizational reward for the practice of responsibility. Honour might yet prove to be worth a re-evaluation.

11
Metavalues

The foregoing discussion will have raised our guard against any simplistic acceptance of organizations as morally neutral or morally positive entities. We have seen how, quite apart from competition among themselves and independently of the idiographic value structures of their administrators and members, they can be morally negative. It may perhaps be more accurate to describe organizations as morally primitive value environments. I mean to say that, without committing the biological fallacy, organizations tend to be governed by value imperatives which would correspond, in the individual, to the lower levels of Maslow's or Herzberg's hierarchy. These imperatives pervade the organization but are most potent and close to the surface of consciousness in the administrative-managerial subsystem. They may be described as *metavalues*.

A metavalue is a concept of the desirable so vested and entrenched that it seems to be beyond dispute or contention. It usually enters as an unspoken or unexamined assumption into the ordinary value calculus of individual or collective life. Examples of metavalues would be wealth or life itself. In a democratic society, democracy is a metavalue; amongst academics, education, rationality, and consistency are common metavalues. It is not so much that metavalues are absolute or quasi-absolute as that they go for the most part unquestioned, *beyond* value, and so intrude unconsciously to affect value behaviour. Let us now consider the principal organizational metavalues.

MAINTENANCE

It has been said that the first law of nature is self-preservation. Extrapolating to the collectivity the first law of organization is survival. The organization must maintain itself. In new and emerging organizations this metavalue is patently obvious, but it can recede from the conscious level as the association, organization, or institution becomes established and secure. Once in existence, an organization does not question its need-to-be. The attendant values of organizational loyalty are rapidly proliferated and form the basis of the value indoctrination of new members. Though threats to the collective interests of organization members may close their ranks and raise the level of consciousness of the maintenance value, it does not follow that the actual best means to survival will be selected. Organizations may sometimes appear to the outside observer to be suicidal—the trade union, for example, which puts its employers and itself out of business—but this only serves to prove that factual rationality is distinct from valuational trans- or subrationality.

For the administrator it goes without saying (it is *beyond* value question) that his first obligation is to maintain the organization. Without the organization there is nothing for him to administer. This does not deny the occasional administrative function of eliminating dysfunctional subsystems. Such elimination would be in the interests of the whole organization, the largest unit of employment of the administrator himself. Katz and Kahn express it as follows: 'Since any organization must survive in order to carry out its basic functions, survival becomes a salient goal for organizational decision makers. [Dynamic forces generated by maintenance structures] have as their implicit, and sometimes explicit, goal the survival of present organizational forms. For many administrators and officials, concern with the preservation of the bureaucracy assumes primary significance. Indeed, the term bureaucracy is often used, not in the Weberian sense, but in the sense of an officialdom absorbed only in the preservation of its structure and in the ease of its own operation' (265, 266).

The maintenance metavalue is nomothetic. It is a fundamental part of the administrator's value bias. To rise above this bias it would be necessary for him to ask the unaskable question, Should my organization exist?

GROWTH

The second metavalue is growth. Organizations seek to expand; their dynamic finds form in extension. Merely to survive and maintain the status quo is not enough. Resources are always limited and the normal condition is competition for their control. This applies to corporate as well as to individual bodies and to public corporations as well as to private. It also applies intraorganizationally, and the study of bureaucracy is replete with instances of dysfunction traceable to this impulse and metavalue. Growth can also be conceived as protective insofar as it augments power and thus protects against threats to survival. In this way it is corollary to the first metavalue.

But organizations are not biological entities. They are coherences of interest and it is this coherence, or economy of incentives as Barnard calls it, which must grow if the metavalue is to be actualized. Barnard accepts the innate propensity for expansion and analyses the metavalue in this way:

> The maintenance of incentives, particularly those relating to prestige, pride of association, and community satisfaction, calls for growth, enlargement, extension. It is, I think, the basic and, in a sense, the legitimate reason for bureaucratic aggrandizement in corporate, governmental, labor, university, and church organizations everywhere observed. To grow seems to offer opportunity for the realization of all kinds of active incentives—as may be observed by the repeated emphasis in all organizations upon size as an index of the existence of desirable incentives, or the alternative rationalization of other incentives when size is small or growth is discouraged. The overreaching which arises from this cause is the source of destruction of organizations otherwise successful, since growth often so upsets the economy of incentives, through its reactions upon the effectiveness and efficiency of organization, that it is no longer possible to make them adequate. (159)

The caution against overexpansion is to be noted. The status of growth as a metavalue is less secure than that of maintenance. From time to time it is consciously acknowledged that bigness does not of itself provide the necessary and sufficient conditions for goodness; and it is well known that growth can be cancerous and dysfunctional. On the other hand, the logic of survival is to place as many bulwarks as possible between target and threat. Many subordinates rather than few can mean more protective cover, sacrificial cover if need be. And organizational expansion, even in non-threatening supportive environments, serves to preclude the birth or growth of potential competitors. Growth can mean power (itself an administrative metavalue) and to gain power is a natural administrative reflex. Therefore, a bias towards growth is corollary to that towards maintenance. To challenge this metavalue is to challenge the second law of organization and the natural tendency of systems.

EFFECTIVENESS AND EFFICIENCY

An organization is effective if it can achieve its purposes, and conversely. It follows that there is an imperative to be effective and that effectiveness is an organizational metavalue. How can this be contested? To point to the factual evidence of many existing ineffective organizations does not refute the metavalue; such evidence merely suggests that there is some measure (intuitive or objective) of organizational success and that on this standard (or metavalue) organizations can be perceived to be deficient. What in personal language is called success, though here with overtones of fame, reputation, and power, is in organizational terms called effectiveness. Effectiveness is the accomplishment of desired ends. As a metavalue it is tautologous, for it means the desirability of accomplishing desired ends, and because of this tautology it goes unexamined. The only way in which it can be challenged, short of re-examining the ends themselves, is by a consideration of what sociologists call latent functions. These are the unforeseen, unintended, or unpredictable side effects which are consequences of any means-end chain of action initiated by the pursuit of goals. Sometimes these latent functions may be foreseen, intended, and tacitly recognized. For example, a conference of administrators may have as its manifest function the reading and discussion of presented papers, but this function may be valuationally outweighed by the concomitant social intercourse and interaction (especially where expense accounts can be billed for the occasion). In such a case the *ad hoc* organization (the conference and its arrangements) is effective if the latent functions are fulfilled and due propriety observed with respect to the manifest functions. The metavalue of effectiveness appears to be the one metavalue which is incontestable—because of tautology—but it can on scrutiny give rise to questions about the sought and unsought consequences of the ends of action.

Efficiency is a term which has caused some confusion in the

classical literature due to its divergent usage by Barnard. Barnard related efficiency to the satisfaction of individual motives. This is consistent with his view of organizations as incentive collectivities. Organizations were for him 'efficient' insofar as they succeeded in eliciting sufficient individual co-operation. The efficiency of a co-operative system would be its capacity to maintain itself by the individual satisfactions it affords.

Simon's usage is more conventional. Efficiency is essentially the ratio of input to output and can be conceived in engineering terms. A transformer is 80% efficient if that is the ratio of wattage delivered to wattage at the input terminals. Monetary measures of efficiency form the bases of economic accountancy. The primary fact of economic life is scarcity of resources and consciousness of this underlies all administrative decisions and establishes a criterion of choice wherein one seeks the largest result or pay-off for any given application of resources. I shall take the term in this ordinary sense and consider it a metavalue because on the face of it no administrator will consciously choose, *ceteris paribus*, the less efficient of two alternatives. But let us look at this great basic assumption of administration more closely.

The efficiency metavalue implies that (a) given alternative means with the same cost attaching to each means, one will seek the maximum return, that is, maximization of ends or (b) given alternative goals with the same end value one will choose ends so as to minimize the cost of means. In both (a) and (b) there are two possible sources of fallacy, the one having to do with the meaning and specification of costs and the other with the meaning and specification of goals or ends. By now it will be obvious that this type of specification presents difficulties (Chapters 3 & 4 above). There are major conceptual obstacles which include the incommensurability of quantification and quality (p and v factors), the imponderability of the p factor in decision making, and the problem of ascertaining all cost and benefit functions. Efficiency as a metavalue is applied forward, to the future; but as a value it is measured backwards, in respect of the past. Perhaps this explains why, from the standpoint of retrospective wisdom, so much inefficiency is to be observed in organizations. But it remains a metavalue, and to challenge it is to open up all the issues of administrative philosophy. An administrator cannot choose to value inefficiency but he can probe, if he wishes, the devious and sometimes intractable implications of the efficiency metavalue.

ORGANIZATIONS AS MORAL PRIMITIVES

I would reiterate that the four metavalues described above refer to organizations rather than to individuals. They are universal organizational values. Taken together, they contribute the desire or volition bases for collective systems, and when conceived as organizational laws they form quasi-moral imperatives or commandments for the administrator: or perhaps one single injunction, 'Thou shalt not destroy thine organization!' And so, by way of the positive corollary, 'Seek its interest always!' and easy stages of increasing identification with us (organization members) and disidentification with them (non-organization members) to, 'What's good for General Motors is good for the country' and, finally, 'My country, right or wrong'. Perhaps, but even without any extrapolation, the conventional wisdom is that the administrator must maintain his organization, must seek its growth wherever opportunity for growth is discerned, must seek the accomplishment of his organization's goals, and throughout must seek these ends as efficiently as possible. This primitive value structure or base has imperative force for the administrator prior to and without regard for his personal value orientation. And this force will apply whether he is actively conscious of it or not. It is in this way that we can consider organizations to be morally 'primitive'; the collectivity is neither person nor biological entity but its structure of collective interest and its constitution as a corporate entity establishes *ipso facto* a value pattern with governing effect on its administrators and this pattern, measured against humane individual standards, can be called elemental, primitive, or unsophisticated.

This does not mean that organizations are of necessity corrupting or degrading to the moral or value life of their members, but that they *can* work this subtly negative influence if their primitive imperatives are allowed to impose themselves, achieve dominance, or go unexamined. An efficient organization effectively maintaining itself, expanding its influence, achieving its goals, can be wondrous to behold and a source of beneficence to those inside and outside it. It can also be a Juggernaut, a moral anathema, an engine of corruption. The prophylactic is fairly simple to prescribe. It is to be found in the periodic re-examination of the metavalues. This will raise for reflection the following questions.

1. Is the organization unjustified in its basic purpose?
2. Is the organization unjustified in its complex of ancillary purposes?
3. *Should* the organization grow? consolidate? reduce? Is the growth pattern valid and defensible?
4. What are the latent functions of the organizational effort and are they valid or defensible?
5. What, so far as reasonable analysis can reveal, is the shape of the non-quantitative cost benefit account? Is the quality of organizational life adequate under its constraints?
6. What consistency exists between the answers to these value questions and (a) Type II morality, (b) the Type I commitments of the administrator?

It is *not* suggested (unless this be directly brought out by the metavalue analysis itself) that a full re-examination of organizational policy and philosophy be undertaken. That is a matter for administrative philosophy at large; the point of metavalue scrutiny is simply to reduce their primitive unconscious influence and re-enter them into the value calculus of administration at a more conscious and sophisticated level.

To this point I have been talking of organizations as moral primitives. It is logically possible, though psychologically unlikely, that there are individual administrators who are similarly primitive. The administrator, too, has his individual metavalue counterparts of *personal* maintenance, growth, efficiency, and effectiveness. To these we can probably add, as corollaries, the instrumental metavalue of power and the end metavalue of success. The private metavalue system is as deserving of periodic re-examination as is the organizational, but it is distinct and can be considered as a separate subset of administrative philosophy. We shall return to this issue in the final chapter.

Metavalues are by definition *good*. The question is whether they are *right*. To even ask that question implies a degree of sophistication, consciousness, and moral complexity which at least augurs to obviate or mitigate any charge of primitiveness.

12
Options and Prognosis

EXTREMES AND CONTINUA

In assessing the philosophical options facing the administrator it will not do to be doctrinaire. Nòr will it serve any very useful purpose to encode the various value orientations under labels such as (say) realism, pragmaticism, or ideal utilitarianism. Conventional labels have their uses, but it is probably only in the very rare case that the round executive peg will fit itself firmly into the square philosophical slot. Moreover, I have tried to avoid systematizing, choosing instead to regard philosophical activity as the business of continuous logical and valuational critique. There may be some agreement on the logical side of this business, but there is much less on the valuational side. Besides, the former may be open to inspection, but the latter sealed from view. This need not be a bad thing; the privacy of values may be legitimate even in the public office, but in any event, there is no real means of enforcing their openness to public inspection. Where this book seeks to persuade, however, is in the ethical necessity of raising the private consciousness of value—with the end of advancing authenticity amongst administrators. This authenticity I have defined is no very original way, but in strict accordance with Barnard, and for that matter with Polonius in Hamlet, as being true to one's own set of values, whatever they may be. Authenticity, then, is the submission to the discipline of 'whatever morality exists within'.

To be sure, this implies some kind of act of faith. One must believe, in a loosely articulated sort of way, that consciousness, or to be more precise, heightened self-consciousness, is good, and will lead to the right either by evolutionary beneficence or by personal character development. I confess to this transrational element and the reader should be cautioned about it if not against it. The self-consciousness of value implies, perhaps even entails, the self-critique of values, and this, I suggest, leads out of any self-righteous dogmatism or equally self-righteous scepticism towards an active search for individual worth. This philosophical activity seems especially deserving of recommendation in cultural times which are characterized by pluralism, moral relativism, and blind ideological commitment when, in Yeats' line, 'The best lack all conviction, while the worst are full of passionate intensity'.

It may help in our initial charting of this work to sketch in the extremes of position which presently exist in the field of administration. Let us try as best we can to avoid emotive labels. At one extreme, then, we can expect to find, in the value sense, non-commitment or even painstaking detachment. The administrator may feel that the philosophers as a whole are non-persuasive or unable to convince, and he may ground himself as best he can upon the facts or what seem to him to be the facts. To support his position he may enlist the findings of organization theory. Plato would express it this way:

> . . . Suppose a man was in charge of a large and powerful animal, and made a study of its moods and wants; he would learn when to approach and handle it, when and why it was especially savage or gentle, what the different noises it made meant, and what tone of voice to use to soothe or annoy it. All this he might learn by long experience and familiarity, and then call it a science, and reduce it to a system and set up to teach it. But he would not really know which of the creature's tastes and desires was admirable or shameful, good or bad, right or wrong; he would simply use the terms on the basis of its reactions, calling what pleased it good, what annoyed it bad. He would have no rational account to give of them, but would call the inevitable demands of the animal's nature right and admirable, remaining quite blind to the real nature of and difference between inevitability and goodness, and quite unable to tell anyone else what it was. . . (1975, 288)

At the other end of the continuum the administrator may be publicly or privately persuaded; he may be 'engaged'. One must now name names, though only for the purposes of illustration. His values may be governed by a system of beliefs to which he has acceded, such as (say) the purportedly rational doctrines of Marxism or the non-rational religion of Christianity (*credo quia absurdum*) or the commitment to success-through-work; it does not matter so long as there are dominant values, principles of the Type I order, which serve to structure and inform the subordinate values in the individual's hierarchy. An example is provided by Thompson, who argues that the contemporary value condition of 'polynormativism' must yield to a general administrative commitment to a 'norm of universalism' which we would equate with the Kantian imperative or golden rule. Modern man, he would insist, must learn to be comfortable with impersonality ... the social value of administrative action is more important than its personal cost (1975, 90–1).

The distinction between these extremes is a qualitative one, psychological as well as philosophical in nature, whereby in the one the will is exercised to refrain from commitment and in the other to embrace it. I would suggest, however, that it is only in technological fantasy or science fiction that a person can achieve any real degree of value neutrality. What is a more realistic continuum, then, is one of sorts or congeries of values ranging from hedonistic individualism through conventionalism to the adoption of principles and systems which extend interest beyond the primitive ego. The types we have postulated in Chapter 6 could apply also to the analysis of individual values: happiness at Type III might be conceived as a surplus of private pleasure, at Type II as Benthamite utilitarianism, the greatest good of the greatest number, and at Type I as some form of love and self-transcendence. If we had the time or the patience for such an exercise, we could also classify and locate within this hierarchy of valuation the various labelled packages of philosophy and the much more numerous and realistic aggregates of daily administrative eclecticism, rational and irrational, including perhaps the *arthasastra* and the *via aurea mediocritas*.

Associated with the philosophical positions are psychological complexes of attitudes and value orientation. Kafka's bureaucrats appear as faceless and disengaged, while Weber's are postulated as impartially benevolent. The administrator who has failed either the organization or himself may linger on to serve time, doing only the things necessary to maintain his position and its perquisites. He moves to the disengaged end of the spectrum. At the other extreme are the involved, the engaged, the committed, the fanatical. It could be argued that both extremes are dangerous: the one leading to apathy, anomie, and ineffectiveness, the other to ruthlessness and the enforcement of will by the leader on the led.

The extremes also appear in the administrative literature in the guise of Theory X and Theory Y or some variation upon these themes; that is, as stereotypes of organizational man. As Miles has shown, the administrator must have some implicit philosophy, some working view-of-man which funds his assumptions and goes to establish the mores and the quality of life in his organization. It is my view that both Theory X and Theory Y give valid but partial perspectives. Both present a face of the larger truth which is more complex and ineluctable. The administrator must take as his first premise the model of man expressed in Theory X and then he must search for a sophistication of it which would incorporate the insights of Theory Y. Such a synthetic Theory Z would envision man as a complex of lower and higher hierarchically ordered aspirations. He would be an end in himself and the ultimate resource for collective organizational life, finding his fulfillment in his work-life and in society, but perhaps having to withdraw from the collective embrace in order to win to those spiritual satisfactions which might constitute his greatest endeavour. Yet this creature comes trailing no clouds of glory, but all the impedimenta of personal indulgence: selfishness, hedonic myopia, and infinite corruptibility. If there is a logical contradiction in this picture and it does not hang well together, my defence is that neither does man himself, and neither do organizations.

Theory Z, of course, is speculative. Its pragmatic verification would be by way of the daily experience and insights of practical administration. It would have to be forged in the heat of action and the cool of administrative reflection. To the extent that it is complex, it invokes a corresponding complexity of morality.

Because the administrator is isolated in the formal leader role from his organizational fellows and because of the facts of power and hierarchy his particular view of man, his philosophy, carries extra weight. Philosophy is not the prerogative of the professional philosophers but the birthright of all men, and it is certain that the organizational leader will have a philosophy in the sense of a more or less conscious set of loosely or tightly articulated value propositions about man, men, and man in relationship to men. The degree of their coherence, clarity, and consistency would be the systematic measure of their quality. And they would constitute administrative as distinct from any other sort of philosophy to the extent that they addressed the concepts discussed in these pages. I have argued that the administrator has a special onus to do this kind of philosophizing and have suggested that there might be leadership advantages in taking on the task.

In the formal role of leader a separation occurs of *man* from *men*. What is created is a man-men relation pervaded by values. In my view the authenticity of the leader stems first from the quality of his private commitment to his own set of values (and these cannot be too divergent from the overall complex of organizational purpose and interest) and second from the relating of these values to the followership. How is this second thing done? Primarily, I suspect, from the insights generated through sensitive participation, observation, interaction, and reflection; by human and humane intercourse. This need not return us to the paragon fallacy nor to the cult of leadership that goes with it. No spectacular behaviour is entailed by these suggestions, and it must always be remembered that the administrator role involves more than leadership. There are plenty of occasions when in fact the best leadership will be followership and when the initiatives will arise elsewhere. But the administrator's relationship to men, itself a function of his man-men philosophy, must be at all times authentic. And I would seek to persuade that, if it is to be thus, man must be recognized as being *at base* intrinsically valuable, an end-in-himself.

It is paradoxical that this essentially Kantian position can be interpreted so as to lead to Thompson's administrative norm of universal impartiality on the one hand, (1975, 91) and to Marxian hive ethics and the supremacy of the collectivity over the individual on the other hand (Gregor, 1973, 140). My own reading would stress the deep-seated radical 'at base' character of intrinsic human worth. Man is an end-in-himself only, as it were, at the *end* . . . in those situations where he finds himself cast against the very limits of his phenomenological reality. Short of this, perhaps Thompson and the Marxists are right. But this very proviso alters the whole colouring and cast of any ethical system which seeks to elevate Type II values to the Type I dimension.

THE CONTINUUM OF INTEREST

There is a continuum which cuts across all those postulated so far. To draw it we take as our basic premise the primacy of self-interest. The ego is then our point of initiation and the line of interest extends from that point outwards to indicate ever larger and wider ranges of interest: extended ego in the family, kin-group, and clan; the work-group; the organization of major employment; the community of work and of leisure, the sub-culture; and finally to society, nation, and culture at large. At each discernible quantum shift along this continuum, conflicts of interest can occur. This is well exemplified in an old Sanskrit dictum (Vividishananda, 1957, 188) which can be adapted as follows: 'For the sake of the family sacrifice the individual, for the sake of the community sacrifice the family, for the sake of the nation sacrifice the community, for the sake of the world sacrifice the nation, and for the sake of the individual soul sacrifice the whole world'. There is a profundity in this wisdom because, while it declares the simple rule of subordination of lesser to larger interests (referred to previously as the nomothetic bias), it also suggests that there is a point at which the intrinsic worth of the individual becomes prior, that is, the individual by virtue of his quality of being an end-in-himself usurps and preempts the nomothetic rule. (P5.05) In our scheme such points could only occur at the Type I level of value and it follows in the practical logic of administration that they were best avoided.

The continuum of interest with its extemes of ego definition can, however, serve a useful purpose as a skeletal structure upon which the administrator can fashion his own private philosophy. We have seen previously how a nomothetic bias is appropriate to administrative value systems. It was then argued that this presumptive bias must be tempered by the value complexities arising from given situations and the administrator's own moral complexity and his philosophy of man. It is futile to wish with Plato for the advent of the philosopher kings, but it is neither unreasonable nor impractical to seek programmes which will move administrative man in the Platonic direction. Any such programme would acknowledge the continuum of interest and would entail at least the following stages.

First, the administrator would seek the self-knowledge of his own values by private reflection, including to the best of his ability the scrutiny of his metavaluational assumptions and constraints. Second, he would review in the manner outlined above the meta-values of his organization and then the overt scope of the organizational values proper. Third, he would analyze for conflict points the extension of the organizational interest into the social, national, and cultural environment and, lastly, he would seek to become as aware as possible of the scope of his own self-interest, now redefined as extended ego in the organization, and in his familial and affective connections. If this contemplative activity does not yield any consciousness of irreconcilable conflict, then no more need immediately be done and there will already have been a gain in self-awareness and sophistication.

When value conflict occurs, as it most certainly will, in the ordinary run of organizational business, its resolution can be approached through use of our value model. The values which are involved are first analyzed in terms of type or level and then decided or settled on the postulate of hierarchy at the lowest level of resolution consistent with authenticity and moral responsibility. Let us pursue this further in the next section (p. 194 *ff.*).

All these elements—value type, authenticity, responsibility—are relative to factual situations, but converge ultimately upon an extremity. At the point of extremity the end of the continuum of interest is reached and the ultimate test of administrative integrity is encountered. Though it be harsh to say at such a point, it might indeed be necessary to 'sacrifice the whole world'. It is somewhat understandable, therefore, that the undertaking of administrative philosophy can engender some hesitancy and reluctance and must be approached with great caution. One must have the faith that ignorance is not bliss and that 'Know Thyself' is a rewarding precept.

There is another, perhaps less philosophical and more psychological, way of expressing these general ideas. We can make use of the concepts of discipline and commitment. The essence of administrative morality could then be thought of as twofold: first, the conscious commitment to the highest level of interest proper to his personality and personal situation (as determined by his own value analysis) and, second, the discipline of translating the resultant values into action and being constrained by them in action. The psychological terms which call for greater clarification, analysis, and understanding are primarily those of discipline and commitment, but would certainly include detachment, compartmentalization, fulfilment, self, identification, self-actualization, and power. To the practical administrative man the blurring of disciplinary lines between the fields of philosophy and psychology is not a matter of the first importance. Let him use whatever means or metaphors serve him best in his analysis of the continuum of interest.

ILLUSTRATIONS

The point made above (p. 193) about settling conflict and deciding issues at the lowest level of value analysis deserves some amplification. Let me attempt to make it clearer by way of some necessarily oversimplified examples.

Let us take first the case of appointing a subordinate (see also Chapter 3 above). We shall assume that the decision rests with the administrator and that all formal procedures have been complied with. He can now bring the three types of value to bear on his decision: his personal predilections and affect about the candidate (III), the expressed views of others and of referent groups (IIb), the evaluation of the short and long term consequences of the new admission to the organizational ranks (IIa), and the raising of any questions of principle, such as the compatibility or incompatibility of the candidate on philosophical, moral, ideological, or major value grounds (I); at which level the decision is then made is a matter for second order judgment. The bases of this latter judgment lie at the roots of moral complexity and may involve many situational factors. In the instance chosen a critical factor would be the significance of the role for the general organizational welfare. If assessed to be of the highest significance, all the levels would be engaged and a candidate acceptable on levels III, IIb, and IIa might yet be rejected for Type I considerations. Conversely, if the role were less significant, a candidate, though disliked personally by the administrator (Type III), might yet be selected by him on the nomothetic grounds of his value to the organization (Type IIa). In the 'easiest' situation, mere preference could be allowed to settle the issue. The 'level of settlement' or the second order value judgment is a matter for the administrator's moral responsibility and his acuity of analysis in the given situation. It is unreasonable, however, to expect to settle every issue at the highest level; the wear and tear upon executive tissue would be excessive, and existential confrontations of the Sir Thomas More or Martin Luther calibre are to be entertained only in the very last resort.

Other examples could be drawn from the area of administrative discretion.[1] Administrative discretion occurs, particularly in the field of public administration (Leys, 1943, 10–23), when the ends of policy are unclear or when the ends are clear but in contention by opposing interests. The first case is well illustrated in public education. Administrators may make inconsistent decisions in this area, but because of the vagueness of policy guidelines the inconsistencies can pass unnoticed. In this type of situation the demands of moral complexity, knowing when to raise issues of principle and when to avoid them, can be intensified, and the temptation to resolve issues at the pragmatic or lower levels greatly persuasive. The problem is further compounded by the fact that two types of administrator, professional and political, are engaged in the *de facto* making of policy.

In the case when ends are clear but in opposition the administrator has the problem of divergent objectives and contending parties. The complication here is to ensure that all the values *and* all the types or levels of value relevant to the case are entered into the conscious deliberations,[2] since opposing parties will seek to conceal or disguise them where this is thought to be advantageous. Thereafter the decision whether to press for resolution by (say) victory on one side or compromise (Type I *vs*. Type IIb) would be the second order value judgment with all its attendant implications. The desirability of the administrator's having a rich personal value structure and commensurate value skills is abundantly clear. And the question to be raised is whether this is best left to informal chance or whether the odds of its occurring can be improved by some formality or training.

PROFESSIONALISM

Not all of those who practise in the field of administration, and perhaps only few, will have had professional preparation in the sense of formal training in the distinctive competencies of organization theory, decision skills, policy making, and leadership. Many will come to their role informally, by the political highroad or the collegial byway, or by accident or chance. Even among those who claim specialist professional expertise it is not the rule (French and British mandarins excepted) that they will have been exposed to philosophy and her methods, much less to a specific philosophy of administration, for such a thing does not presently exist. This book is at best its prolegomena. Yet the arguments in favour of this exposure now seem to be powerful and the need for an administrative philosophy compelling.

Modern man is an organizational man, and as such he is *administered* man. It is this which justifies a philosophy of administration—together with the fact that while administration has a logic it is too complex as a field of study and practice to be considered a science. Such philosophy would not at this time serve administrative thought as does logic mathematics or as the philosophy of science serves science, but much as the philosophy of education serves to inform educational practice.

Moreover, examination of the body of knowledge in administration reveals the discernible marks of pathology. Neither the theory nor the practice of administration is entirely healthy. If one were to take man and his welfare as the basic measure of things, then the existence of administering and administered men in large complex organizations poses problems of the first philosophical magnitude, among which would be included the problem of responsibility, the problem of justice, and the problem of organizational morality. Questions about the moral component of leadership and about the reconciliation of metavalues are also indicative of the need for value sophistication.

I have taken the position that within our set of meanings the administrator is a philosopher-in-action by *force majeure* and that administration is in large part the clarification, declaration, and objectification of value propositions. Certain components of philosophy therefore have significance for the administrator, and I would identify these more specifically as follows:

1. a concern for language and meaning since the administrative universe is semantic,
2. some of the disciplines of formal logic since the administrative universe is increasingly technological,

3. general critical skills since the administrative universe is increasingly fallacy-ridden and,
4. a major concern with value.

This last presupposes some model of the universe and some theory of man.

The administrator may come by these acquisitions informally; great is the credit due to him if he does, but it were better if they were available as a recognized condition of professional status. Formally or informally their advantages are marked: at the least these skills will assist in the elucidation of the decisional calculus and at the best they can contribute to the sense of purpose, peace of mind, and spiritual strength of the individual administrator. Any supplanting of confusion by enlightened conviction and any rightful gain of energy or charisma is desirable in administration.

I would see three phases recurring continuously throughout the administrative career. First, initial commitment to the role and the organization. This phase represents the ordinary level of involvement. Second, an activity of disengagement or reflection which is philosophically contemplative in character but necessary in order to consider and assess the logic and values of the organizational process and purpose. Third, a subsequent recommitment and reinvolvement with the organizational life at a higher and more fully reasoned level. The function of a philosophy of administration as a component of professional training would be quite simply to ease and facilitate these labours. This professional component should also be made accessible to the amateur and collegial types who make up such a large part of the administrative body. It would be a professional obligation to see to this accessibility, for it is aimed at improving the quality of organizational life, and it would be a responsibility of non-professional administrators to avail themselves of it and contribute towards the work.

At present no distinctive philosophy of administration exists. Nor is political philosophy very helpful. As La Porte puts it: 'What attention has been given by political philosophers appears to be mostly in the mode of peevish criticism or wholesale rejection of complex organizations as a legitimate form of human association. . . .' (Marini, 1971, 33). Neither does a distinctive profession of administration exist. Yet the seeds and nuclei of both an administrative philosophy and an administrative profession are to be found everywhere, and most notably in the academic schools of administration and management. The emergent development argued for here must be grounded in a recognition of administration as a critical set of behaviours which cannot be reduced to a science but which constitute a basic humanism to which present emphases on social science and quantitative methods are tributary. The propositions and themes developed in this book may also contribute to the mapping of that humanism, but the emergence of a philosophy of administration as a critical base for a recognized administrative profession can properly come about only from the collective efforts of administrative practitioners, theorists, philosophers, and social scientists. The materials for this work are all around and the need for it inexorable. It is critical to the quality of modern life.

13
Propositions towards a Philosophy of Administration

The body of knowledge in administrative science as it presently stands is such that theorists and practitioners can easily become disenchanted with themselves and with each other. Self (1972: 50) has castigated it as a 'weak and tasteless synthetic brew' of scientific administration, human relations, and systems theory, and has suggested that academics and practitioners are only tenuously linked by the 'pragmatic Deweyist American faith' that social science will ultimately 'pay off'. Whatever might be the true scientific status of administrative thought, and indeed the semantic association with science may be largely honorific, it is certain that its *philosophical* status is in yet worse repair (Hodgkinson, 1975). And this is curious when one considers that the set of behaviours encompassed by administration are so pervasive and potent in the affairs of men and so contributory to the quality of life. Moreover, the general recognition of the importance of the a-factual element of value and the emphatic concern of Barnard (1972: 261–95) with the topic of morality would seem to presage more in the way of administrative philosophy than has actually been forthcoming. It is not unreasonable to contend that administration is too serious an activity to be left either to the unsynthesized and endless inquiry of quantitative methodology or to the pragmatic indifference of administrators themselves.

Throughout this book I have argued for two ends which can be simply described as, first, the restoration of communion between philosophers and administrators and, second, the raising of the level of philosophical consciousness (pre-eminently *value* consciousness) on the part of administrators themselves. It is time now to consign the first of these aims to the reaction of learned colleagues entrenched in each of the two encampments and it thus passes effectively beyond my control. For the sake of the second aim,

however, and for the administrative reader who wishes to exercise
his own powers of critical reflection, I would like to try to draw
together the various threads of argument woven into this study in a
form which, while concise, may serve to provoke that reflective
critique on the part of the reader which can sharpen and sophisti-
cate his private philosophy. One is reminded at this point of a seg-
ment of an interview with the eminent authority on the philosophy
of science, Sir Karl Popper:

> Interviewer: So your thesis is this: we are all practising philosophers in
> the sense that we all hold philosophical theories and act on them. But
> usually we are not aware that what we are doing is uncritically accepting
> the truth of a theory.
>
> Sir Karl: Yes.
>
> I: And some of the theories are true, you say, while others are not only
> false but harmful. And you say the real task for philosophy is to examine
> critically our often unconscious philosophical prejudices and to correct
> them where correction is needed.
>
> SK: Exactly.   (Magee, 1973)

The propositions set out below seek to refer to certain realities of
administrative life which are not easily amenable or accessible to
scientific methodologies. The term reality is crucial. It is probably
advantageous for us to think in terms not of *a* reality, singular, but in
terms of three sorts of reality, plural. The triple reality is consistent
and comparable with the value model of Chapter 6 above. In this
scheme Reality III would be the empirical domain of science, the
deterministic world of cause and effect, the world of hard edges,
tangibilities, and the stuff and furniture of experience. Here propositions can be predictive and verifiable, taking the form of 'laws'
perhaps, such as $I = E/R$ or $e = mc^2$. It is a reality we all have to
live in and, generally, the more science can tell us about it the
better.

The second reality, Reality II, would be the appropriate province
of *social* science. Here propositions are less rigorously shaped, more
probabilistic, cast in such forms as 'Organizations which have a high
degree of goal specificity are more likely to have a high degree of
effectiveness than organizations which have a low degree of goal

specificity.' Or 'B = f (P,E)': Behaviour is a function of personality and environment, or, 'If I fail to pay my workers they will cease to contribute to the goals of my enterprise'. In this reality there are degrees of freedom; its realm is only partly determined. It is in part imponderable and the propositions of its 'language' may be called hypothetical. Again, and in general, the more verified or unfalsified propositions that social science can deliver about this reality the better.

Finally we must acknowledge and construe Reality I, the phenomenological realm of individual experience which, at least in potential, is voluntaristic or free. Its commergence with the shared realities of II and III will produce quite different *mise-en-scène* for the psychotic or normal adult, for a child, indeed for any two persons. Propositions touching upon this realm therefore, while constrained by the 'lower' or 'harder' realities and falsifiable by them, are more evocative or philosophical: they function only through the eye of the beholder and the mind of the reader and are dependent for their ultimate worth and validity upon the value orientation, life experience, and phenomenological status of the recipient. They are, as it were, raw material for philosophy, and their function is as much affective as cognitive; the term proposition as used here can be defined as a 'message that potentially or actually produces changes in the familiarity, knowledge, or understanding of its receiver' (Ackoff and Emory, 1972, 249).

The propositions are numbered and the numbering system (*pace* Wittgenstein, 1922) seeks to reflect logical contiguity and significance. For example, propositions beginning with the numbers 1.12 are related, but 1.12111 is more peripheral than the intermediate assertions 1.121 and 1.1211. Generally, the shorter the length of a number the greater the significance of the statement for the entire corpus. The propositions are ordered in seven series which can be roughly categorized under the following rubrics. Series 1 treats of the nature of administration as philosophy while series 2 is concerned with administration as a profession and practical activity. Series 3 treats of the nature of organizations and the field of administrative action. Series 4 is directed to the nature of man as organization man and to the quality of life in organizations. Series 5 is especially concerned with the moral aspect of administration. Series 6 deals with the aspects of power, authority, and leadership.

The final aggregation, Series 7, dealing as it does with the phenomenon of value, is the only grouping which is not directed specifically to the profession of administration, though it deals, of course, with a central concept in any administrative philosophy. The numbers in brackets appended to each proposition refer to the chapter in which the proposition was generated and can be used by way of review reference if the reader is so inclined.

It is inevitable that this or any such system will be biased by its author's value presumptions; inevitable also that the reader will bring to it his own assumptions and biases, but an ordering of premisses in this way does have the compensating factor of allowing each reader to bring to the conceptual matrix his own wealth of experience, knowledge, and insight. It is out of these last, provoked perhaps by propositional logic, but tempered by sensitivity and sophistication, that any qualitative non-positivistic philosophy of administration must in the end be constructed.

PROPOSITIONS 1–7.7

ADMINISTRATION AS PHILOSOPHY

1   Administration is philosophy-in-action. (1)

1.1   Administration is a generalism. (1)

1.11   To form purposes, for oneself or others, is to philosophize. (1)

1.111   Intellectual understanding of organizational purpose is unevenly distributed; it is the prerogative of administration. (8)

1.12   Philosophy is an activity—the activity of logic and the activity of making value judgments. (1)

1.121   Philosophy is also a view of man. (1)

1.1211   To do philosophy is the right of all men, and the special obligation of administrators. (12)

1.12111 The philosophy of administration will take its first model from the field of education. (12)

1.122   Administrators possess models-of-man. These are concepts and working tools, philosophical in nature, explicit or implicit, of man and the world, by which they organize their administrative action and reflection. (1)

1.1221   Administrators must learn how to listen to the philosophers and the philosophers must learn how to speak to them. If there is no dialogue here, there is no hope. (12)

1.1222   The boundary between a psychology and a philosophy of administration is ill-defined. Discipline and commitment would be central terms for them both. (12)

1.123   Administration has a reflective aspect as well as an active aspect. (1)

1.1231   The reflective aspect is dualistic and dialectical. (1)

1.1232   The main philosophical need in administration is for value sophistication. This entails logical critique. (12)

1.1233   Reflective analysis and critique is the way in which the administrator does philosophy. His subjects are himself, his organization, and the world. (12)

1.12331 The administrator cannot help being a philosopher-in-action, but he can help the quality of his philosophy. (12)

1.2   A philosophy of administration must be concerned with the analysis and investigation of administrative concepts, the language of administration. (1)

1.201   In the first analysis, a philosophy of administration must be constrained and determined by cultural context and ideology. (1)

1.202   In the last analysis, a philosophy of administration must go beyond cultural context and ideology. (1)

1.203   Administrative philosophy must concern itself with the *Realpolitik* of power and with its psychomechanics. (5)

1.2031   The philosopher of administration must know two things: where the values are and where the power lies. (9)

1.2032   Administration is schizoidal. Discipline wars with indulgence, self-assertion with self-sacrifice. (8)

1.2033   Detachment and commitment, consistency and inconsistency, to be engaged or disengaged: these are the extremes of administrative philosophy and psychology. Their function is to direct our attention to the middle ground. (12)

1.204   How to make the contemplative act and the active reflect? A problem for administrative philosophy. (9)

1.2041   Philosophical activity can be dangerous. No prize without price. (12)

1.21   Organization theory can only pose the problem for administrative philosophy. (1)

1.211   Until social science becomes philosophy it can tell us nothing about how organizations should form their goals. (8)

1.212   Philosophy begins in the dirt. (9)

1.2121   The administrative philosopher is a physician of organizational culture. (7)

1.22   Language is the basic administrative tool. (5)

1.221   Language cloaks power and *has* power. (5)

1.2211   Administrative utterances are in the imperative mood. (5)

1.222   The administrator must be dialectician and rhetorician. (5)

1.3   Administration has a decisional character. (1)

1.31   Decision is the distinctive administrative act. (3)

1.32   Rational decision is a mode of problem solving. (3)

1.321   Decisional data are dualistic; factual and valuational. (3)

1.3211   Administrative science would reduce uncertainty while administrative philosophy would clarify values. But each must trespass upon the other's territory. (3)

1.3212   Decisional logic is dualistic and dialectical. (3)

1.322   The quantification of ranked preferences, that is, the translation of ordinals into cardinals, would enable and permit a decisional calculus, if it were possible. But then the resultant decision would need *justifying*. And this is beyond quantitative calculus. (3)

1.33   In the final analysis all decisions are binary. That is, they reflect an either—or. (3)

1.34   The basic decision process is analytic and imputational. Analysis explores alternatives, imputation assigns values and probabilities. (3)

1.341   The art of analysis depends upon skills of perception, the ability to discern the tactical factors of the situation. The art of imputation depends upon skills of conception, the ability to discern strategic factors. Both arts invoke imagination and the latter invokes will. (3)

1.342   True decisions are open and extralogical. Only calculations can be logical. Therefore, machines can never decide. (3)

1.3421   Rationality is subordinate to intention. Intention sets the limits within which rationality may be expressed. (3)

1.3422   Rationality is always constrained but rarely extinguished. It is a necessary but not sufficient condition for decision making. A norm. (3)

1.3423   No true decision process can be designed so as to exclude entirely the personality of the decider. (3)

1.35   Decisions are both possibility-determined and possibility-determining. They create futures. This is philosophy-in-action. (3)

1.351   Uncertainty and value set the limits to decision possibility. (3)

1.3511   The only limits to decisional possibility (and to administrative philosophy) are those set by the imagination and the will. (3)

1.36   Policy goes beyond logic. (4)

1.3601   Policy is strategic decision making. (4)

1.361   Policy is organizational man's claim on the future. (4)

1.362   Policy contains an irreducible element of gambling. This is because of the omnipresence of uncertainty in the affairs of men. Hence policy making is metalogical. (4)

1.363   Metamorphic changes in the organizational life are envisioned and realized by way of ideology—before the fact. (4)

1.3631   After the fact, metamorphic changes can be seen to be the result of historical determinism. (4)

1.3632   Incrementalism is the mean between calculation and inspiration. (4)

1.4   Administration has a communicative character. (1)

1.5   Administration is a humanism. It is not a science. (1)

1.51   It is commonplace that the self-interest of one can be a cost to the self-interest of others. But what is meant by *self*? This concept enshrouds the core of the problem. (9)

1.511   The administrator must acknowledge the primacy of self-interest. It is the point of origin for administrative philosophy. (9)

1.512   The commitment to self-interest can be subrational or transrational. It can be elevated by the quality of courage and devotion to the value of truth. (9)

1.52   Machiavellianism is philosophically and psychologically unsound—though more honoured in the observance than the breach. (9)

ADMINISTRATION AS PROFESSION AND PRACTICE

2   We are all either administered or administering. (1)

2.01   The relations between superior and subordinate are funded by a wealth of unexamined assumptions. (7)

2.011   Once aware of the administrative assumptions we wish the best assumptions to be applied to ourselves—though not necessarily to others. (7)

2.02   The essence of conservative practice is to assume the worst. (7)

2.03   The essence of political skill is the concealment of manipulation. (7)

2.1   Administration secures services *from* men *for* organizations. (1)

2.101   Administration begins where automation ends. It is something men do to men. (1)

2.102   Two strategic factors operate in organizations: the nomothetic and the idiographic. Both seek their expression in the organization's goals but the values of the latter are elastic, of the former inelastic. (8)

2.103   True purpose is usually unenunciated and rhetoric is essential to value behaviour. The administrator accedes to this. (8)

2.11   Determining structure ('drawing the line') is the key adminis-
          trative power perogative. (2)

2.12   To *advise* can be to *command*. (2)

2.121   Participatory decision making improves the possibilities for
          consensus and manipulation. The process becomes logically
          aberrant only when it obscures intentions. To the extent that it
          retards imagination it is not aberrant, only inefficient and
          ineffective. (3)

2.1211   Will or hedonic compulsion can override reason; therefore, the
          rational administrator and the bureaucrat may be weak. (7)

2.122   Decision makers (participants) are to be distinguished from
          decision takers (executives). (3)

2.123   The organizational analogue to the legal corporation is the
          decision making group. (10)

2.1231   Committees: a sometime mode of responsible irresponsibility.
          (10)

2.124   Areas of discretion in the decisional life of the organization
          afford the possibility of the regeneration of value—Or degen-
          eration. (12)

2.13   In any complex organization *administration* is distanced from
          action. (2)

2.2   Administration mediates between organization and environ-
          ment. (1)

2.21   The administration of an organization is its diplomacy. (1)

2.211   Administrative rhetoric will seek to make organizational wel-
          fare appear as extra-organizational good. (8)

2.212   The administrator is bound by the metavalues. He can exceed
          or transcend but not deny them. (11)

2.213   The negotiator seeks to conceal values, the arbitrator to reveal
          them, the administrator to understand them. (12)

2.214   Value skills are best left to chance—the democratic answer. To
          education—the Platonic answer. (12)

2.22   The fiction of agency is dangerous. (10)

2.3   There is a continuum from administration to management and the former is logically prior to the latter. (1)

2.31   The precinct of administration is ends, of management, means. (1)

2.32   Both administration and management pervade the organization. (1)

2.321   Whoever makes policy is engaged in administrative behaviour. In this way managers become administrators. (4)

2.322   Administrative work loads can be organized so as to prevent reflection. Busyness is correlated with superficiality. (9)

2.3221   Compartmentalization is necessary but its dangers can be overlooked. These are lack of authenticity, unimaginativeness, and freneticism. (9)

2.4   Administration is a discernible though putative profession. (1)

2.401   Administration appeals to the unfitted while it repels the fitted; the Platonic dilemma. (9)

2.4011   It would be reasonable to assume that most administrators are neither psychopaths nor saints. But it would be conservative to assume that there is a bias in the negative direction. (9)

2.40111   Men may seek administrative office to prevent its being held by others who are worse. (9)

2.41   An administrative profession must entail some special administrative competence. (1)

2.411   Equity requires rewards commensurate to contribution. In all organizations is the administrator's contribution the greatest? In most? (9)

2.4111   Dramaturgy is compensation for incompetence by competent 'performance'. (9)

2.412   Administrative expertise is the specialty of generalism. But it does not follow that everyone is an administrative expert. (5)

2.413   Administrative professionalism will relegitimize the principle of hierarchy. (9)

2.414   Administration lacks theory; it is not a discipline but an interdisciplinary nexus. (9)

2.42   Administration is a profession in which many amateurs are engaged. (4)

2.421   Some administrators are professional, some political, and some a combination of both. (4)

2.422   If administration is a practical affair then the intellectual is suspect. He is in the way. And if it is a political affair he is more than in the way—he is dangerous. (9)

2.423   We require of our doctors that they study but we do not do so of our administrators. (12)

2.5   Administration is a perpetual becoming in which the future is more pressing than the present. (7)

2.6   A career ladder has a ratchet effect. Descent is devalued and deterred. (9)

2.61   Cliquism is a defence against careerism, a form of self-insurance. (9)

2.62   The principle of hierarchy prevents functional recycling. (9)

2.621   Skilled non-administrative function neither implies nor entails skilled administrative function (the Peter principle). But neither does it not imply nor entail it. (9)

ORGANIZATIONS—THE FIELD OF ADMINISTRATIVE ACTION

3   Human organizations are collectivities whose necessary and sufficient conditions are purposes, men, and techniques. (1)

3.01   Organizations are the fields of administrative action. Administrators create, preserve, and destroy organizations. (1)

3.0101   A corporation is a legal fiction; an organization is a conceptual fiction. Lawyers and administrators are the agents of phantasy. (10)

3.02   In the private sector the profit motive is a necessary but not a sufficient condition for organization. In the public sector the service motive is a necessary but not a sufficient condition for organization. (1)

3.03   Organizations generate a value culture. This culture reinterprets (transvalues) the values of society. (7)

3.031   When the work of an organization contends against deep-
          seated values in its larger culture, it must be transvalued.
          Hence the glorification of the military, the dictator, the
          administrator. Hence too the professionalism of the surgeon,
          the undertaker, the police. (9)

3.1   Organizations are evaluated upon criteria which are extrane-
          ous to organizations and administration. These criteria are
          metavalues. (1)

3.101   As chess is amoral so is rational administration. (10)

3.1011   Organizations are morally primitive. When defined by their
          metavalues. (11)

3.102   Metavalues go beyond value; undisputed, unexamined. (11)

3.1021   There are individual and organizational metavalues; the latter
          have the force of the collectivity and hence an initial pretension
          to righteousness. (11)

3.1022   The metavalue prophylactic is periodic analysis. (11)

3.11   Metavalues pervade the monitoring process. (7)

3.12   Efficiency is a metavalue. (8)

3.121   Efficiency is a metavalue for the future and a value for the past.
          (11)

3.1211   Efficiency is the ratio of output to input. This statement is itself
          inefficient; it says much less than it intends. (11)

3.122   The prime fact (and the ovum of value) is the scarcity of
          resources. (11)

3.123   The lure of efficiency leads to the fallacy of quantification.
          Some costs and some ends are non-quantifiable. True account-
          ing is always incomplete. (11)

3.124   The metavalue of effectiveness is tautologous and trivial but it
          points to the ends of action. (11)

3.1241   It is not enough to be effective; one seeks also to be efficiently
          effective. (11)

3.13   Military organizations, like religions, are dependent upon
          transrational values. Loyalty is their metavalue. (9)

3.131   Collectivities cannot be punished; organizations are immune from retribution. (9)

3.14   The first law of organization is maintenance. (11)

3.141   Organizations do not question their need to exist. They need to exist because they do exist. (11)

3.15   The second law of organization is growth. (11)

3.151   Growth (up to diminishing returns) is a kind of maintenance, a mode of survival. (11)

3.1511 Growth of organizations is growth of interest. And this implies the growth of power. (11)

3.2   The basic organizational tension is between the one and the many. Organizations are fundamentally dualistic and dialectical. (2)

3.21   The dialectic of organizational value is unending but biased. (8)

3.3   Organizations are patterns of energy and information flow. (2)

3.31   Energy and information are the dynamic and static aspects respectively of the one referent of flow, the organizational event. (2)

3.311   Negentropy is directly and positively related to information. (2)

3.4   Organizations are purposive and problem solving. If there be no purpose or problem the organization will tend to create them. (2)

3.401   The organizational purpose (problem) may be inchoate. (2)

3.402   The organizational purpose cannot remain static. It is constantly being modulated by events. (4)

3.4021 Multiplicity of ends and vagueness of general purpose will increase with organizational size and complexity. (8)

3.41   The universe is purposive but inscrutable. Organizational purposes and individual purposes are scrutable. (6)

3.411   An organization is a state of inadequacy. It strains to close the gap between what is and what can be. To have a goal is to be dissatisfied, by definition. (7)

3.5   Organizations are not organisms nor are organizations qualitatively equivalent to the sum of their parts. (2)

3.501 Organizations are irrational. (8)

3.6   Organizations presuppose hierarchy. Hierarchy is archetypical. (2)

3.61   Organizations have a hierarchy of status and a hierarchy of purpose. (2)

3.611 To unite the organizational hierarchies in a one-to-one ratio would yield an ideal logical form. (2)

3.6111 Status co-ordinates are not necessarily purposive coordinates. (2)

3.6112 To correlate the organizational hierarchies with the organizational reward system would again be logically ideal. (2)

3.7   Organizations are flow fields of decision process. (3)

ORGANIZATIONAL MAN

4   Man shapes his life through organizations. (1)

4.01   Man lives in and by organizations. Directly or indirectly we are all organization members. (1)

4.02   Organizational purpose is external, impersonal, objective, but for the member it is internal, personal, subjective. Organizational purpose modulates individual purpose. And, to a lesser extent, conversely. (8)

4.03   Organizations have a double meaning—inward to their members, outward to the world. The administrator has to reconcile these perspectives, and to do so rationality is not enough. (8)

4.031 Organizations exist for the welfare of their members. This is the basic truth. (8)

4.1   As organization member man is a quantifiable variable and a non-quantifiable variable. Which aspect preponderates is dependent upon the working context of administrative propositions. (1)

4.2   Human work motivations are dualistic and dialectical. (1)

4.201 At base men are moved by fear—a defensible assumption. (7)

4.2011 Men seek power as an antidote to fear; but if fear grows correlatively then the cure enlarges the disease. (7)

4.202 Men are powerfully moved by group pressures. Great is the power of the group. But greater still is the power of the man moved by his true will. (7)

4.203 The organization can be a source of joy. To some men it can give their meaning and purpose in life. (7)

4.21 Technologically, there must be one best way of performing work. (1)

4.22 Humanistically, there is no one best way of performing work. (1)

4.23 Theory X and Theory Y are not contradictories; *both* are true. (12)

4.231 The nature of man is mixed and ineluctable; the necessary generalities of a Theory Z must always be inconsistent approximations, continually reassessed by each administrator. (12)

4.3 We speak of organizational 'life', 'vitality', 'morale', 'climate'. Such concepts are functions of administration. That is, the quality of organizational life depends on administration. (2)

4.31 The essence of the organizational quasi-life is symbolic. It is a matter of the manipulation of symbols. (2)

4.32 Policy dictates the organizational game. The rules of that game must have some persistence. But they are never immutable. (4)

4.321 Ceremonial seeks to motivate at the transrational level. At the rational level it is absurd; at the subrational level it gives pleasure or incurs pain. (8)

4.4 Organization members surrender a part of their autonomy simply by being members (Barnard, Simon); they lose the right, and the habit, of making certain decisions. (3)

4.5 Organizations are abstractions, unconscious, and without will. (2)

4.51 Organizations exhibit quasi-consciousness and quasi-will. (2)

4.511   Organizations are quasi-moral and quasi-immortal. (2)

4.52   Vested organizational interest is a species of neofeudalism. (7)

ADMINISTRATIVE MORALITY

5   There is a moral aspect to administration. (1)

5.01   Administrative decisions bear a special moral charge. They are made for and about *others*. (3)

5.011   Role incumbency need not reduce moral responsibility. For the administrator it exalts it. (10)

5.02   Administrators lack the value autonomy of their subordinates insofar as they are constrained by the nomothetic dimension. (7)

5.03   The administrator has a natural affinity for the work ethic. (7)

5.04   Supervision has an ethical connotation. Its imperative lies in the collective good. It must look outside the organization as well as in. (7)

5.05   The simplest rule of administrative morality is, 'submit the lesser to the larger interest'. But this must be tempered and sophisticated. (12)

5.1   The concept of responsibility invokes the moral aspect of administration. (1)

5.11   Collectivities author but do not own their acts. (10)

5.111   Apparat degenerates value. (10)

5.12   The administrator cannot be a mere agent of the collectivity. This would be the lapse into management—irresponsibility. (10)

5.13   Responsibility is transitive: from x to y for z. But $x = y$ is possible and z may be a part of x. (10)

5.131   The system of law is a language game of responsibility. It is not moral. Though it may seek its ground in morality. (10)

5.14   Responsibility requires some act of will. It goes beyond mechanical accountability. (10)

5.141   Morality reduces to the individual. Ultimately only the individual is responsible. (10)

5.142   Authenticity is a function of value commitment. (12)

5.15   The factors of moral responsibility are value structure, value complexity, value strength, ego, will, role, situation, and sophistication. (10)

5.151   The problem of the moral economics of organization is to ensure that the gains to the status of man accruing from membership outweigh the losses deriving from role incumbency and instrumentality. (10)

5.2   The problem of administration is the reconciliation of the nomothetic and idiographic dimensions. (Getzels and Guba) The problem of the organization is the superimposition of the former on the latter.
        The problem of administrative philosophy is the justification of the former in terms of the latter. (5)

5.3   Man is an end in himself. So human commitment and human relations become the components of leadership authenticity. (12)

5.4   The ultimate ground of decision is consciousness. That is, intention. Responsibility runs with each decision. (3)

5.41   Purposiveness translates the future into the present, and conversely, by way of decision. (3)

5.42   Any decision process can be subverted. Subversion does not entail irrationality. But illogic follows from confusion of intent. (3)

5.43   The raising of value consciousness is an ethical imperative. (12)

5.5   An *ought* cannot be derived from an *is* (Moore). No factual proposition can prove a value proposition. (3)

5.51   Right is to good as desirable to desired. (6)

5.511   Desire is satisfied by *its* extinction, the desirable by *my* extinction, that is, by loss of ego in the nomothetic domain. (6)

5.512   Lower values seek to replace higher. They are transvalued either by extinction of desire (psychology) or the will to the desirable (philosophy). (6)

5.5121   Moral conflict, which is the normal administrative condition, is the unending war between assertion and self-sacrifice. (6)

5.6   Individual interest is always tripartite: self (including the extended self), organization (including other organizations), society (including mankind at large.) (4)

5.601   Self-interest is never simple. (10)

5.61   Identification of individual and organizational interest need not be reciprocal; it may be intransitive. (7)

5.611   The progression of interest is from self to society, through the organization. (7)

5.6111   Totalitarianism seeks unification of the progression of interest while pluralism seeks its integration. (7)

5.62   If all is relative and preferential, then self-seeking is the simplest strategy. Self-interest fills the vacuum created by positivism. (7)

5.621   Opportunism is the first organizational value sickness; executive succession is congealed opportunism. (7)

5.7   Compassion, empathy, and sympathetic imagination are necessary conditions of administrative morality. (4)

5.71   Humane comprehension varies inversely with distance from action. (4)

5.72   The language of policy making requires continuous philosophical, that is, moral scrutiny. (4)

5.721   Ends as desirable must be distinguished from ends as projected. The latter subtend and subsume the associated means. (4)

5.7211   Means and ends are always intertwined. Their disentanglement is a problem in administrative philosophy. (4)

5.7212   While ends can dictate means they cannot justify them. Each means is an end in itself. (7)

5.8   Conscience is that which informs us first of collective responsibility and then of higher responsibilities still. (6)

5.81   The highest and the lowest of values are idiographic; between lies the realm of value belonging to the nomothetic mass. (6)

5.811   Management has a natural affinity for the middle realm of value. (6)

5.8111   It is but a step from the moral to the mortal. Safety lies in amorality. (6)

5.82   There is a point, the Luther point, at which the administrator must fight his organization, or leave it, or go down the paths of unauthenticity. (8)

5.83   The chief fruit of administrative philosophy is moral complexity and sophistication. (10)

5.831   Between Machiavelli and Plato let us choose the latter. Better. Let us not choose but assimilate the former to the latter. (12)

5.832   Commitment should be renewed and refined throughout the administrative career. This is done by philosophy. (12)

5.833   Will supervenes reason. (6)

5.9   The nature of administration is such that it rewards the skills of guile. The arts of concealment and dissembling can be advantageous. Or they can be necessary. (9)

5.901   As disbelief can be suspended in the theatre, so conscience can be suspended in the organization. (9)

5.91   Ambition and love of power motivate the administrator. The question is, Can these values be civilized? (9)

5.92   Careerism conduces to irresponsibility since responsibilities can be shed by *moving*: onward, upward, outward. (9)

5.921   When career progress is paced by seniority and guarded by tenure the dangers are irresponsibility, impotence, and anomie. (9)

5.93   The principle of *quid pro quo* is universal and eternal. All things have their price. But the price is subject to negotiation. And one gives in order to receive. More than one gave. (9)

5.9311   One binds by gifts. Donation supplements structure and the administrator is a merchant of reciprocity. (9)

POWER, AUTHORITY, LEADERSHIP

6   Power is the first term in the administrative lexicon. (5)

6.01   Influence is incommensurable. It arises spontaneously from the interaction of human actors. It is irresponsible. (5)

6.011   Patterns of influence overflow organizational boundaries. (5)

6.1   Administrative power is a function of the will. The contest of wills is the pragmatic test of power. (5)

6.11   The metavalue of Machiavellianism is success. Defined in terms of power. (9)

6.111   For the careerist there is no immobility save that provided by defeat. Success feeds ambition. (9)

6.12   If one has power be of a mind to wield it. Skilful display augments power, unskilful display diminishes it. (9)

6.121   There is such a thing as the judicious rage, the calculated loss of control. (9)

6.122   The arts of the courtier govern the dealings with superiors. (9)

6.13   Ambiguity and ambivalence favour deceit. (9)

6.1301   At the least one must appear to be honest, committed, credible. (9)

6.131   Where there is opposition seek to divide it. And redivide the divisions. (9)

6.132   Beware of friendliness in the realms of power. There is no need to beware of friendship. It does not exist. (9)

6.1321   A rival's success must be diminished. (9)

6.14   The law game and the organization game rest upon the sanctions of power. (10)

6.2   Authority is legitimized power. (5)

6.201   Logically, authority is self-justifying. Anti-authoritarianism is therefore nihilistic or else it is a claim for more authority. (5)

6.21   Authority stems from the membership not from the administration, it rests on perception. That is, upon the values of the perceiver. (5)

6.2101   In the first analysis administrators are far from impotent. The zone of acceptance may be wider than they believe. (9)

6.2102   Administrative authority is a convenient and necessary fiction. In the last analysis administrators are impotent. (5)

6.22   The legitimacy of authority rests on its connection with the organizational purpose. (5)

6.221   Illicit authority thrives upon obscurity of purpose. (5)

6.222   Technological professionalism threatens traditional authority (Victor Thompson), and leads to countervailing administrative professionalism. (5)

6.2221   Rewards follow authority: authority follows expertise; expertise follows purpose. (This is a normative not a factual proposition.) (5)

6.3   Authority transcends logic. (5)

6.4   The term leadership is an incantation for the bewitchment of the led. (5)

6.401   Technical competence and role authority are necessary but insufficient conditions for leadership. (5)

6.41   Leadership is an event, not an attribute of a personality. It is a description given to a dynamic complex of action. (5)

6.4101   The best leadership is often followership. (12)

6.411   Because leadership is a complex intrinsic property of a situation it cannot be detached, isolated, and traded in the market place. (5)

6.42   Leadership is the conjunction of technical competence and moral complexity. (Barnard) (5)

6.4201   Meritocracy is logically preferable to democracy. (5)

6.421   Leaders embody collective values. The sanctity of these values may entail their concealment, and the leader's inaccessibility. Or the values may call for display, and the leader's visibility. (5)

6.422   The essence of leadership is to know when to raise and when to avoid moral issues (Broudy). (6)

6.43   Charisma plays upon our lust for purpose. The charismatic leader will give hope and meaning to our lives. (5)

6.431   There is no aspect of administration more dangerous than that which forges the link between power, charisma, and men. (5)

6.432   Organizational complexity persuades us of the need for a para-
         gon to deal with it. We then persuade ourselves that the new
         leader must be a paragon and we invest him with a robe as well
         as an office. (9)

6.433   The moral leader is charismatic. (10)

6.5   Hypothesis: Organizational climate and leadership quality are
         functions of the administrator's morality. (10)

VALUES

7   The world of fact is given, the world of value made. (6)

7.01   We discover facts and impose values. (6)

7.011   Facts must go undefined. (6)

7.012   Values are special kinds of facts; but never true or false. (6)

7.0121   We cannot distil value from the scenario of events. But we can
         always project value upon it. That is our will. (6)

7.0122   There is nothing at all valuable or beautiful or good *out there*,
         only *in here*. (6)

7.02   What is good is different from what is right. (11)

7.1   Desire taints all things; there is no immaculate perception or
         conception. And yet value is other than its field of manifesta-
         tion. This is a great mystery. (6)

7.11   Valuation preceeds rationality. One can only be rational within
         the limits set by value. (8)

7.2   Values are concepts of the desirable with motivating force. (6)

7.21   Our value system is an expression of our psychological integ-
         rity. The more values we sustain the more our need for system.
         (6)

7.211   One can choose what the world calls evil and call it, privately,
         good. To do so rightly would be moral. (10)

7.212   Morality, an individual matter, governs relations with others.
         (10)

7.213   Ethics is an aid to moral navigation. We can sail without it if we
         wish. But we ignore it at some peril. (10)

7.22   Values stem from the self, from others, and from that which is neither self nor others. (6)

7.23   Rank is the essence of value; hierarchy is the essence of universal order. (6)

7.231   Hierarchy implies the possibility of degradation. (6)

7.2311 Values run down. They are born, live and die. Like us they are nurtured within the bosom of societies; and finally rejected. (6)

7.24   Value conflict is to be resolved at the lowest level. (12)

7.241   First order valuation is the identification and analysis of the values in a case. (12)

7.242   Second order valuation is the determination of the values to be used in trying the case. (12)

7.3   Needs are discrepancies between perceived and conceived states of affairs. They are sources of value. (6)

7.4   Motives are sources of value. They may be in the dark or in the light. In the first case they push us and we call them drives, in the second they pull us and we call them reasons. (6)

7.41   To approve none of our motives is to be animal, to approve them all is to be a god. To go beyond morality is to be superman or beast. (6)

7.5   Attitudes are the first public manifestations of value, they structure our attention to the world. (6)

7.6   Interest is the active value orientation of an individual or group. It is value referred to fact. (6)

7.7   Consciousness is intrinsically valuable; the means to its own end. (12)

FUNCTIONS OF THE PROPOSITIONS

The propositions just enunciated are connotative messages transmitted with the intent of exciting resonances, but also with the intention of frustrating, and in so doing provoking that dilemmatic type of cerebral action which occasionally leads us to the flash of insight. Certainly these philosophical propositions do not seek to be exhaustive, definitive, dogmatic. They are organized into a logical complex not to provide a 'model' but with the purpose of producing change or potential change in the familiarity or knowledge or understanding of their recipients. They are thus a form of meaning stimuli whose function will vary with the nature of the audience. For students of administration, whether they be practitioners *in situ* or aspirants to administrative office, they are intended to deepen understanding and provoke some insight into the moral complexities of organizational life. For theorists, scholars, researchers, and empiricists, they are intended to act as a counter-irritant against the compulsion towards behaviourism, denotation, and operational definition; not to deter the scientific thrust, but to heighten the awareness of the subtleties and complexities of the human factor. Finally, for philosophers of administration, if such there be, they are intended to motivate towards interest in the organizational conditions of human life and the clarification of the logic of those conditions.

Notes

CHAPTER ONE

1. Save for a glancing reference in his introduction, p. 6.
2. See Finer (1952, 174) for a latter-day adaptation of POSD-CORB. He forms APOSDCORB wherein the A refers to an 'attuning' of the executive to the purpose and ethos of the organization.
3. Maslow's language makes use of the term *needs* rather than values. (See Chapter 6)
4. Shakespeare's historical plays are replete with administrative insights as are C. P. Snow's novels of the British bureaucracy. *The Caine Mutiny* is a classical American example.

CHAPTER TWO

1. Miller's anthropological example of the Algonquin Indians would be illustrative (1955, 271).
2. Cf. also for the concept of influence, Franklin, 1975, 153.
3. Administrative expertise is conventionally directed to the maintenance and preservation of organizations rather than their *destruction*. However, social scientists have been concerned with the latter as a weapon in international polity. The evidence for this assertion is, regrettably, classified at the time of writing, but if destructive techniques are available, their existence would tend to strengthen the relation between organization theory and administrative competence.

CHAPTER THREE

1. The reduction to *one* candidate is chosen for purposes of illustration. The underlying logic implies that each and every candidate would be subjected to the same *form* of analysis in the complex process of iterative selection and comparison.
2. We could as well assume, of course, other possibilities, e.g. 0.8 indicating an 80% choice of success and a 20% choice of failure. The figure selected is chosen to reflect the not uncommon 'toss up' situation.
3. A very dubious presumption unless one is careful to include the psychological factors of imagination, intuition, and conation under the term rationality. More strictly, if both players are perfectly rational the games should logically be drawn, a situation not atypical of master level chess.
4. The advent of the computer has in its own way invoked Kaplan's 'law of the hammer'. This states that when a small boy discovers the use of a hammer he tends to find that all objects need hammering. (Kaplan, 1964, 28)
5. Opinions differ as to whether the evaluator should remain aloof from the decision making process, the arguments hinging about objectivity versus involvement (Stake, 1967, 523–40; Tyler *et al.*, 1967).

CHAPTER FOUR

1. Dror (1964) has criticized the strategy as being inertial and unsuited to a context of large scale and rapid change. *Per contra* it might be defended as a method of *coping* with such a context.
2. Braybrooke and Lindblom (1963) present a cogent case for the reconciliation of Bentham's utilitarianism (and hedonistic calculus) with public policy making.
3. Parsons (1960) presents the sociological argument for qualitative breaks.

CHAPTER FIVE

1. It is difficult to make a precise distinction but I would like to reserve the term 'legitimate' for 'morally valid at large' while *legitimized* would imply 'morally valid from the standpoint of the organization or its administration'.
2. Barnard's comments about the flouting of law, even under totalitarian regimes, are interesting (161). Tyrannical government by decree (cf. some modern African states) is not necessarily any more authoritative (or managerially competent) than more democratic forms and this is so because of the *logic* of authority described above.
3. Katz and Kahn (1966, 463) argue for a democratic as opposed to an authoritarian base for authority structure and refer to the former as 'the only answer to the nightmare of totality'. But they are not criticizing authority as such.
4. For example, and in a specific domain, the Kellogg Foundation grants to the Cooperative Program in Educational Administration.
5. Halpin's treatment of the concept of authenticity (1966, 203–224) is one notable exception to this generalization. Selznick (1957) is also suggestive in his notion of the institutionalization of value.

CHAPTER SIX

1. Neither Wittgenstein nor Russell define facts; the former implicitly leaves them undefined (1922, 1961) while the latter explicitly asserts their axiomatic status (1973, p. 276).
2. This is not inconsistent with contemporary attempts at definition of this difficult concept. Cf. e.g. Lambert and Lambert, 1965, 50; Woodruff, 1942, 33.
3. We shall not specify a value number, leaving the quantity vague. Rokeach, however, specifies 32; 16 instrumental and 16 terminal values (1968, 1973). Scott (1965) specifies 12. I would guess that the number chosen is variable with cultural and linguistic sophistication.

4. Marxists might claim social class as a grounding of value but the scheme I propose would subsume this explanation under consensus while Marxism itself as a ground for value would be subsumed under principle.
5. It might well be expedient for (say) a committed logical positivist to disguise his value bases as Type IIa or even Type I but he himself would be covertly aware of their true Type III foundation.
6. This is a second-order value judgment the grounding of which is itself postulated or axiomatic. If it does not in turn raise the problem of *regressus ad infinitum* it is so far as I can see only because of the difficulty or limitation of such conception, as with the case of imagining and comprehending multi-dimensional spaces of greater than three or four dimensions. I do not know what an n-order value judgment would look like.
7. It should be noted that I am not putting forward a *law* of moral entropy but *postulating a tendency*.

CHAPTER SEVEN

1. Miles uses this term throughout but his work is applicable to administration as well as management.
2. These remarks could be applied, for example, to the problems facing democratic governments as a result of terrorism. The terrorists gain power advantages utterly disproportionate to their strictly technical or managerial power position.

CHAPTER NINE

1. Plato is talking of *political* leadership roles but the sense applies, *mutatis mutandis*, to administrators of the three types recognized in this book.

CHAPTER TEN

1. Granted that the personality component will vary with role, professional artists and administrators having more personality latitude than machinists and sergeants-major. The principle is unaltered and there would be a 'personality-surplus' even in the most liberal of organizational roles.
2. Bureauticism is a play upon neuroticism; the idea being that certain personalities cannot adjust to the impersonal attitudes and demands of rational bureaucracy.

CHAPTER TWELVE

1. Areas of discretion occur for managers as well as administrators. Their distinguishing marks are a lack of clarity about means or ends and a passing of the decision 'buck'.
2. Leys (Mailick and Van Ness, 1962, 81–93) gives an interesting suggestion for ensuring the consideration of six key Type I values: Happiness, lawfulness, harmony, survival, integrity, and loyalty together with their philosophical correspondences.

Bibliography

Abbott, Max B. and Lovell, John T., eds. *Change Perspectives in Educational Administration*. Auburn: U. Ala., 1965.

Ackoff, R. L. and Emery, F. E. *Purposive Systems*. Tavistock: London, 1972.

Alderfer, C. P. 'A New Theory of Human Needs.' *Organizational Behaviour and Human Performances*, 1969, 4, 142.

Arendt, H. *Eichmann in Jerusalem*. New York: Viking, 1963.

Argyris, Chris. *Personality and the Organization*. New York: Harper & Bros., 1957.

———. *Understanding Organizational Behaviour*. Dorsey, 1960.

———. *Management and Organizational Development*. New York: McGraw-Hill, 1971.

———. 'Personality and Organization Theory Revisited.' *Administrative Science Quarterly*, 1973.

Ayer, Alfred Jules. *Language, Truth and Logic*. London: Gollancz, 1946.

Bailey, J. J. and O'Connor, R. J. 'Operationalizing Incrementalism: Measuring the Muddles,' *Public Administration Review*, 1975, 35: 60.

Bakke, E. Wright, in von Bertalanffy, L., and Rapoport, A., eds. *General Systems* Yearbook. Soc. for Gen. Systems Research., 1960.

Barnard, Chester I. *The Functions of the Executive*. Cambridge, Mass.: Harvard U. P., 1972.

Blake, R. R., Mouton, J. S., *et al*. 'Breakthrough in Organiztion Development,' *Harvard Business Review*, Nov–Dec. 1964.

Blau, Peter M., and Schoenherr, Richard A. *The Structure of Organizations*. New York: Basic Books, 1970.

Blau, P., and Scott, W. *Formal Organizations*. San Francisco: Chandler, 1972.

Boulding, Kenneth E. 'General Systems Theory—Skeleton of a Science,' *Management Science*, 1956.

Braybrooke, David and Lindblom, Charles E. *A Strategy of Decision. Policy Evaluation as a Social Process.* Free Press Glencoe. New York, 1963, p. 78.

————. 'A Strategy of Decision,' rev. *American Sociological Review*, 1964, 29B: 930.

Brittan, S. *The Treasury under the Tories.* Harmondsworth: Penguin, 1964.

Broudy, Harry S. 'Conflicts in Values' in Ohm, R. E., and Monahan, W. G., eds. *Educational Administration: Philosophy in Action.* U. of Oklahoma, 1965.

Carey, Alex. 'The Hawthorne Studies: A Radical Criticism,' *American Sociological Review*, Vol. 32, 403–416.

Carlson, S. *Executive Behaviour: A Study of the Work Load and the Working Methods of Managing Directors.* Stockholm: Strombergs, 1951.

de Chardin, P. Teilhard. *The Phenomenon of Man.* New York: Harper, 1959.

Clark, Kenneth. *The Pathos of Power.* New York: Harper and Row, 1969.

Clayre, Alisdair. *Work and Play.* London: Weidenfeld and Nicholson, 1975.

Collins, O. F., and Moore, D. G. *The Organization Makers.* New York: Appleton, 1970.

Cooper, D. E. 'Collective Responsibility,' *Philosophy*, 1968, 43, 258–268.

Dalton, Melville. 'Conflicts between Line and Staff Managerial Officers,' *American Sociological Review*, 1950, Vol. 15, 342–51.

Dror, Y. 'Muddling Through—'Science' or Inertia?' *Public Administration Review*, 1964, 24:153.

Dubin, Robert. 'Industrial Workers' Worlds: A Study of the "Central Life Interests" of Industrial Workers,' *Social Problems*, 1956, V. 4, 136.

Dunsire, A. *Administration, The Word and the Science.* Martin Robertson and Halsted Press, 1973.

Etzioni, A. *A Comparative Analysis of Complex Organizations.* New York: Free Press, 1961.

———. *Modern Organizations.* New Jersey: Prentice-Hall, 1964.

———. *The Active Society: A Theory of Societal and Political Processes.* New York: 1968.

Fayol, H. *Administration, industrielle et générale.* Paris: 1916. tr. J. A. Coubrough, London: Pitman, 1929.

Fiedler, F. E. *A Theory of Leadership Effectiveness.* New York: McGraw-Hill, 1966.

Filmer, P., Phillipson, M., Silverman, D., and Walsh, D. *New Directions in Sociological Theory.* London: Collier-MacMillan, 1972.

Finer, Herman. *Administration and the Nursing Services.* New York: MacMillan, 1952.

Follett, M. P. *Creative Experience.* London: Longmans, 1924.

Franklin, Jerome L. 'Down the Organization: Influence Processes across Levels of Hierarchy,' *Administrative Science Quarterly*, Jan. 1975, 153.

French, Wendell L. and Bell, Cecil H. *Organization Development.* New Jersey: Prentice-Hall, 1973.

Fromm, Erich *The Anatomy of Human Destructiveness.* Greenwich, Conn: Fawcett, 1973.

Gantt, H. L. *Industrial Leadership.* New Haven: Yale U. P., 1916.

———. *Organizing for Work.* Harcourt, Brace, and Howe, N.Y. 1919.

Georgiu, P. 'The Goal Paradigm and Notes Towards a Counter Paradigm,' *Administrative Science Quarterly*, 1973, Sep. 18:291.

Getzels, Jacob W. and Guba, Egon. 'Social Behaviour and the Administrative Process,' *School Review*, 1957, Winter 423.

Gilbreth, Frank B., and Lilian M. *Fatigue Study.* London: Routledge, 1916.

———. *Applied Motion Study.* New York: Sturgess and Walton, 1917.

Goldhamer, Herbert, and Shils, Edward A. 'Types of Power and Status,' *American Journal of Sociology*, 1939, XIV 171.

Golembiewski, Robert T. *Men, Management and Morality.* New York: McGraw-Hill, 1965.

Gore, W. J., and Silander, F. S. 'A Bibliographical Essay on Decision Making,' *Administrative Science Quarterly*, 1959, Vol. 4.

Granger, Robert L. *Educational Leadership*. Intext, Pa.: Scranton, 1971.

Greenfield, T. Barr. *Theory in the Study of Organizations and Administrative Structures*. Canadian Assoc. for Study of Educational Administration (paper) 1974; also in *Educational Administration: International Challenges*. London: Athlone Press, 1975.

Gregor, A. J. 'Classical Marxism and the Totalitarian Ethic' in Laszlo, E., and Wilbur, J. B., *Value Theory in Philosophy and Social Science*. New York: Gordon and Beach. 1973.

Griffiths, Daniel E. *Administrative Theory*. New York: Appleton-Century-Crofts, 1959.

Gulick, Luther, and Urwick, L., eds. *Papers on the Science of Administration*. New York: Inst. of Pub. Admin. Columbia U., 1937.

Haas, J. E. and Drabek, T. E. *Complex Organizations*. New York: Macmillan, 1973.

Halpin, Andrew W. *Theory and Research in Administration*. New York: MacMillan 1966.

Herzberg, F. 'The Motivation-Hygiene Concept and Problems of Manpower,' *Personnel Administration*, 1964, 27 I 3.

———. *Work and the Nature of Man*. Cleveland: World Pub. 1966.

———. 'One more time: How do you motivate employees?' *Harvard Business Review*, 1968, 46, 53–62.

Hodgkinson Christopher, 'Why Democracy Won't Work,' *Phi Delta Kappan*, 1973, LIV 5 316.

———. 'Philosophy, Politics, and Planning. An Extended Rationale for Synthesis' *Educational Administration Quarterly*, 1975, Winter XI 11.

Homans, G. C. *The Human Group*. New York: Harcourt Brace, 1950.

House, R. J., and Wigdor, L. A. 'Herzberg's Dual-Factor Theory of Job Satisfaction and Motivation,' *Personnel Psychology*, 1967, 20:369.

Kant, Immanuel, tr. Abbott, T. K. *Critique of Practical Reason*. New York: Longmans Green, 1909.

Kaplan, Abraham, *The Conduct of Inquiry*. San Francisco: Chandler, 1964.

Katz, Daniel, and Kahn, Robert L. *The Social Psychology of Organizations*. New York: Wiley, 1966.

Keeling, D. *The Administrative Process in Britain*. Methuen, 1970.

Kohlberg, L. 'Sequences in the Development of Moral Thought,' *Vita Humana*, 1963, 6:11.

Ladd, John. 'Morality and the Ideal of Rationality in Formal Organizations,' *The Monist*, 1970, Vol. 54, 488–516.

Lambert, William W., and Lambert, Wallace E. *Social Psychology*. New Jersey: Prentice-Hall, 1965.

Laszlo, Ervin. *Introduction to Systems Philosophy*. New York: Harper, 1972.

Leavitt, Harold J. *Managerial Psychology*. U. of Chicago, 3rd ed. 1972.

Lerner, D., and Lasswell, H. D., eds. *The Policy Sciences*. Palo Alto, 1951.

Lessem, R. 'A Philosophy of Organizations,' *Systematics* Pt. I Sep. 1972 Vol. 10; Pt. II Sep. 1973 Vol. II

Lewis, R. and Stewart, R. *The Boss*. London: Phoenix House, 1958.

Leys, Wayne A. R. 'Ethics and Administrative Discretion,' *Public Administration Review*, 1943: 3, 10.

———. 'The Value Framework of Decision Making' in Mailick, S., and van Ness, E. H., eds. *Concepts and Issues in Administrative Behaviour*. New Jersey: Prentice-Hall, 1972.

Likert, R. *New Patterns of Management*. New York: McGraw-Hill, 1961.

———. *The Human Organization*. New York: McGraw-Hill, 1967.

Lindblom, Charles E. 'The Science of Muddling Through,' *Public Administration Review*, 1959, Spring, 155–169.

Litchfield, G. H. 'Notes on a General Theory of Administration,' *Administrative Science Quarterly*, 1956, Jan.

Lorenz, K., tr. Wilson, M. *On Aggression*. New York: Harcourt and Brace, 1966.

Machiavelli, N. *The Prince*. London: Routledge, 1886.

Magee, Bryan. *Modern British Philosophy*. St. Albans: Paladin, 1973.

March, J. G., and Simon, H. A. *Organizations*. New York: Wiley, 1958.

Marini, *Toward a New Public Administration: The Minnowbrook Perspective*. San Francisco: Chandler, 1971.

Maslow, A. H. 'A Theory of Human Motivation,' *Psychological Review*, 1943, 50, 370.
―――. *Motivation and Personality* New York: Harper, 1954.
―――. *Eupsychian Management*. Irwin, III.: Homewood, 1965.
―――. *Toward a Psychology of Being*. 2nd. ed. New York: van Nostrand, 1968.
Mayo, Elton. *The Human Problems of an Industrial Civilization*. New York: MacMillan, 1933.
―――. *The Social Problems of an Industrial Civilization*. London: Routledge and Kegan Paul, 1949.
McClelland, D. C., Atkinson, J. W., Clark, R. A., Lovell, E. L. *The Achievement Motive* New York: Appleton-Century, 1953.
―――. *The Achieving Society*. New Jersey: Van Norstrand, 1961
McGregor, D. *The Human Side of Enterprise*. New York: McGraw-Hill, 1960.
McGregor, C., and Bennis, W. G., eds. *The Professional Manager*. New York: McGraw-Hill, 1967.
Merton, R. K. Gray, A. P., Hockey, B., Sevin, H. *Reader in Bureaucracy*. New York: Free Press, 1952.
Michels, R. tr. Paul, E. and Paul, C. *Political Parties*. New York: Free Press, 1949.
Miles, Raymond E. *Theories of Management*. New York: McGraw-Hill, 1975.
Milgram, S. 'Behavioral Study of Obedience,' *Journal of Abnormal and Social Psychology*, 1963, 67:371.
―――. *Obedience to Authority*. New York: Harper & Row, 1974.
Miller, J. 'Two Concepts of Authority' *American Anthropologist*, 1955 LVII; 271,
Miller, James G. 'Living Systems: Cross-Level Hypotheses,' *Behavioural Science*, 1965 10 No. 4.
Mintzberg, Henry. *The Nature of Managerial Work*. New York: Harper & Row, 1973.
Mooney, J. D. *The Principles of Organization*. New York: Harper & Bros, 1937.
Moore, G. E. *Principia Ethica*. Cambridge U. P., 1903.
Morphet, Edgar L., Johns, Roe L., Reller, Theodore L. *Educational Organization and Administration* 2nd ed. New Jersey: Prentice-Hall, 1967.

Noustadt, R. E. *Presidential Power: The Politics of Leadership*. New York: Wiley, 1960.

Oakeshott, M. J. *Hobbes on Civil Association*. Oxford: Basil Blackwell, 1975.

Ouchi, William G., and Dowling, James B. 'Defining the Span of Control,' *Administrative Science Quarterly*, 1974, Sep. 357.

Parsons, T. *The Structure of Social Action*. Glencoe: Free Press, 1937.

———. *The Social System*. New York: Free Press, 1951.

———. *Structure and Process in Modern Societies*. New York: Free Press, 1960.

Parsons, T., and Shils, E. A., eds. *Toward a General Theory of Action*. New York: Harper, 1962.

Passmore, John. *A Hundred Years of Philosophy*, 2nd ed. Harmondsworth: Penguin, 1968.

Perrow, C. *Organizational Analysis: a Sociological View*. Belmont, Calif., 1970.

Peters, R. S., ed. *Nature and Conduct*. London: MacMillan, 1975.

Piaget, J. *The Moral Judgment of the Child*. London: Kegan Paul, 1932.

Pollard, Harold R. *Developments in Management Thought*. London: Heinemann, 1974.

Plato. *The Republic*. Harmondsworth: Penguin Classics, 2nd ed. rev. 1974.

Rathe, A. W., ed. *Gantt on Management*. New York: Amer. Mgmt. Assoc., 1961.

Rather, D. and Gates, G. P. *The Palace Guard*. New York: Warner, 1975.

Reddin, W. J. *Managerial Effectiveness*. New York: McGraw-Hill, 1970.

Report of First Division Association 'Professional Standards in the Public Service,' *Public Administration*, Vol. 50, 1972, 167–182.

Rokeach, M. *Beliefs, Attitudes, and Values*. San Francisco: Jossey-Bass, 1968.

———. *The Nature of Human Values*. New York: Free Press, 1973.

Russell, Bertrand. *An Inquiry into Meaning and Truth*. London: Penguin University Books, 1973.

———. *Power*. London: Unwin, 1975.

Satprakashananda, Swami. *Methods of Knowledge*. London: Allen and Unwin, 1965.

Sayles, L. R. *Managerial Behaviour: Administration in Complex Organizations*. New York: McGraw-Hill, 1964.

Schneider, B., and Alderfer, C. P. 'Three Studies of Measures of Need Satisfaction in Organizations,' *Administrative Science Quarterly*, 1973, 18:489.

Schneider, J., and Locke, E. A. 'A Critique of Herzberg's Incident Classification System and a Suggested Revision,' *Organizational Behaviour and Human Performance*, 1971, 6:441.

Schutz, W. C. 'What makes Groups Productive?' *Human Relations*, 1955, Nov., 429–31.

Scott, William A. *Values and Organizations*. Chicago: Rand McNally, 1965.

Self, Peter. *Administrative Theories and Politics*. London: Allen & Unwin, 1972.

Selznick, P. *Leadership in Administration*. Evanston, Ill.: Row, Peterson, 1957.

Shannon, Claude E., and Weaver, Warren. *The Mathematical Theory of Communication*. Urbana, Ill., 1949.

Shartle, C. L. 'Leadership and Executive Performance,' *Personnel*, 1949, 25: 370–80.

———. *Executive Performance and Leadership*. New Jersey: Prentice-Hall, 1956.

Simon, Herbert A. *Administrative Behaviour*. New York: Free Press, 2nd. ed. 1957, 1965.

Simon, H., Smithburg, D., Thompson, V. *Public Administration*. New York: Knopf, 1950.

Sisson, C. H. *The Spirit of British Administration*. London: Faber & Faber, 1959.

Skinner, B. F. *Beyond Freedom and Dignity*. New York: Knopf, 1971.

Snow, C. P. *Science and Government*. Oxford, 1961.

Spencer, Herbert. *Principles of Sociology*. London, 1910.

Stake, Robert E. 'The Countenance of Educational Evaluation,' *Teachers College Record*, 1967, Vol. 68, 523.

Steers, Richard M., and Porter, Lyman W. *Motivation and Work Behaviour*. New York: McGraw-Hill, 1975.

Stewart, R. *Managers and their Jobs*. London: MacMillan, 1967.

Stieglitz, H. *The Chief Executive—and his Job*. Nat. Indl. Conf. Bd. New York: Study No. 214, 1969.

Stogdill, Ralph M. 'Personal Factors associated with Leadership,' *Journal of Psychology*, 1948, 25, 1, 35–71.

Stogdill, R. M., and Coons, A. E., eds. *Leader Behaviour: Its Description and Measurement*. Ohio State U. 1957.

Stufflebeam, D. L. *et al*. *Educational Evaluation and Decision Making*. Itasca, Ill.: Peacock, 1971.

Subramaniam, V. 'Fact and Value in Decision Making,' *Public Administrative Review* 1963, 23, 232–237.

———. 'The Fact-Value Distinction as an Analytical Tool,' *Indian Journal of Public Administration*, Vol. 17, 1971.

Suppes, P. 'The Philosophical Relevance of Decision Theory,' *Journal of Philosophy*, Vol. 57, 1961.

Taylor, F. W. *Shop Management*. New York: Harper Bros., 1911.

———. *The Principles of Scientific Management*. Harper & Bros. New York 1915.

———. *Scientific Management*. London: Harper & Bros, 1964.

Thompson, Victor A. *Modern Organization*. New York: Knopf, 1961.

———. *Without Sympathy or Enthusiasm. The Problem of Administrative Compassion*. U. of Alabama Press, 1975.

Tribe, Lawrence H. 'Policy Science: Analysis or Ideology,' *Philosophy and Public Affairs*, 1972, Fall 66–110.

Tyler, Ralph, Gagne, Robert, Scriven, Michael. *Perspectives of Curriculum Evaluation*. Chicago: Rand McNally, 1967.

Vickers, Sir Geoffrey. *The Art of Judgment*. London, 1965.

———. *Value Systems and Social Process*. London: Penguin, 1970.

Vividishananda, Swami. *A Man of God*. Madras: Sri Ramakrishna Math, 1957.

Vollmer, H. M. *Employer Rights and the Employment Relationship*. U. of Calif., 1960.

von Bertalanffy, L. 'The Theory of Open Systems in Physics and Biology' *Science*, 1950, III, 23–28.

———. 'General Systems Theory,' *General Systems* (Yearbook 1) 1956, 1–10.

———. *General Systems Theory*. New York., 1968.

Vroom, V. H. *Work and Motivation*. New York: Wiley, 1964.

Waldo, Dwight. 'Organization Theory: An Elephantine Problem,'

Public Administration Review, 1961, Autumn, Vol. XXI 210.

Weber, M., tr. Parsons. *The Protestant Ethic and the Spirit of Capitalism*. New York: Scribner, 1930.

———. tr. A. M. Henderson, T. Parsons. *The Theory of Social and Economic Organization*. New York: Free Press, 1947.

Whyte, W. *The Organization Man*. New York: Doubleday, 1957.

Wiener, Norbert. *The Human Use of Human Beings: Cybernetics and Society*. New York: Garden City, 1954.

Wiles, David K. 'Politics and Planning: A Rationale for Synthesis in Educational Administration,' *Educational Administration Quarterly*, 1974, Winter X.1 44.

Wittgenstein, L. *Philosophical Investigations*. Oxford: Basil Blackwell, 1953.

———. *Tractatus Logico-Philosophicus*. Oxford: Routledge and Kegan Paul, 1961, 1922.

———. *On Certainty*. Basil Blackwell, 1969.

Woodruff, A. D. 'Personal Values and the Direction of Behaviour,' *School Review* 1942, 50, 32–42.

Wright, M. 'The Professional Conduct of Civil Servants,' *Public Administration*, Vol. 51, 1973, 1–16.

Zimmer, Heinrich. *Philosophies of India*. New York: Bollingen Foundation, 1951.

Index